Theory and Resistance in Education

Critical Perspectives in Social Theory
A SERIES EDITED
by Stanley Aronowitz & Roslyn Bologh

THEORY AND RESISTANCE IN EDUCATION

A Pedagogy for the Opposition

Henry A. Giroux

Bergin & Garvey Publishers, Inc.
Massachusetts

First published in 1983 by
Bergin & Garvey Publishers, Inc.
670 Amherst Road
South Hadley, Massachusetts 01075

Printed in the United States of America

89   056   9876543

Library of Congress Cataloging in Publication Data

Giroux, Henry A.
Theory and resistance in education.
(Critical perspectives in social theory)
Bibliography: p.
Includes index.
1. Giroux, Henry A.   2. Education—Philosophy.
3. Positivism.   4. Socialization.   I. Title.
II. Series
LB885.G472T48   1983   370'.1   83-2698
ISBN 0-89789-031-0
ISBN 0-89789-032-9 (pbk.)

For Jeanne
For Paulo and Elsa
For Donaldo
For Roger and Wendy
For Stanley
For David

Contents

Foreword

By PAULO FREIRE

There is, I believe, a certain coherence between the pedagogical stand I have been taking throughout the years and the manner in which I write forewords. Thus, the few I have written are more of an attempt at challenging the possible readers to engage themselves in a critical reading rather than conducting a rigorous analysis of the text. Not that I consider it to be inappropriate to spell out to the readers all my reactions to the book, as its first reader, but because I prefer the role of someone who, through challenging, invites others to establish a relationship of conviviality with the book.

My close contact with the restless thought of Henry Giroux started some time ago, during a Swiss summer afternoon in my office, two or three years before my return to Brazil after sixteen years of exile. A paper of his, with the author's name withheld, was sent to me by a journal with a cover letter requesting my opinion, since the paper discussed my work. The seriousness of the writing, its clarity, its rigor—all had a deep impact upon me. I read it and reread it with the same seriousness with which it had been written. Afterwards, I wrote to the editor of the journal stating that, in my view, the article should have been published "the day before yesterday."

I also expressed in my letter the pleasure that I would take in some day meeting the author of the manuscript. A few days later, I received a letter from Henry, accompanied by some of his writings. After reading them, my first impression was greatly reinforced—these works contained an undeniable power of thinking.

Since that time we have never ceased to correspond, and the more I read Giroux's work the more I became convinced of how impossible it is "to come in contact" with him as a person or with his work without reacting. That is, his thought does not allow those who approach him to remain indifferent. His view and defense of what has been called radical pedagogy are in themselves inherently radical. Nothing in Giroux brings him close to a sectarian understanding of the world, just as there is no room in his thought for the "springing" of false dichotomies.

Giroux knows very well that to be in the world and with the world means exactly to continuously experience the dialectics between subjectivity and objectivity. He also knows that one of the most difficult things is to live in the world without falling into the temptation of either overestimating subjectivity to the detriment of objectivity or overestimating the latter over the former. His passion, and my own, is neither subjective idealism nor mechanistic objectivism, but critical immersion in history. This is the raison d'etre of the radical pedagogy he proposes.

This book by Henry Giroux deals with this crucial problem in an ample and profound manner, in an easy style that is never simplistic. *Theory and Resistance in Education* is a book of great importance and should be read by anyone interested in education, social theory, and critical practice.

Introduction

By STANLEY ARONOWITZ & ROSLYN BOLOGH

The past decade has witnessed a virtual explosion of American interest in social theory. A panoply of Marxism, neo-Weberianism, poststructuralism and several others have been taken up by intellectuals as means to critique the dominant pluralist traditions of American social science, humanistic studies, and philosophy. On the one hand, neo-Marxism and, more broadly, social theory itself has become more respectable, even though empiricism and positivism still hold sway in most universities. On the other hand, the battles have intensified among the dissidents: orthodox Marxism opposes the Frankfurt school's critical theory; French structuralist and poststructuralist thought condemns the others as impossibly "essentialist": that is, argues that Marxism as such remains in the thrall of Western *logos* positing the "economic" as the determination, in the last instance, of all social phenomena. In short, the explosion of social theories occurs in fits and starts, its uneven path strewn with new categories for intellectuals to chew, spit out, or digest.

Despite the confusion and the lack of a hegemonic discourse among the new social theorists, the work is increasingly rich in its critique of contemporary society. Virtually no space has been permitted to remain unfilled. Radicals of both Marxist and other critical persuasions have entered even the most sacred conservative academic precincts, such as economics, geography, political science, and literature. In some instances, the new social theory and critical studies have constituted a storm center to which the disciplines feel obliged to respond. In other cases, the professions have regrouped around their own counterattacking ideologues—for example, in history, the revisionists found themselves beleaguered at the end of the 1970s.

The series "New Perspectives in Social Theory" is intended as an intervention in the debate among those engaged in working in the new social theory. In each volume, writers will attempt to make original contributions to the debate rather than remain locked into prevailing assumptions, most of which are ensconced in antinomies. For example, Henry Giroux's work on education provides the general reader as well as the education specialist with a broad survey of the leading ideas of the new sociology of education, as well as with a critique of main trends within the field. Anyone who consults Giroux's wide-ranging analysis is bound to come away with a critical view of education theory in the past decade. In contrast to most writers in the field, Giroux is by no means confined to theoretical and historical work in education itself. He shows an astonishing range of references, a broad sweep that includes the Frankfurt school (to which he is deeply indebted), the work of French education theorists such as Pierre Bourdieu, the powerful ideology critique of Italian Marxist Antonio Gramsci (whose categories hegemony, "common sense," and the place of education and intellectuals in the formation of political blocs informs Giroux's understanding of the role of schools in society). In this book, the reader is about to encounter a veritable feast of theoretical rumination, but rumination always brought to bear on the place of schools in our culture, the active political role of schools in shaping that culture, and, most important of all, the prospects for changing our schools.

But Giroux goes further. His work suggests new directions in the theory of American education, particularly its ideological, intellectual, and political aspects. As he argues, the two leading positions among the critics of American education—pluralism and "reproduction" theories—are opposite sides of the same general orientation. Both assume that the purpose of American schools, however unintended, is to prepare students for the world of work. In both paradigms citizenship education, a leading ideological tenet of liberal schooling, is clearly subordinate to the vocational value of the curriculum.

Giroux is especially concerned to demonstrate that reproduction theories, which posit a rigid socialization model geared to the labor market or the perpetuation of leading ideological precepts of American society, have failed to offer an alternative model of the actual course of educational development to the mainstream of pluralist thought—because both theories are based on the same assumptions. Giroux challenges both traditions by arguing that schools are complex organizations whose relation to the larger society is mediated by, among other things, social movements; these have their own agendas, which help determine the configuration of school life. Further, he shows that the sites of social and ideological struggle, particularly the classroom, are spaces of genuine change, modification, unintended consequences. Giroux's thesis is that resistance is more than response to the authoritarian curriculum—which, in recent times, no longer even invokes a democratic purpose. Resistance is a symptom of an incipient alternative agenda, an agenda which, in many cases, is not evident to the actors themselves. Students do not merely refuse the compulsory ideologies and their practices, they form a separate culture and public sphere within which a different set of practices is reproduced. For Giroux, it is not a question of alternative socialization, as formulated in Paul Willis's excellent study of an English comprehensive high school. Nor does resistance turn back on itself and simply reproduce the occupational hierarchy, as Willis claims. What Giroux wants to show is that while these variants of ideological and social reproduction are going on, something else is also happening in the interminable struggle of students against school authority. Although Giroux does not go so far as to claim that students can triumph against the nearly insurmountable odds offered by the social structure, he argues that the "surplus" resistance presented by students opens up tiny but significant spaces for new forms of power.

In this, the first volume of the New Perspectives series, Giroux helps to clarify the purpose of the series. "New Perspectives in Social Theory" aims to stir controversy by valorizing as well as offering trenchant critique of what is new and exciting in social theory. In *Theory and Resistance*, we believe Giroux has performed this difficult task admirably.

Preface

This book was written during a trying time. On the national level, political hopes and dreams for a better future have been replaced by publicity gimmicks and advertisements for a creeping authoritarianism. The moral questions that once informed issues regarding human needs and welfare have been overshadowed by technical questions about balancing budgets and increasing military stockpiles. Leftist academics are being slowly purged from the universities, while many of their colleagues disappear into the security of their tenured positions and refuse to resist or challenge the academic assassins who act without compassion or reflection. The script is grim, and the historical logic that informs it raises alarm. Such a scenario is not meant to prompt despair or cynicism; instead it points to the necessity to organize collectively and to fight harder. It also implies that the struggle will be a long and arduous one, and that in time the seeds of a new society may or may not bloom. In other words, one has to struggle against the new authoritarianism and hope that such an effort will pay off in the future. The dialectic between the reality and the promise cannot be escaped, it can only be ignored, and then only by those who have the economic and political power to close their doors and hide from the carnage they create, but never actually see or touch. This is the age of clean killers.

To struggle for economic and social democracy is to take risks. It is impossible to escape this logic. In my own case, I made the mistake of thinking that all major universities generally provided a setting where a critical dialogue could be constructed, oppositional views aired, or, for that matter, where alternative positions could be taught. It now appears that there are very few universities left in the United States where academic freedom is taken seriously. The message, of course, is not strictly a personal one, though that is not to be discounted since actions that violate the principles of academic freedom always disrupt lives in a deeply painful way. What is more important is that the message is a political one, and it speaks to the need for educators, teachers, community people, and others to develop, where possible, political, cultural, and educational collectives that provide both the space and the support necessary for them to survive and to struggle with dignity and power. There are no safe avenues any longer. There are only fleeting possibilities for us to think through the past, to examine the sedimented histories that constitute who we are, and to insert ourselves into the present so as to struggle for a better society. This book makes a small contribution to that effort. It provides no final answers: only the politicians and the game shows do that, and both of them are rigged. The book simply raises questions, invokes a new discourse for educators, and points to new relations and modes of analysis for understanding and changing schools and the larger society. The rest is open-ended.

I am deeply grateful to the following people for reading all or parts of this manuscript and for providing me with moral and/or intellectual sustenance: Richard Bates, Geoff Whitty, Madeleine Arnot, Dick Dyro, Susan Crow, Philip Wexler, Maxine Greene, Bette Weneck, Steve Ellenwood, Jeanne Brady, Judy Schickendanz, Jim Giarelli, Len Barton, Jurg Jenzer, Tom Pandiscio, Kathleen Weiler, Don Lazere, David Purpel, Walter Feinberg, Tom Popkewitz, Pat Bizzell, Bruce Herzberg, Paulo Freire, Philip Corrigan, Paul Olson, Paul Breines, Roger and Wendy Simon, Ulf Lundgren, Donaldo Macedo, Michael Apple, Ralph Page, George Wood, Jim Walker, Jean Brenkman, Cleo Cherry-Holmes, and Ray Barbery. I am also grateful for the support I have received from my sister, Linda Barbery, and her husband, Al Barbery. I am deeply indebted to Stanley Aronowitz, who ruined my summer by asking for a number of editorial changes in the manuscript, all of which greatly improved the text. A special thanks goes to Rosa. Needless to say, I am ultimately responsible for the final form this book has taken.

Earlier versions of some of the material used in this book have appeared in *Theory and Research in Social Education, McGill Journal of Education, Curriculum Inquiry, Humanities in Society,* and *Interchange.* Chapter 5 copyright © 1980 by Ontario Institute for Studies in Education; first published by John Wiley & Sons, Inc.

Henry A. Giroux
Miami University
Oxford, Ohio

SECTION ONE

Theory & Critical Discourse

Since the established universe of discourse is that of an unfree world, dialectical thought is necessarily destructive, and whatever liberation it may bring is liberation in thought, in theory. However, the divorce of thought from action, of theory from practice, is itself part of an unfree world. No thought and no theory can undo it; but theory may help to prepare the ground for their possible reunion, and the ability of thought to develop a logic and language of contradiction is a prerequisite for this task {Marcuse 1960}.

IN THIS BRIEF PARAGRAPH, MARCUSE MANAGES TO CAPTURE BOTH THE spirit and the challenge that presently confront radical pedagogy. Its spirit is rooted in an aversion to all forms of domination, and its challenge centers around the need to develop modes of critique fashioned in a theoretical discourse that mediates the possibility for social action and emancipatory transformation. Such a task will not be easy, particularly at the present historical juncture, informed as it is by a long tradition of ideological discourse and social practices that promote modes of historical, political, and conceptual illiteracy.

The following section attempts to develop a theoretical discourse that seriously engages the challenge implicit in Marcuse's statement. It does so by positing an argument for a theory of radical pedagogy that takes as its first task the development of a new language and set of critical concepts. In this case, it calls for a discourse that acknowledges as a central concern the categories of history, sociology, and depth psychology. At the same time, it attempts to fashion these categories into a mode of analysis that grounds human agency and structure within a context that reveals how the dynamics of domination and contestation mediate the specific forms they take under concrete historical circumstances. In essence, this section attempts to rescue the critical potential of radical educational discourse while simultaneously enlarging the concept of the political to include those historical and socio-cultural institutions and practices that constitute the realm of everyday life. In more specific terms, this means developing analyses of schooling that draw upon a critical theory and discourse that interrelate modes of inquiry drawn from a variety of social science disciplines. On the other hand, this section attempts to construct a theoretical foundation to extend the notion of critique into relations and dimensions of schooling and social activity often ignored by both traditional and radical educators.

The questions underlying the modes of analysis used in this section are important ones: how do we make education meaningful by making it critical, and how do we make it critical so as to make it emancipatory. The starting point for pursuing these questions is historical in nature and suggests a brief commentary on how the issue has been treated in traditional and radical analyses.

Educational traditionalists generally ignore the issue. In both conservative and liberal versions of schooling, theory has been firmly entrenched in the logic of technocratic rationality and has been anchored in a discourse that finds its quintessential expression in the attempt to find universal principles of education that are rooted in the ethos of instrumentalism or self-serving individualism. At the same time, these accounts have suppressed questions of the relations among power, knowledge, and ideology. In effect, traditional educational theory has ignored not only the latent principles that shape the deep grammar of the existing social order, but also those principles that underlie the development and nature of its own view of the world. Schools, in these perspectives, are seen merely as instructional sites. That they are also cultural and political sites is ignored, as is the notion that they represent arenas of contestation and struggle among differentially empowered cultural and economic groups.

Needless to say, various modes of radical educational theory and practice have emerged in the last few decades to challenge the traditionalist paradigm. We have witnessed structuralist accounts that focus on macro-issues concerning those social, economic, and political determinants of schooling that have aimed at capital accumulation and the reproduction of the labor force. Characteristic of these investigations are accounts of schools as part of an "ideological state apparatus," the ultimate function of which is to constitute the ideological conditions for the maintenance and reproduction of capitalist relations of production, i.e., the creation of a labor force that will passively comply with the dictates of capital and its institutions. We have also seen the development of historical and sociological accounts of the way in which the structure of the workplace is replicated through daily routines and practices that shape classroom social relations, that is, the hidden curriculum of schooling. More recently, we have accounts of schooling that illuminate how cultural resources are selected, organized, and distributed in schools so as to secure existing power relations.

I shall argue in this section that all of these positions have failed to provide an adequate basis for developing a radical theory of pedagogy. The traditionalists have failed because they have refused to make problematic the relations among schools, the larger society, and issues of power, domination, and liberation. There is no room in their discourse for the fundamental categories of praxis: categories such as subjectivity, mediation, class, struggle, and emancipation. While radical educators do make the relations among schools, power, and society an object of critical analysis, they do so at the theoretical expense of falling into either a one-sided idealism or an equally one-sided structuralism. In other words, there are, on the one hand, radical educators who collapse human agency and struggle into a celebration of human will, cultural experience, or the construction of "happy" classroom social relations. On the other hand, there are radical views of pedagogy that cling to notions of structure and domination. Such views not only argue that history is made behind the backs of human beings, but also imply that within such a context of domination human agency virtually disappears. The notion that human beings produce history—including its constraints—is subsumed in a discourse that often portrays schools as prisons, factories, and administrative machines functioning smoothly to produce the interests of domination and inequality. The result has often been modes of analysis that collapse into an arid functionalism or equally disabling pessimism.

It is at this juncture that the work of the Frankfurt School becomes important. Within the theoretical legacy of critical theorists such as Adorno, Horkheimer, and Marcuse there is a sustained attempt to develop a theory and mode of critique that aims at both revealing and breaking with the existing structures of domination. Crucial to this perspective are an analysis and a call for the integration of the processes of emancipation and the struggle for self-emancipation. History, psychology, and social theory interface in an attempt to rescue the human subject from the logic of capitalist administration. Political education (not necessarily schooling) takes on a new dimension within the context of this work. As Marcuse points out:

> It is precisely the preparatory character of [education] which gives it its historical significance: to develop, in the exploited, the consciousness (and the unconscious) which would loosen the hold of enslaving needs over their existence—the needs which perpetuate their dependence on the system of exploitation. Without this rupture, which can only be the result of political education in action, even the most elemental, the most immediate force of rebellion may be defeated, or become the mass basis of counterrevolution [Marcuse 1969].

Central to the work of the Frankfurt School is an examination of the degree to which the logic of domination has been extended into the sphere of everyday life, the public sphere, and the mode of production itself. What critical theory provides for educational theorists is a mode of critique and a language of opposition that extends the concept of the political not only into mundane social relations but into the very sensibilities and needs that form the personality and psyche. The achievements of the critical theorists are their refusal to abandon the dialectic of agency and structure (i.e., the open-endedness of history) and their development of theoretical perspectives that treat seriously the claim that history can be changed, that the potential for radical transformation exists.

It is against this theoretical landscape that I shall examine the various analyses of the hidden curriculum and reproductive theories of schooling that have emerged in the last few decades in the United States and Europe. Whereas the Frankfurt School provides a discourse that illuminates the social, political, and cultural totality in which schools develop, the various analyses of schooling provide a referent point from which to assess both the strengths and limitations of such work. Moreover, it is precisely in the interface of the work of the Frankfurt School and the various theories of schooling under analyses in this section that the theoretical elements for a radical theory of pedagogy begin to appear. It is to this task that I will now turn.

1

Critical Theory
& Educational Practice

Introduction

This chapter attempts to contribute to the search for a theoretical foundation upon which to develop a critical theory of education. Within the parameters of this task, the notion of critical theory has a two-fold meaning. First, critical theory refers to the legacy of theoretical work developed by certain members of what can be loosely described as "the Frankfurt School." What this suggests is that critical theory was never a fully articulated philosophy shared unproblematically by all members of the Frankfurt School. But it must be stressed that while one cannot point to a single universally shared critical theory, one can point to the common attempt to assess the newly emerging forms of capitalism along with the changing forms of domination that accompanied them. Similarly, there was an attempt on the part of all the members of the Frankfurt School to rethink and radically reconstruct the meaning of human emancipation, a project that differed considerably from the theoretical baggage of orthodox Marxism. Specifically, I argue in this chapter for the importance of original critical theory and the insights it provides for developing a critical foundation for a theory of radical pedagogy. In doing so, I focus on the work of Adorno, Horkheimer, and Marcuse. This seems to be an important concern, especially since so much of the work on the Frankfurt School being used by educators focuses almost exclusively on the work of Jurgen Habermas.

Second, the concept of critical theory refers to the nature of self-conscious critique and to the need to develop a discourse of social transformation and emancipation that does not cling dogmatically to its own doctrinal assumptions. In other words, critical theory refers to both a "school of thought" and a process of critique. It points to a body of thought that is, in my view, invaluable for educational theorists; it also exemplifies a body of work that both demonstrates and simultaneously calls for the necessity of ongoing critique, one in which the claims of any theory must be confronted with the distinction between the world it examines and portrays, and the world as it actually exists.

The Frankfurt School took as one of its central values a commitment to penetrate the world of objective appearances and to expose the underlying social relationships they often conceal. In other words, penetrating such appearances meant exposing through critical analysis social relationships that took on the status of things or objects. For instance, by examining notions such as money, consumption, distribution, and production, it becomes clear that none of these represents an objective thing or fact, but rather all are historically contingent contexts mediated by relationships of domination and subordination. In adopting such a perspective, the Frankfurt School not only broke with forms of rationality that wedded science and technology into new forms of domination, it also rejected all forms of rationality that subordinated human consciousness and action to the imperatives of universal laws. Whether it be the legacy of Victorian European positivist intellectual thought or the theoretical edifice developed by Engels, Kautsky, Stalin, and other heirs of Marxism, the Frankfurt School argued against the suppression of "subjectivity, consciousness, and culture in history" (Breines 1979–80). In so doing it articulated a notion of negativity or critique that opposed all theories that celebrated social harmony while leaving unproblematic the basic assumptions of the wider society. In more specific terms, the Frankfurt School stressed the importance of critical thinking by arguing that it is a constitutive feature of the struggle for self-emancipation and social change. Moreover, its members argued that it was in the contradictions of society that one could begin to develop forms of social inquiry that analyzed the distinction between *what is* and *what should be*. Finally, it strongly supported the assumption that the basis for thought and action should be grounded, as Marcuse argued just before his death, "in compassion, [and] in our sense of the sufferings of others." (Habermas 1980)

In general terms, the Frankfurt School provided a number of valuable insights for studying the relationship between theory and society. In so doing, its members developed a dialectical framework by which to understand the mediations that link the institutions and activities of everyday life with the logic and commanding forces that shape the larger social totality. The characteristic nature of the form of social inquiry that emerged from such a framework was articulated by Horkheimer when he suggested that members of the Institute for Social Research explore the question of "the interconnection between the economic life of society, the psychic development of the individual, and transformations in the realm of culture . . . including not only the so-called spiritual contents of science, art, and religion, but also law, ethics, fashion, public opinion, sport, amusement, life style, etc." (Horkheimer 1972).

The issues raised here by Horkheimer have not lost their importance with time; they still represent both a critique and a challenge to many of the theoretical currents that presently characterize theories of social education. The necessity for theoretical renewal in the education field, coupled with the massive number of primary and secondary sources that have been translated or published recently in English, provide the opportunity for American- and English-speaking pedagogues to begin to appropriate the discourse and ideas of the Frankfurt School. Needless to say, such a task will not be easily accomplished, since both the complexity of the language used by members of the School and the diversity of the positions and themes they pursued demand a selective and critical reading of their works. Yet their critique of culture, instrumental rationality, authoritarianism, and ideology, pursued in an interdisciplinary context, generated categories, relationships, and forms of social inquiry that constitute a vital resource for developing a critical theory of social education. Since it will be impossible in the scope of this chapter to analyze the diversity of themes examined by the Frankfurt School, I will limit my analysis to the treatment of rationality, theory, culture, and depth psychology. Finally, I will discuss the implications of these for educational theory and practice.

History and Background of the Frankfurt School

The Institute for Social Research (*Das Institute für Sozialforshung*), officially created in Frankfurt, Germany, in February, 1923, was the original home of the Frankfurt School. Established by a wealthy grain merchant named Felix Weil, the Institute came under the directorship of Max Horkheimer in 1930. Under Horkheimer's directorship, most of the members who later became famous joined the Institute. These included Erich Fromm, Herbert Marcuse, and Theodor Adorno. As Martin Jay points out in his now-famous history of the Frankfurt School: "If it can be said that in the early years of its history the Institute concerned itself primarily with an analysis of bourgeois society's socio-economic substructure, in the years after 1930 its prime interests lay in its cultural superstructure" (Jay 1973).

The change in the Institute's theoretical focus was soon followed by a shift in its location. Threatened by the Nazis because of the avowedly Marxist orientation of its work and the fact that most of its members were Jews, the Institute was forced to move for a short time in 1933 to Geneva, and then in 1934 to New York City, where it was housed in one of Columbia University's buildings. Emigration to New York was followed by a stay in Los Angeles in 1941, and by 1953 the Institute was re-established in Frankfurt, Germany.

The strengths and weaknesses of the Frankfurt School project become intelligible only if seen as part of the social and historical context in which it developed. In essence, the questions it pursued and the forms of social inquiry it supported represent both a particular moment in the development of Western Marxism and a critique of it. Reacting to the rise of Fascism and Nazism, on the one hand, and to the failure of orthodox Marxism, on the other, the Frankfurt School had to refashion and rethink the meaning of domination and emancipation. The rise of Stalinism, the failure of the European or Western working class to contest capitalist hegemony in a revolutionary manner, and the power of capitalism to reconstitute and reinforce its economic and ideological control forced the Frankfurt School to reject the orthodox reading of Marx and Engels, particularly as developed through the conventional wisdom of the Second and Third Internationals. It is particularly in the rejection of certain doctrinal Marxist assumptions, developed under the historical shadow of totalitarianism and through the rise of the consumer society in the West, that Horkheimer, Adorno, and Marcuse attempted to construct a more sufficient basis for social theory and political action. Certainly, such a basis was not to be found in standard Marxist assumptions such as (a) the notion of historical inevitability, (b) the primacy of the mode of production in shaping history, and (c) the notion that class struggle as well as the mechanisms of domination take place primarily within the confines of the labor process. For the Frankfurt School, orthodox Marxism assumed too much while simultaneously ignoring the benefits of self-criticism. It had failed to develop a theory of consciousness and thus had expelled the human subject from its own theoretical calculus. It is not surprising, then, that the focus of the Frankfurt School's research deemphasized the area of political economy to focus instead on the issues of how subjectivity was constituted and how the spheres of culture and everyday life represented a new terrain of domination. It is against this historical and theoretical landscape that we can begin to abstract categories and modes of analysis that speak to the nature of schooling as it presently exists, and to its inherent potential for developing into a force for social change.

Rationality and the Critique of Instrumental Reason

Fundamental to an understanding of the Frankfurt School's view of theory and of its critique of instrumental reason is its analysis of the heritage of Enlightenment rationality. Echoing Nietzsche's earlier warning about humanity's unbounded faith in reason, Adorno and Horkheimer voiced a trenchant critique of modernity's unswerving faith in the promise of Enlightenment rationality to rescue the world from the chains of superstition, ignorance, and suffering. The problematic nature of such a promise marks the opening lines of *Dialectic of Enlightenment:* "In the most general sense of progressive thought the Enlightenment has always aimed at liberating men from fear and establishing their sovereignty. Yet the fully enlightened earth radiates disaster triumphant" (Adorno & Horkheimer 1972).

Faith in scientific rationality and the principles of practical judgement did not constitute a legacy that developed exclusively in the seventeenth and eighteenth centuries, when people of reason united on a vast intellectual front in order to master the world through an appeal to the claims of reasoned thought. According to the Frankfurt School, the legacy of scientific rationality represented one of the central themes of Western thought and extended as far back as Plato (Horkheimer 1974). Habermas, a later member of the Frankfurt School, argues that the progressive notion of reason reaches its highest point and most complex expression in the work of Karl Marx, after which it is reduced from an all-encompassing concept of rationality to a particular instrument in the service of industrialized society. According to Habermas:

> On the level of the historical self-reflection of a science with critical intent, Marx for the last time identifies reason with a commitment to rationality in its thrust against dogmatism. In the second half of the nineteenth century, during the course of the reduction of science to a productive force in industrial society, positivism, historicism, and pragmatism, each in turn, isolate one part of this all-encompassing concept of rationality. The hitherto undisputed attempts of the great theories to reflect on the complex of life as a whole is henceforth itself discredited as dogma. . . . The spontaneity of hope, the art of taking a position, the experience of relevance or indifference, and above all, the response to suffering and oppression, the desire for adult autonomy, the will to emancipation, and the happiness of discovering one's identity—all these are dismissed for all time from the obligating interest of reason [Habermas 1973].

Marx may have employed reason in the name of critique and emancipation, but it was still a notion of reason limited to an overemphasis on the labor process and on the exchange rationality that was both its driving force and ultimate mystification. Adorno, Horkheimer, and Marcuse, in contrast to Marx, believed that "the fateful process of rationalization" (Wellmer 1974) had penetrated all aspects of everyday life, whether it be the mass media, the school, or the workplace. The crucial point here is that no social sphere was free from the encroachments of a form of reason in which "all theoretical means of transcending reality became metaphysical nonsense" (Horkheimer 1974).

In the Frankfurt School's view, reason has not been permanently stripped of its positive dimensions. Marcuse, for instance, believed that reason contained a critical element and was still capable of reconstituting history. As he put it, "Reason represents the highest potentiality of man and existence; the two belong together" (Marcuse 1968a). But if reason was to preserve its promise of creating a more just society, it would have to demonstrate powers of critique and negativity. According to Adorno (1973), the crisis of reason takes place as society becomes more rationalized; under such historical circumstances, in the quest for social harmony, it loses its critical faculty and becomes an instrument of the existing society. As a result, reason as insight and critique turns into its opposite—irrationality.

For the Frankfurt School, the crisis in reason is linked to the more general crises in science and in society as a whole. Horkheimer argued in 1972 that the starting point for understanding "the crisis of science depends on a correct theory of the present social situation." In essence, this speaks to two crucial aspects of Frankfurt School thought. First, it argues that the only solution to the present crisis lies in developing a more fully self-conscious notion of reason, one that embraces elements of critique as well as of human will and transformative action. Second, it means entrusting to theory the task of rescuing reason from the logic of technocratic rationality or positivism. It was the Frankfurt School's view that positivism had emerged as the final ideological expression of the Enlightenment. The victory of positivism represented not the high point but the low point of Enlightenment thought. Positivism became the enemy of reason rather than its agent, and emerged in the twentieth century as a new form of social administration and domination. Friedman sums up the essence of this position:

> To the Frankfurt School, philosophical and practical positivism constituted the end point of the Enlightenment. The social function of the ideology of positivism was to deny the critical faculty of reason by allowing it only the ground of utter facticity to operate upon. By so doing, they denied reason a critical moment. Reason, under the rule of positivism, stands in awe of the fact. Its function is simply to characterize the fact. Its task ends when it has affirmed and explicated the fact. . . . Under the rule of positivism, reason inevitably stops short of critique [Friedman 1981].

It is in its critique of positivistic thought that the Frankfurt School makes clear the specific mechanisms of ideological control that permeate the consciousness and practices of advanced capitalist societies. It is also in its critique of positivism that it develops a notion of theory that has major implications for educational critics. But the route to understanding this concept necessitates that one first analyze the Frankfurt School's critique of positivism, particularly since the logic of positivist thought (though in varied forms) represents the major theoretical impetus currently shaping educational theory and practice.

The Frankfurt School defined positivism, in the broad sense, as an amalgam of diverse traditions that included the work of Saint-Simon and

Comte, the logical positivism of the Vienna Circle, the early work of Wittgenstein, and the more recent forms of logical empiricism and pragmatism that dominate the social sciences in the West. While the history of these traditions is complex and cluttered with detours and qualifications, each of them has supported the goal of developing forms of social inquiry patterned after the natural sciences and based on the methodological tenets of sense observation and quantification. Marcuse provides both a general definition of positivism as well as a basis for some of the reservations of the Frankfurt School regarding its most basic assumptions:

> Since its first usage, probably in the school of Saint-Simon, the term "positivism" has encompassed (1) the validation of cognitive thought by experience of facts; (2) the orientation of cognitive thought to the physical science as a model of certainty and exactness; (3) the belief that progress in knowledge depends on this orientation. Consequently, positivism is a struggle against all metaphysics, transcendentalisms, and idealisms as obscurantist and regressive modes of thought. To the degree to which the given reality is scientifically comprehended and transformed, to the degree to which society becomes industrial and technological, positivism finds in the society the medium for the realization (and validation) of its concepts—harmony between theory and practice, truth and facts. Philosophic thought turns into affirmative thought; the philosophic critique criticizes within the societal framework and stigmatizes non-positive notions as mere speculation, dreams or fantasies [Marcuse 1964].

Positivism, according to Horkheimer, presented a view of knowledge and science that stripped both of their critical possibilities. Knowledge was reduced to the exclusive province of science, and science itself was subsumed within a methodology that limited "scientific activity to the description, classification, and generalization of phenomena, with no care to distinguish the unimportant from the essential" (Horkheimer 1972). Accompanying this view are the ideas that knowledge derives from sense experience and that the ideal it pursues takes place "in the form of a mathematically formulated universe deducible from the smallest possible number of axioms, a system which assures the calculation of the probable occurrence of all events" (ibid).

For the Frankfurt School, positivism did not represent an indictment of science; instead it echoed Nietzsche's insight that "It is not the victory of science that is the distinguishing mark of our nineteenth century, but the victory of the scientific method over science" (Nietzsche 1966). Science, in this perspective, was separated from the question of ends and ethics, which were rendered insignificant because they defied "explication in terms of mathematical structures" (Marcuse 1964). According to the Frankfurt School, the suppression of ethics in positivist rationality precludes the possibility for self-criticism, or, more specifically, for questioning its own normative structure. Facts become separated from values, objectivity undermines critique, and the notion that essence and appearance may not coincide is lost in the positivist view of the world. The latter point becomes particularly clear in the Vienna Circle pronouncement: "The view that thought is a means of knowing more about the world than may be directly observed . . . seems to us entirely mysterious" (Hahn 1933). For Adorno, the idea of value freedom was perfectly suited to a perspective that was to insist on a universal form of knowledge while simultaneously refusing to inquire into its own socio-ideological development and function in society.

According to the Frankfurt School, the outcome of positivist rationality and its technocratic view of science represented a threat to the notion of subjectivity and critical thinking. By functioning within an operational context free from ethical commitments, positivism wedded itself to the immediate and "celebrated" the world of "facts." The question of essence—the difference between the world as it is and as it could be—is reduced to the merely methodological task of collecting and classifying facts. In this schema, "Knowledge relates solely to what is, and to its recurrence" (Horkheimer 1972). Questions concerning the genesis, development, and normative nature of the conceptual systems that select, organize, and define the facts appear to be outside the concern of positivist rationality.

Since it recognizes no factors behind the "fact," positivism freezes both human beings and history. In the case of these, the issue of historical development is ignored since the historical dimension contains truths that cannot be assigned "to a special fact-gathering branch of science" (Adorno, quoted in Gross 1979). Of course, positivism is not impervious to history, or to the relationship between history and understanding, at any rate. On the contrary, its key notions of objectivity, theory, and values, as well as its modes of inquiry, are paradoxically a consequence of and a force in the shaping of history. In other words, positivism may ignore history but it cannot escape it. What is important to stress is that fundamental categories of socio-historical development are at odds with the positivist emphasis on the immediate, or more specifically with that which can be expressed, measured, and calculated in precise mathematical formulas. Russell Jacoby (1980) points concisely to this issue in his claim that "the natural reality and natural sciences do not know the fundamental historical categories: consciousness and self-consciousness, subjectivity and objectivity, appearance and essence."

By not reflecting on its paradigmatic premises, positivist thought ignores the value of historical consciousness and consequently endangers the nature of critical thinking itself. That is, inherent in the very structure of positivist thought, with its emphasis on objectivity and its lack of theoretical grounding with regard to the setting of tasks (Horkheimer 1972), are a number of assumptions that appear to preclude its ability to judge the complicated interaction of power, knowledge, and values and to reflect critically on the genesis and nature of its own ideological presuppositions. Moreover, by situating itself within a number of false dualisms (facts *vs.* values, scientific knowledge *vs.* norms, and description *vs.* prescription) positivism dissolves the tension between potentiality and actuality in all spheres of social existence. Thus, under the guise of neutrality, scientific knowledge and all theory become rational on the grounds of whether or not they are efficient, economic, or correct. In this case, a notion of methodological correctness subsumes and devalues the complex philosophical concept of truth. As Marcuse points out, "The fact that a judgement can be correct and nevertheless without truth, has been the crux of formal logic from time immemorial" (quoted in Arato & Gebhardt 1978).

For instance, an empirical study that concludes that native workers in a colonized country work at a slower rate than imported workers who perform the same job may provide an answer that is correct, but such an answer tells us little about the notion of domination or the resistance of workers under its sway. That the native workers may slow down their rate as an act of resistance is not considered here. Thus, the notions of intentionality and historical context are dissolved within the confines of a limiting quantifying methodology.

For Adorno, Marcuse, and Horkheimer, the fetishism of facts and the belief in value neutrality represented more than an epistemological error; more importantly, such a stance served as a form of ideological hegemony that infused positivist rationality with a political conservatism that made it an ideological prop of the status quo. This is not to suggest, however, an intentional support for the status quo on the part of all individuals who work within a positivist rationality. Instead, it implies a particular relationship to the status quo; in some situations this relationship is consciously political, in others it is not. In other words, in the latter instance the relationship to the status quo is a conservative one, but it is not self-consciously recognized by those who help to reproduce it.

A big problem when it comes to change

The Frankfurt School's Notion of Theory

According to the Frankfurt School, any understanding of the nature of theory has to begin with a grasp of the relationships that exist in society between the particular and the whole, the specific and the universal. This position appears in direct contradiction to the empiricist claim that theory is primarily a matter of classifying and arranging facts. In rejecting the absolutizing of facts, the Frankfurt School argued that in the relation between theory and the wider society mediations exist that give meaning not only to the constitutive nature of a fact but also to the very nature and substance of theoretical discourse. As Horkheimer writes, "The facts of science and science itself are but segments of the life process of society, and in order to understand the significance of facts or of science, generally one must possess the key to the historical situation, the right social theory" (Horkheimer 1972).

This speaks to a second constitutive element of critical theory. If theory is to move beyond the positivist legacy of neutrality, it must develop the capacity of meta-theory. That is, it must acknowledge the value-laden interests it represents and be able to reflect critically on both the historical development or genesis of such interests and the limitations they may present within certain historical and social contexts. In other words, "methodological correctness" does not provide a guarantee of truth, nor does it raise the fundamental question of why a theory functions in a given way under specific historical conditions to serve some interests and not others. Thus, a notion of self-criticism is essential to a critical theory.

A third constitutive element for a critical theory takes its cue from Nietzsche's dictum that "A great truth wants to be criticized, not idolized" (quoted in Arato & Gebhardt 1978). The Frankfurt School believed that the critical spirit of theory should be represented in its unmasking function. The driving force of such a function was to be found in the Frankfurt School's notions of immanent criticism and dialectical thought. Immanent critique is the assertion of difference, the refusal to collapse appearance and essence, the willingness to analyze the reality of the social object against its possibilities. As Adorno wrote:

> Theory . . . must transform the concepts which it brings, as it were, from outside into those which the object has of itself, into what the object, left to itself, seeks to be, and confront it with what it is. It must dissolve the rigidity of the temporally and spatially fixed object into a field of tension of the possible and the real: each one in order to exist, is dependent upon the other. In other words, theory is indisputably critical [Adorno et al. 1976].

Dialectical thought, on the other hand, speaks to both critique and theoretical reconstruction (Giroux 1981a). As a mode of critique, it uncovers values that are often negated by the social object under analysis. The notion of dialectics is crucial because it reveals "the insufficiencies and imperfections of 'finished' systems of thought. . . . It reveals incompleteness where completeness is claimed. It embraces that which is in terms of that which is not, and that which is real in terms of potentialities not yet realized" (Held 1980). As a mode of theoretical reconstruction, dialectical thought points to historical analysis in the critique of conformist logic, and traces out the "inner history" of the latter's categories and the way in which these are mediated within a specific historical context. By looking at the social and political constellations stored in the categories of any theory, Adorno (1973) believed their history could be traced and their existing limitations revealed. As such, dialectical thought reveals the power of human activity and human knowledge as both a product of and force in the shaping of social reality. But it does not do so to proclaim simply that humans give meaning to the world. Instead, as a form of critique, dialectical thought argues that there is a link between knowledge, power, and domination. Thus it is acknowledged that some knowledge is false, and that the ultimate purpose of critique should be critical thinking in the interest of social change. For instance, as I mentioned earlier, one can exercise critical thought and not fall into the ideological trap of relativism, in which the notion of critique is negated by the assumption that all ideas should be given equal weight. Marcuse points to the connection between thought and action in dialectical thought:

> Dialectical thought starts with the experience that the world is unfree; that is to say, man and nature exist in conditions of alienation, exist as "other than they are." Any mode of thought which excludes this

contradiction from its logic is faulty logic. Thought "corresponds" to reality only as it transforms reality by comprehending its contradictory structure. Here the principle of dialectic drives thought beyond the limits of philosophy. For to comprehend reality means to comprehend what things really are, and this in turn means rejecting their mere factuality. Rejection is the process of thought as well as of action. . . . Dialectical thought thus becomes negative in itself. Its function is to break down the self-assurance and self-contentment of common sense, to undermine the sinister confidence in the power and language of facts, to demonstrate that unfreedom is so much at the core of things that the development of their internal contradictions leads necessarily to qualitative change: the explosion and catastrophe of the established state of affairs [Marcuse 1960].

According to the Frankfurt School, all thought and theory are tied to a specific interest in the development of a society without injustice. Theory, in this case, becomes a transformative activity that views itself as explicitly political and commits itself to the projection of a future that is as yet unfulfilled. Thus, critical theory contains a transcendent element in which critical thought becomes the precondition for human freedom. Rather than proclaiming a positivist notion of neutrality, critical theory openly takes sides in the interest of struggling for a better world. In one of his most famous early essays comparing traditional and critical theory, Horkheimer spelled out the essential value of theory as a political endeavour:

> It is not just a research hypothesis which shows its value in the ongoing business of men; it is an essential element in the historical effort to create a world which satisfies the needs and powers of men. However extensive the interaction between the critical theory and the special sciences whose progress the theory must respect and on which it has for decades exercized a liberating and stimulating influence, the theory never aims simply at an increase of knowledge as such. Its goal is man's emancipation from slavery [Horkheimer 1972].

Finally, there is the question of the relationship between critical theory and empirical studies. In the ongoing debate over theory and empirical work, we recognize recycled versions of the same old dualisms in which one presupposes the exclusion of the other. One manifestation of this debate is the criticism that the Frankfurt School rejected the value of empirical work, a criticism that is also being lodged currently against many educational critics who have drawn upon the work of the Frankfurt

School. Both sets of criticisms appear to have missed the point. It is certainly true that for the Frankfurt School the issue of empirical work was a problematic one, but what was called into question was its universalization at the expense of a more comprehensive notion of rationality. In writing about his experiences as an American scholar, Adorno spelled out a view of empirical studies that was representative of the Frankfurt School in general:

> My own position in the controversy between empirical and theoretical sociology . . . I may sum up by saying that empirical investigations are not only legitimate but essential, even in the realm of cultural phenomena. But one must not confer autonomy upon them or regard them as a universal key. Above all they must terminate in theoretical knowledge. Theory is no mere vehicle that becomes superfluous as soon as data are in hand [Adorno 1969].

By insisting on the primacy of theoretical knowledge in the realm of empirical investigations, the Frankfurt School also wanted to highlight the limits of the positivist notion of experience, where research had to confine itself to controlled physical experiences that could be conducted by any researcher. Under such conditions, the research experience is limited to simple observation. As such, abstract methodology follows rules that preclude any understanding of the forces that shape both the object of analysis as well as the subject conducting the research. By contrast, a dialectical notion of society and theory would argue that observation cannot take the place of critical reflection and understanding. That is, one begins not with an observation but with a theoretical framework that situates the observation in rules and conventions that give it meaning while simultaneously acknowledging the limitations of such a perspective or framework. The Frankfurt School's position on the relation between theory and empirical studies thus helps to illuminate its view of theory and practice.

But a further qualification must be made here. While critical theory insists that theory and practice are interrelated, it nonetheless cautions against calling for a specious unity, for as Adorno points out:

> The call for the unity of theory and practice has irresistably degraded theory to the servant's role, removing the very traits it should have brought to that unity. The visa stamp of practice which we demand of all theory became a censor's place. Yet whereas theory succumbed in the vaunted mixture, practice became nonconceptual, a piece of the

politics it was supposed to lead out of; it became the prey of power [Adorno 1973].

Theory, in this case, should have as its goal emancipatory practice, but at the same time it requires a certain distance from such practice. Theory and practice represent a particular alliance, not a unity in which one dissolves into the other. The nature of such an alliance might be better understood by illuminating the drawbacks inherent in the traditional anti-theoretical stance in American education, in which it is argued that concrete experience is the great "teacher."

Experience, whether on the part of the researcher or others, contains no inherent guarantees to generate the insights necessary to make it transparent to the self. In other words, while it is indisputable that experience may provide us with knowledge, it is also indisputable that knowledge may distort rather than illuminate the nature of social reality. The point here is that the value of any experience "will depend not on the experience of the subject but on the struggles around the way that experience is interpreted and defined" (Bennet 1980b). Moreover, theory cannot be reduced to being perceived as the mistress of experience, empowered to provide recipes for pedagogical practice. Its real value lies in its ability to establish possibilities for reflexive thought and practice on the part of those who use it; in the case of teachers, it becomes invaluable as an instrument of critique and understanding. As a mode of critique and analysis, theory functions as a set of tools inextricably affected by the context in which it is brought to bear, but it is never reducible to that context. It has its own distance and purpose, its own element of practice. The crucial element in both its production and use is not the structure at which it is aimed, but the human agents who use it to give meaning to their lives.

In short, Adorno, Horkheimer, and Marcuse provided forms of historical and sociological analysis that pointed to the promise as well as to the limitations of the existing dominant rationality as it developed in the twentieth century. Such an analysis took as a starting-point the conviction that for self-conscious human beings to act collectively against the modes of technocratic rationality that permeated the workplace and other socio-cultural spheres, their behaviour would have to be preceded and mediated by a mode of critical analysis. In other words, the pre-condition for such action was a form of critical theory. But it is important to stress that in linking critical theory to the goals of social and political emancipation, the Frankfurt School redefined the very notion of rationality. Rationality was no longer merely the exercise of critical thought, as had been its earlier Enlightenment counterpart. Instead, rationality now became the nexus of thought and action in the interest of liberating the community or society as a whole. As a higher rationality, it contained a transcendent project in which individual freedom merged with social freedom.

The Frankfurt School's Analysis of Culture

Central to the Frankfurt School's critique of positivist rationality was its analysis of culture. Rejecting the definition and role of culture found in both traditional sociological accounts and orthodox Marxist theory, Adorno and Horkheimer (1972) were noteworthy in developing a view of culture that assigned it a key place in the development of historical experience and everyday life. On the other hand, the Frankfurt School rejected the mainstream sociological notion that culture existed in an autonomous fashion, unrelated to the political and economic life-processes of society. In their view, such a perspective neutralized culture and in so doing abstracted it from the historical and societal context that gave it meaning. For Adorno the conventional view was shot through with a contradiction that reduced culture to nothing more than a piece of ideological shorthand:

> [The conventional view of culture] overlooks what is decisive: the role of ideology in social conflicts. To suppose, if only methodologically, anything like an independent logic of culture is to collaborate in the hypostasis of culture, the ideological *proton pseudos*. The substance of culture . . . resides not in culture alone but in relation to something external, to the material life-process. Culture, as Marx observed of juridical and political systems, cannot be fully "understood either in terms of itself . . . or in terms of the so-called universal development of the mind." To ignore this . . . is to make ideology the basic matter and to establish it firmly [Adorno 1967a].

On the other hand, while orthodox Marxist theory established a relationship between culture and the material forces of society, it did so by reducing culture to a mere reflex of the economic realm. In this view, the primacy of economic forces and the logic of scientific laws took precedence over issues concerning the terrain of everyday life, consciousness, or sexuality (Aronowitz 1981a). For the Frankfurt School, changing socioeconomic conditions had made traditional Marxist categories of the 1930s and 1940s untenable. They were no longer adequate for understanding the integration of the working class in the West or the political effects of technocratic rationality in the cultural realm.

Within the Frankfurt School perspective the role of culture in Western society had been modified with the transformation of critical Enlightenment rationality into represssive forms of positivist rationality. As a result of the development of new technical capabilities, greater concentrations of economic power, and more sophisticated modes of administration, the rationality of domination increasingly expanded its influence to spheres outside of the locus of economic production. Under the sign of Taylorism and scientific management, instrumental rationality extended its influence from the domination of nature to the domination of human beings. As such, mass-cultural institutions such as schools took on a new role in the first half of the twentieth century as "both a determinant and fundamental component of social consciousness" (Aronowitz 1976). According to the Frankfurt School, this meant that the cultural realm now constitutes a central place in the production and transformation of historical experience. Like Gramsci (1971), Adorno and Horkheimer (1972) argued that domination has assumed a new form. Instead of being exercised primarily through the use of physical force (the army and police), the power of the ruling classes was now reproduced through a form of ideological hegemony; that is, it was established primarily through the rule of consent, and mediated via cultural institutions such as schools, family, mass media, churches, etc. Briefly put, the colonization of the workplace was now supplemented by the colonization of all other cultural spheres (Aronowitz 1973; Enzenberger 1974; Ewen 1976).

According to the Frankfurt School, culture, like everything else in capitalist society, had been turned into an object. Under the dual rationalities of administration and exchange the elements of critique and opposition, which the Frankfurt School believed inherent in traditional culture, had been lost. Moreover, the objectification of culture did not simply result in the repression of the critical elements in its form and content; such objectification also represented the negation of critical thought itself. In Adorno's words: ". . . Culture in the true sense did not simply accommodate itself to human beings; . . . it always simultaneously raised a protest against the petrified relations under which they lived, thereby honoring them. Insofar as culture becomes wholly assimilated to and integrated into those petrified relations, human beings are once more debased" (Adorno 1975).

As far as the Frankfurt School was concerned, the cultural realm had become a new locus of control for that aspect of Enlightenment rationality in which the domination of nature and society proceeded under the guise of technical progress and economic growth. For Adorno and Horkheimer (1972) culture had become another industry, one which not only produced goods but also legitimated the logic of capital and its institutions. The term "culture industry" was coined by Adorno as a response to the reification of culture, and it had two immediate purposes. First, it was coined in order to expose the notion that "culture arises spontaneously from the masses themselves" (Lowenthal 1979). Second, it pointed to the concentration of economic and political determinants that control the cultural sphere in the interest of social and political domination. The term "industry" in the metaphor provided a point of critical analysis. That is, it pointed not only to a concentration of political and economic groups who reproduced and legitimated the dominant belief and value system, it also referred to the mechanisms of rationalization and standardization as they permeated everyday life. In other words, "the expression 'industry' is not to be taken literally. It refers to the standardization of the thing itself—such as the Western, familiar to every movie-goer—and to the rationalization of distribution techniques . . . [and] not strictly to the production process" (Adorno 1975).

At the core of the theory of culture advanced by Horkheimer, Adorno, and Marcuse was an attempt to expose, through both a call for and demonstration of critique, how positivist rationality manifested itself in the cultural realm. For instance, they criticised certain cultural products such as art for excluding the principles of resistance and opposition that once informed their relationship with the world while simultaneously helping to expose it (Horkheimer 1972). Likewise, for Marcuse (1978), "the truth of art lies in its power to break the monopoly of established reality (i.e., of those who established it) to define what is real. In this rupture . . . the fictitious world of art appears as true reality." The Frankfurt School argued that in a one-dimensional society art collapses, rather than highlights, the distinction between reality and the possibility of a higher truth or better world. In other words, in the true spirit of positivist harmony, art becomes simply a mirror of the existing reality and an affirmation of it. Thus, both the memory of a historical truth or the image of a better way of life are rendered impotent in the ultra-realism of Warhol's Campbell-soup painting or the Stakhanovite paintings of socialist realism.

Dictates of positivist rationality and the attendant mutilation of the power of imagination are also embodied in the techniques and forms that shape the messages and discourse of the culture industry. Whether it be in the glut of interchangeable plots, gags, or stories, or in the rapid pace of the film's development, the logic of standardization reigns supreme. The message is conformity, and the medium for its attainment is amusement, which proudly packages itself as an escape from the necessity of critical thought. Under the sway of the culture industry, style subsumes substance and thought is banished from the temple of official culture. Marcuse states this argument superbly:

> By becoming components of the aesthetic form, words, sounds, shapes, and colors are insulated against their familiar, ordinary use and function; . . . This is the achievement of style, which *is* the poem, the novel, the painting, the composition. The style, embodiment of the aesthetic form, in subjecting reality to another order, subjects it to the laws of beauty. True and false, right and wrong, pain and pleasure, calm and violence become aesthetic categories within the framework of the oeuvre. Thus deprived of their [immediate] reality, they enter a different context in which even the ugly, cruel, sick become parts of the aesthetic harmony governing the whole [Marcuse 1972].

Inherent in the reduction of culture to amusement is a significant message which points to the root of the ethos of positivist rationality— the structural division between work and play. Within that division, work is confined to the imperatives of drudgery, boredom, and powerlessness for the vast majority; culture becomes the vehicle by which to escape from work. The power of the Frankfurt School's analysis lies in its exposure of the ideological fraud that constitutes this division of labor. Rather than being an escape from the mechanized work process, the cultural realm becomes an extension of it. Adorno and Horkheimer write:

> Amusement under late capitalism is the prolongation of work. It is sought-after as an escape from the mechanized work process, and to recruit strength in order to be able to cope with it again. But at the same time mechanization has such power over a man's leisure and happiness and so profoundly determines the manufacture of amusement goods, that his experiences are after-images of the work process itself. The ostensible content is merely a faded background; what sinks in is

an automatic succession of standardized operations [Adorno & Hork-heimer 1972].

The most radical critique of the division of labour among the three theorists under study finds its expression in the work of Herbert Marcuse (1955, 1968b). Marcuse (1968b) claims that Marxism has not been radical enough in its attempt to develop a new sensibility that would develop as "an instinctual barrier against cruelty, brutality, ugliness." Marcuse's (1955) point is that a new rationality taking as its goal the erotization of labour and "the development and fulfillment of human needs" would necessitate new relations of production and organizational structures under which work could take place. This should not suggest that Marcuse abandons all forms of authority or that he equates hierarchical relationships with the realm of domination. On the contrary, he argues that work and play can interpenetrate each other without the loss of either's primary character. As Agger points out:

> Marcuse is . . . saying that . . . work and play converge without abandoning the "work" character of work itself. He retains the rational organization of work without abandoning the Marxian goal of creative praxis. As he notes . . . "hierarchical relationships are not unfree per se." That is, it depends upon the kind of hierarchy which informs relationships. . . . Marcuse . . . suggests two things: in the first place, he hints at a theory of work which rests upon the merger of work and play components. His views in this regard are captured in his vision of the "erotization of labor." In the second place, Marcuse hints at a form of organizational rationality which is nondominating [Agger 1978].

According to Marcuse (1964) science and technology have been inte-grated under the imprint of a dominating rationality that has penetrated the world of communicative interaction (the public sphere) as well as the world of work. It is worth mentioning, by contrast, Habermas's (1973) argument that science and technology in the sphere of work are necessarily limited to technical considerations, and that the latter organization of work represents the price an advanced industrial order must pay for its material comfort. This position has been challenged by a number of theorists, including Aronowitz (1981), who astutely argues that Habermas separates "communications and normative judgments from the labor pro-cess" and thus "cede[s] to technological consciousness the entire sphere of rational purposive action (work)." In further opposition to Habermas,

Marcuse (1964) argues that radical change means more than simply the creation of conditions that foster critical thinking and communicative competence. Such change also entails the transformation of the labor process itself and the fusion of science and technology under the guise of a rationality stressing cooperation and self-management in the interest of democratic community and social freedom.

While there are significant differences among Adorno, Horkheimer, and Marcuse in their indictment of positivist rationality and in their respective notions about what constitutes an aesthetic or radical sensibility, their views converge on the existing repressiveness underlying positivist rationality and on the need for the development of a collective critical consciousness and sensibility that would embrace a discourse of opposition and non-identity as a precondition of human freedom. Thus, for them, criticism represents an indispensable element in the struggle for emancipation, and it is precisely in their call for criticism and a new sensibility that one finds an analysis of the nature of domination that contains invaluable insights for a theory of education. The analysis, in this case, includes the Frankfurt School's theory of depth psychology, to which I will now briefly turn.

The Frankfurt School's Analysis of Depth Psychology

As I have pointed out previously, the Frankfurt School faced a major contradiction in attempting to develop a critical tradition within Marxist theory. On the one hand, the historical legacy since Marx had witnessed increased material production and the continued conquest of nature in both the advanced industrial countries of the West and the countries of the socialist bloc as well. In both camps, it appeared that despite economic growth the objective conditions that promoted alienation had deepened. For example, in the West the production of goods and the ensuing commodity fetishism made a mockery of the concept of the Good Life, reducing it to the issue of purchasing power. In the socialist bloc, the centralization of political power led to political repression instead of political and economic freedom as had been promised. Yet in both cases the consciousness of the masses failed to keep pace with such conditions.

For the Frankfurt School it became clear that a theory of consciousness and depth psychology was needed to explain the subjective dimension of liberation and domination. Marx had provided the political and economic grammar of domination, but he relegated the psychic dimension to a secondary status, believing that it would follow any significant changes in the economic realm. Thus it was left to the Frankfurt School, especially Marcuse (1955, 1964, 1968b, 1970), to analyse the formal structure of consciousness in order to discover how a dehumanized society could continue to maintain its control over its inhabitants, and how it was possible that human beings could participate willingly at the level of everyday life in the reproduction of their own dehumanization and exploitation.[1] For answers, the Frankfurt School turned to a critical study of Freud.

For the Frankfurt School, Freud's metapsychology provided an important theoretical foundation for revealing the interplay between the individual and society. More specifically, the value of Freudian psychology in this case rested with its illumination of the antagonistic character of social reality. As a theoretician of contradictions, Freud provided a radical insight into the way in which society reproduced its powers both in and over the individual. As Jacoby puts it:

> Psychoanalysis shows its strength; it demystifies the claims to liberated values, sensitivities, emotions, by tracing them to a repressed psychic, social, and biological dimension. . . . It keeps to the pulse of the psychic underground. As such it is more capable of grasping the intensifying social unreason that the conformist psychologies repress and forget: the barbarism of civilization itself, the barely suppressed misery of the living, the madness that haunts society [Jacoby 1975].

The Frankfurt School theorists believed that it was only in an understanding of the dialectic between the individual and society that the depth and extent of domination as it existed both within and outside of the individual could be open to modification and transformation. Thus, for Adorno, Horkheimer, and Marcuse, Freud's emphasis on the constant struggle between the individual desire for instinctual gratification and the dynamics of social repression provided an indispensable clue to understanding the nature of society and the dynamics of psychic domination and liberation. Adorno points to this in the following comments:

> The only totality the student of society can presume to know is the antagonistic whole, and if he is to attain to totality at all, then only in contradiction. . . . The jarring elements that make up the individual, his "properties," are invariable moments of the social totality. He is, in the strict sense, a monad, representing the whole and its contradic-

tions, without however being at any time conscious of the whole
[Adorno 1967b].

To explore the depth of the conflict between the individual and society,
the Frankfurt School accepted with some major modifications most of
Freud's most radical assumptions. More specifically, Freud's theoretical
schema contained three important elements for developing a depth psychology. First, Freud provided a formal psychological structure for the
Frankfurt School theorists to work with. That is, the Freudian outline
of the structure of the psyche with its underlying struggle between Eros
(the life instinct), Thanatos (the death instinct), and the outside world
represented a key conception in the depth psychology developed by the
Frankfurt School.

Secondly, Freud's studies on psychopathology, particularly his sensitivity to humanity's capacity for self-destructiveness and his focus on the
loss of ego stability and the decline of the influence of the family in
contemporary society added significantly to the Frankfurt School analyses   *mastery*
of mass society and the rise of the authoritarian personality. For the
Frankfurt School, the growing concentration of power in capitalist society,
along with the pervasive intervention of the state in the affairs of everyday
life, had altered the dialectical role of the traditional family as both a
positive and negative site for identity formation. That is, the family had
traditionally provided, on the one hand, a sphere of warmth and protection
for its members, while, on the other hand, it also functioned as a repository
for social and sexual repression. But under the development of advanced
industrial capitalism, the dual function of the family was gradually giving
way, and it began to function exclusively as a site for social and cultural
reproduction.

Finally, by focusing on Freud's theory of instincts and metapsychology,
the Frankfurt School devised a theoretical framework for unraveling and
exposing the objective and psychological obstacles to social change. This
issue is important because it provides significant insights into how depth
psychology might be useful for developing a more comprehensive theory
of education. Since Adorno shared some major differences with both
Horkheimer and Marcuse regarding Freud's theory of instincts and his
view of the relationship between the individual and society, I will treat
their respective contributions separately.

Adorno (1968) was quick to point out that while Freud's denunciation
of "man's unfreedom" over-identified with a particular historical period

and thus "petrified into an anthropological constant," it did not seriously detract from his greatness as a theoretician of contradictions. That is, in spite of the limitations in Freudian theory, Adorno—and Horkheimer as well—firmly believed that psychoanalysis provided a strong theoretical bulwark against psychological and social theories that exalted the idea of the "integrated personality" and the "wonders" of social harmony. True to Adorno's (1968) view that "Every image of man is ideology except the negative one," Freud's work appeared to transcend its own shortcomings because at one level it personified the spirit of negation. Adorno (1967b, 1968) clearly exalted the negative and critical features of psychoanalysis and saw them as major theoretical weapons to be used against every form of identity theory. The goals of identity theory and revisionist psychology were both political and ideological in nature, and it was precisely through the use of Freud's metapsychology that they could be exposed as such. As Adorno put it:

> The goal of the well-integrated personality is objectionable because it expects the individual to establish an equilibrium between conflicting forces, which does not obtain in existing society. Nor should it, because these forces are not of equal moral merit. People are taught to forget the objective conflicts which necessarily repeat themselves in every individual instead of helped to grapple with them [Adorno 1968].

While it was clear to the Frankfurt School that psychoanalysis could not solve the problems of repression and authoritarianism, they believed that it did provide important insights into how "people become accomplices to their own subjugation" (Benjamin, J. 1977). Yet beneath the analyses put forth on psychoanalysis by Adorno (1967b, 1968, 1972, 1973) and Horkheimer (1972) there lurked a disturbing paradox: while both theorists went to great lengths to explain the dynamics of authoritarianism and psychological domination, they said very little about those formal aspects of consciousness that might provide a basis for resistance and rebellion. In other words, Horkheimer and Adorno, while recognizing that Freudian psychology registered a powerful criticism of existing society in exposing its antagonistic character, failed to extend this insight by locating in either individuals or social classes the psychological or political grounds for a self-conscious recognition of such contradictions and the ability of human agents to transform them. Consequently, they provided a view of Freudian psychology that consigned Freud to the ambiguous status of radical as well as prophet of gloom.

If Adorno and Horkheimer viewed Freud as a revolutionary pessimist, Marcuse (1955) read him as a revolutionary utopian. That is, though he accepts most of Freud's most controversial assumptions, his interpretation of them is both unique and provocative. In one sense, Marcuse's (1955, 1968a&b, 1970) analysis contained an original dialectical twist in that it pointed to a utopian integration of Marx and Freud. Marcuse (1955) accepted Freud's view of the antagonistic relations between the individual and society as a fundamental insight, but he nevertheless altered some of Freud's basic categories, and in doing so situated Freud's pessimism within a historical context that revealed its strengths as well as limitations. In doing so, Marcuse was able to illuminate the importance of Freud's metapsychology as a basis for social change. This becomes particularly clear if we examine how Marcuse (1955, 1968a&b, 1970) reworked Freud's basic claims regarding the life and death instincts, the struggle between the individual and society, the relationship between scarcity and social repression, and, finally, the issues of freedom and human emancipation.

Marcuse (1955, 1964) begins with the basic assumption that inherent in Freud's theory of the unconscious and his theory of the instincts could be found the theoretical elements for a more comprehensive view of the nature of individual and social domination. Marcuse points to this possibility when he writes:

> The struggle against freedom reproduces itself in the psyche of man as the self-repression of the repressed individual, and his self-repression in turn sustains his masters and their institutions. It is this mental dynamic which Freud unfolds as the dynamic of civilization. . . . Freud's metapsychology is an ever-renewed attempt to uncover, and to question, the terrible necessity of the inner connection between civilization and barbarism, progress and suffering, freedom and unhappiness—a connection which reveals itself ultimately as that between Eros and Thanatos [Marcuse 1955].

For Marcuse (1955, 1970) Freudian psychology, as a result of its analysis of the relationship between civilization and instinctual repression, posited the theoretical basis for understanding the distinction between socially necessary authority and authoritarianism. That is, in the interplay between the need for social labor and the equally important need for the sublimation of sexual energy, the dynamic connection between domination and freedom, on the one hand, and authority and authoritarianism, on the other, starts to become discernible. Freud presented the conflict between the individual's instinctual need for pleasure and the society's demand for repression as an insoluble problem rooted in a trans-historical struggle; as a result, he pointed to the continuing repressive transformation of Eros in society, along with the growing propensity for self destruction. Marcuse (1970) believed that the "Freudian conception of the relationship between civilization and the dynamics of the instincts [was] in need of a decisive correction." That is, whereas Freud (1949) saw the increased necessity for social and instinctual repression, Marcuse (1955, 1970) argued that any understanding of social repression had to be situated within a specific historical context and judged as to whether such systems of domination exceeded their bounds. To ignore such a distinction was to forfeit the possibility of analyzing the difference between the exercise of legitimate authority and illegitimate forms of domination. Marcuse (1955) deemed that Freud had failed to capture in his analyses the historical dynamic of organized domination, and thus had given to it the status and dignity of a biological development that was universal rather than merely historically contingent.

While Marcuse (1955) accepts the Freudian notion that the central conflict in society is between the reality principle and the pleasure principle, he rejects the position that the latter had to adjust to the former. In other words, Freud believed that "the price of civilization is paid for in forfeiting happiness through heightening of the sense of guilt" (Freud 1949). This is important because at the core of Freud's notion that humanity was forever condemned to diverting pleasure and sexual energy into alienating labor was an appeal to a trans-historical "truth": that scarcity was inevitable in society, and that labor was inherently alienating. In opposition to Freud, Marcuse argued that the reality principle referred to a particular form of historical existence when scarcity legitimately dictated instinctual repression. But in the contemporary period such conditions had been superceded, and as such abundance, not scarcity, characterized or informed the reality principle governing the advanced industrial countries of the West.

In order to add a more fully historical dimension to Freud's analysis, Marcuse (1955) introduced the concepts of the performance principle and of surplus-repression. By arguing that scarcity was not a universal aspect of the human condition, Marcuse (1955, 1970) claimed that the moment had arrived in the industrial West when it was no longer necessary to submit men and women to the demands of alienating labor. The existing reality principle, which Marcuse (1955) labeled the performance principle, had outstripped its historical function, i.e., the sublimation of Eros in the interest of socially necessary labor. The performance principle, with its emphasis on technocratic reason and exchange rationality, was, in Marcuse's (1955) terms, both historically contingent and socially repressive. As a relatively new mode of domination, it tied people to values, ideas, and social practices that blocked their possibilities for gratification and happiness as ends in themselves.

In short, Marcuse (1955) believed that inherent in Marx's view of societal abundance and in Freud's theory of instincts was the basis for a new performance principle, one that was governed by principles of socially necessary labor and by those aspects of the pleasure principle that integrated work, play, and sexuality. This leads us to Marcuse's second important idea, the concept of surplus-repression. The excessiveness of the existing nature of domination could be measured through what Marcuse labeled as surplus-repression. Distinguishing this from socially useful repression, Marcuse claims that:

> Within the total structure of the repressed personality, surplus-repression is that portion which is the result of specific societal conditions sustained in the specific act of domination. The extent of this surplus-repression provides the standard of measurement: the smaller it is, the less repressive is the stage of civilization. The distinction is equivalent to that between the biological and the historical sources of human suffering [Marcuse 1955].

According to Marcuse (1955, 1970), it is within this dialectical interplay of the personality structure and historically conditioned repression that the nexus exists for uncovering the historical and contemporary nature of domination. Domination in this sense is doubly historical: first, it is rooted in the historically developed socio-economic conditions of a given society; further, it is rooted in the sedimented history or personality structure of individuals. In speaking of domination as a psychological as well as a political phenomenon, Marcuse did not give a *carte blanche* to wholesale gratification. On the contrary, he agreed with Freud that some forms of repression were generally necessary. What he objected to was the unnecessary repression that was embodied in the ethos and social practices that characterized social institutions like school, the workplace, and the family.

For Marcuse (1964), the most penetrating marks of social repression are generated in the inner history of individuals, in the "needs, satisfactions, and values which reproduce the servitude of human existence." Such needs are mediated and reinforced through the patterns and social routines of everyday life, and the "false" needs that perpetuate toil, misery, and aggressiveness become anchored in the personality structure as second nature; that is, their historical character is forgotten, and they become reduced to patterns of habit.

In the end, Marcuse (1955) grounds even Freud's important notion of the death instinct (the autonomous drive that increasingly leads to self-destruction) in a radical problematic. That is, by claiming that the primary drive of humanity is pleasure, Marcuse redefines the death instinct by arguing that it is mediated not by the need for self-destruction—although this is a form it may take—but by the need to resolve tension. Rooted in such a perspective, the death instinct is not only redefined, it is also politicized as Marcuse argues that in a non-repressive society it would be subordinated to the demands of Eros. Thus, Marcuse (1955, 1964) ends up supporting the Frankfurt School's notion of negative thinking, but with an important qualification. He insists on its value as a mode of critique, but maintains equally that it is grounded in socio-economic conditions that can be transformed. It is the promise of a better future, rather than despair over the existing nature of society, that informs both Marcuse's work and its possibilities as a mode of critique for educators.

Towards a Critical Theory of Education

While it is impossible to elaborate in any detail on the implications of the work of the Frankfurt School for a theory of radical pedagogy, I can point briefly to some general considerations. I believe that it is clear that the thought of the Frankfurt School provides a major challenge and a stimulus to educational theorists who are critical of theories of education tied to functionalist paradigms based on assumptions drawn from a positivist rationality. For instance, against the positivist spirit that infuses existing educational theory and practice, whether it takes the form of the Tyler model or various systems approaches, the Frankfurt School offers an historical analysis and a penetrating philosophical framework that indict the wider culture of positivism, while at the same time providing insight into how the latter becomes incorporated within the ethos and practices of schools. Though there is a growing body of educational literature that is critical of positivist rationality in schools, it lacks the theoretical sophistication characteristic of the work of Horkheimer, Adorno, and Marcuse. Similarly, the importance of historical consciousness as a fundamental dimension of critical thinking in the Frankfurt School perspective creates a valuable epistemological terrain upon which to develop modes of critique that illuminate the interaction of the social and the personal as well as of history and private experience. Through this form of analysis, dialectical thought replaces positivist forms of social inquiry. That is, the logic of predictability, verifiability, transferability, and operationalism is replaced by a dialectical mode of thinking that stresses the historical, relational, and normative dimensions of social inquiry and knowledge. The notion of dialectical thinking as critical thinking, and its implications for pedagogy, become somewhat clear in Jameson's comment that "[D]ialectical thinking is . . . thought about thinking itself, in which the mind must deal with its own thought process just as much as with the material it works on, in which both the particular content involved and the style of thinking suited to it must be held together in the mind at the same time" (Jameson 1971).

What we get here are hints of what a radical view of knowledge might look like. In this case, it would be knowledge that would instruct the oppressed about their situation as a group situated within specific relations of domination and subordination. It would be knowledge that would illuminate how the oppressed could develop a discourse free from the distortions of their own partly mangled cultural inheritance. On the other hand, it would be a form of knowledge that instructed the oppressed in how to appropriate the most progressive dimensions of their own cultural histories, as well as how to restructure and appropriate the most radical aspects of bourgeois culture. Finally, such knowledge would have to provide a motivational connection to action itself; it would have to link a radical decoding of history to a vision of the future that not only exploded the reifications of the existing society, but also reached into those pockets of desires and needs that harbored a longing for a new society and new forms of social relations. It is at this point that the link between history, culture, and psychology becomes important.

It is with regard to the above that the notion of historical understanding in the work of the Frankfurt School makes some important contributions to the notion of radical pedagogy. History, for Adorno and others connected with critical theory, had a two-fold meaning and could not be interpreted as continuous pattern unfolding under the imperatives of "natural" laws. On the contrary, it had to be viewed as an emerging open-ended phenomenon, the significance of which was to be gleaned in the cracks and tensions that separated individuals and social classes from the imperatives of the dominant society. In other words, there were no laws of history that prefigured human progress, that functioned independently of human action. Moreover, history became meaningful not because it provided the present with the fruits of "interesting" or "stimulating" culture, but because it became the present object of analyses aimed at illuminating the revolutionary possibilities that existed in the given society. For the radical educator, this suggests using history in order "to fight against the spirit of the times rather than join it, to look backward at history rather than 'forward' " (Buck-Morss 1977). To put it another way, it meant, as Benjamin claimed "to brush history against the grain" (Benjamin 1974).

Not only does such a position link historical analysis to the notions of critique and emancipation, it also politicizes the notion of knowledge. That is, it argues for looking at knowledge critically, within constellations of suppressed insights (dialectical images) that point to the ways in which historically repressed cultures and struggles could be used to illuminate radical potentialities in the present. Knowledge in this instance becomes an object of analysis in a two-fold sense. On the one hand, it is examined for its social function, the way in which it legitimates the existing society. At the same time it could also be examined to reveal in its arrangement, words, structure, and style those unintentional truths that might contain "fleeting images" of a different society, more radical practices, and new forms of understanding. For instance, almost every cultural text contains a combination of ideological and utopian moments. Inherent in the most overt messages that characterize mass culture are elements of its antithesis. All cultural artifacts have a hidden referent that speaks to the initial basis for repression. Against the image of the barely clad female model selling the new automobile is the latent tension of misplaced and misappropriated sexual desire. Within the most authoritative modes of classroom discipline and control are fleeting images of freedom that speak to very different relationships. It is this dialectical aspect of knowledge that needs to be developed as part of a radical pedagogy.

Unlike traditional and liberal accounts of schooling, with their emphasis on historical continuities and historical development, critical theory points educators toward a mode of analysis that stresses the breaks, discontinuities, and tensions in history, all of which become valuable in that they highlight the centrality of human agency and struggle while simultaneously revealing the gap between society as it presently exists and society as it might be.

The Frankfurt School's theory of culture also offers new concepts and categories for analysing the role that schools play as agents of social and cultural reproduction. By illuminating the relationship between power and culture, the Frankfurt School provides a perspective on the way in which dominant ideologies are constituted and mediated via specific cultural formations. The concept of culture in this view exists in a particular relationship to the material base of society. The explanatory value of such a relationship is to be found in making problematic the specific content of a culture, its relationship to dominant and subordinate groups, as well as the socio-historical genesis of the ethos and practices of legitimating cultures and their role in constituting relations of domination and resistance. For example, by pointing to schools as cultural sites that embody conflicting political values, histories, and practices, it becomes possible to investigate how schools can be analyzed as an expression of the wider organization of society. Marcuse's (1964) study of the ideological nature of language, Adorno's (1975) analysis of the sociology of music, Horkheimer's (1972) method of dialectical critique and W. Benjamin's (1969, 1977) theory of cognition, all provide a number of valuable theoretical constructs through which to investigate the socially produced nature of knowledge and school experience.

The centrality of culture in the work of the Frankfurt School theorists (despite the differing opinions among its members) points to a number of important insights that illuminate how subjectivities get constituted both within and outside of schools. Though their analysis of culture is somewhat undialectical and clearly underdeveloped, it does provide a foundation for a greater elaboration and understanding of the relationship between culture and power, while simultaneously recognizing the latter as important terrain upon which to analyze the nature of domination and of resistance. By urging an attentiveness to the suppressed moments of history, critical theory points to the need to develop an equal sensitivity to certain aspects of culture. For example, working-class students, women, Blacks, and others need to affirm their own histories through the use of a language, a set of social relations, and body of knowledge that critically reconstructs and dignifies the cultural experiences that make up the tissue, texture, and history of their daily lives. This is no small matter, since once the affirmative nature of such a pedagogy is established, it becomes possible for students who have been traditionally voiceless in schools to learn the skills, knowledge, and modes of inquiry that will allow them to critically examine the role society has played in their own self-formation. More specifically, they will have the tools to examine how this society has functioned to shape and thwart their aspirations and goals, or prevented them from even imagining a life outside the one they presently lead. Thus it is important that students come to grips with what a given society has made of them, how it has incorporated them ideologically and materially into its rules and logic, and what it is that they need to affirm and reject in their own histories in order to begin the process of struggling for the conditions that will give them opportunities to lead a self-managed existence.

While it is true that Adorno, Marcuse, and Horkheimer placed heavy emphasis on the notion of domination in their analyses of culture, and in fact appeared to equate mass culture with mass manipulation, the value of their analyses rests with the mode of critique they developed in their attempt to reconstruct the notion of culture as a political force, as a powerful political moment in the process of domination. There is a paradox in their analyses of culture and human agency—that is, a paradox emerged in their emphasis on the overwhelming and one-sided nature of mass culture as a dominating force, on the one hand, and their relentless insistence on the need for critique, negativity, and critical mediation on the other. It is within this seeming contradiction that more dialectical notions of power and resistance have to be developed, positions that recognize wider structural and ideological determinations while recognizing that human beings never represent simply a reflex of such constraints. Human beings not only make history, they also make the constraints; and needless to say, they also unmake them. It needs to be remembered that power is both an enabling as well as a constraining force, as Foucault (1980) is quick to point out.

It must be stressed that the ideological justification of the given social order is not to be found simply in modes of interpretation that view history as a "natural" evolving process, or in the ideologies distributed through the culture industry. It is also found in the material reality of those needs and wants that bear the inscription of history. That is, history is to be found as "second nature" in those concepts and views of the world that make the most dominating aspects of the social order appear to be immune from historical socio-political development. Those aspects of reality that rest on an appeal to the universal and invariant often slip from historical consciousness and become embedded within those historically specific needs and desires that link individuals to the logics of conformity and domination. There is a certain irony in the fact that the personal and political join in the structure of domination precisely at those moments where history functions to tie individuals to a set of assumptions and practices that deny the historical nature of the political. "Second nature" represents history that has hardened into a form of social amnesia (Jacoby 1975), a mode of consciousness that "forgets" its own development. The significance of this perspective for radical pedagogy is that it points to the value of a depth psychology that can unravel how the mechanisms of domination and the possible seeds of liberation reach into the very structure of the human psyche. Radical pedagogy is much too cognitive in its orientation, and it needs to develop a theory of domination that incorporates needs and wants. Radical pedagogy lacks a depth psychology as well as appreciation for a sensibility that points to the importance of the sensual and imaginative as central dimensions of the schooling experience. The Frankfurt School's notion of depth psychology, especially Marcuse's work, opens up new terrain for developing a critical pedagogy. It speaks to the need to fashion new categories of analysis that will enable educators to become more knowledgeable about how teachers, students, and other educational workers become part of the system of social and cultural reproduction, particularly as it works through the messages and values that are constituted via the social practices of the hidden curriculum (Giroux 1981c). By acknowledging the need for a critical social psychology, educators can begin to identify how ideologies get constituted, and they can then identify and reconstruct social practices and processes that break rather than continue existing forms of social and psychological domination.

The relevance of Marcuse's analysis of depth psychology for educational theory becomes obvious in the more recent work of Pierre Bourdieu (1977a, 1977b). Bourdieu argues that the school and other social institutions legitimate and reinforce through specific sets of practices and discourses class-based systems of behavior and dispositions that reproduce the existing dominant society. Bourdieu extends Marcuse's insights by pointing to a notion of learning in which a child internalizes the cultural messages of the school not only via the latter's official discourse (symbolic mastery), but also through the messages embodied in the "insignificant" practices of daily classroom life. Bourdieu (1977b) is worth quoting at length on this issue:

> [Schools] . . . set such a store on the seemingly most insignificant details of dress, bearing, physical and verbal manners. . . . The prin-

ciples embodied in this way are placed beyond the grasp of consciousness, and hence cannot be touched by voluntary, deliberate transformation,
cannot even be made explicit. . . . The whole trick of pedagogic reason
lies precisely in the way it extorts the essential while seeming to demand
the insignificant: in obtaining respect for forms and forms of respect
which constitute the most visible and at the same time the best hidden
manifestations to the established order [Bourdieu 1977b].

Unlike Bourdieu, Marcuse believes that historically conditioned needs
that function in the interest of domination can be changed. That is, in
Marcuse's view (1955) any viable form of political action must begin with
a notion of political education in which a new language, qualitatively
different social relations, and a new set of values would have to operate
with the purpose of creating a new environment "in which the non-
aggressive, erotic, receptive faculties of man, in harmony with the consciousness of freedom, strive for the pacification of man and nature."
(Marcuse 1969). Thus the notion of depth psychology developed by the
Frankfurt School not only provides new insights into how subjectivities
are formed or how ideology functions as lived experience, it also provides
theoretical tools to establish the conditions for new needs, new systems
of values, and new social practices that take seriously the imperatives of
a critical pedagogy.

Conclusion

In conclusion, I have attempted to present selected aspects of the work
of critical theorists such as Adorno, Horkheimer, and Marcuse that provide
theoretical insights for developing a critical theory of education. Specifically, I have focused on their critique of positivist rationality, their view
of theory, their critical reconstruction of a theory of culture, and, finally,
on their analysis of depth psychology. It is within the context of these
four areas that radical educators can begin the task of reconstructing and
applying the insights of critical theory to schooling. Of course, the task
of translating the work of the Frankfurt School into terms that inform
and enrich radical educational theory and practice will be difficult. This
is especially true since any attempt to use such work will have to begin
with the understanding that it contains a number of shortcomings and
moreover cannot be imposed in grid-like fashion onto a theory of radical
pedagogy. For example, the critical theorists I have discussed did not

develop a comprehensive theoretical approach for dealing with the patterns of conflict and contradictions that existed in various cultural spheres. To the contrary, they developed an unsatisfactory notion of domination and an exaggerated view of the integrated nature of the American public; they constantly underestimated the radical potential inherent in working-class culture; and they never developed an adequate theory of social consciousness. That is, in spite of their insistence, on the importance of the notion of mediation, they never explored the contradictory modes of thinking that characterize the way most people view the world. Of course, the latter selection does not exhaust the list of criticisms that could be made against the work of the critical theorists under analysis here. The point is that critical theory needs to be reformulated to provide the opportunity to both critique and elaborate its insights beyond the constraints and historical conditions under which they were first generated. It must be stressed that the insights critical theory has provided have not been exhausted. In fact, one may argue that we are just beginning to work out the implications of their analyses. The real issue is to reformulate the central contributions of critical theory in terms of new historical conditions, without sacrificing the emancipatory spirit that generated them.

2

Schooling & the Politics
of the Hidden Curriculum

In the previous chapter, I argued that the foundation for a critical pedagogy could, in part, be located in the categories of social and cultural
critique found in the work of theorists such as Adorno, Horkheimer, and
Marcuse. The need for such a critical discourse is evident in the various
debates that have emerged in the last fifteen years around the notion of
the hidden curriculum. That is, the debates on the hidden curriculum
have been important not only because they point to aspects of school life
that link schools to the wider society, but also because they have pointed
to the need to generate a new set of categories in which to analyze the
function and mechanisms of schooling. But as important as the debates
on the hidden curriculum have been in helping us to understand the
nature of schooling, it appears that such debates have reached their theoretical limits. In other words, if the concept of the hidden curriculum
is to continue to serve as a valuable theoretical tool for radical educators,
it will have to be resituated in a more critical discourse and become more
attentive to the mode of critique and social theory developed by the
Frankfurt School. Such a task will be difficult, but is imperative that it
42   be accomplished in order to develop a foundation for critical pedagogy.

Some of the issues involved in such a task can be gleaned in an examination of the specific debates that have emerged around the concept of the hidden curriculum.

In the last few years, the character of the discourse on schooling has been considerably transformed. In the face of financial cutbacks, economic recession, and a shrinking job market, progressive and radical critiques of schooling have been reduced to a whisper, being replaced by the rhetoric of cost-efficiency experts. Administrators and teachers now spend long hours developing curriculum models based on the rather narrow principles of control, prediction, and measurement. The pedagogy of critical inquiry and ethical understanding has given way to the logic of instrumental reason, with its directed focus on the learning of discrete competencies and basic skills. Moreover, in the wake of these changes political issues are translated into technical problems, and the imperatives of critique and negation give way to a mode of thinking in which "basic human dilemmas are transformed into puzzles for which supposedly easy answers can be found"(Apple 1979).

Within this grim predicament, the ideological and material forces that link schools to the dominant industrial order no longer appear to be constrained by the principles of social justice that informed liberal pedagogy in the 1960s and 1970s. During that period, educational reformers were at least able to speak with some impact in arguing that our youth "ought to be educated not for the present but for a better future condition of the human race, that is for the idea of humanity" (Marcuse 1972). Now, important business spokespersons such as William Simon and David Packard urge major corporations to provide financial aid to unversities and colleges, not on the basis of their academic reputations, but instead on the basis of whether "schools, departments, institutes or faculties are sympathetic to the free enterprise system" (Vogel 1979). Similarly, the increasing industrialization of schooling is obvious in the recent efforts of major corporations to establish endowed Chairs of Free Enterprise in a number of major universities throughout the United States. The disregard that these efforts display for the conditions that safeguard academic freedom is matched only by the messianic fervor of their intent to spread the beliefs and values of the business community. For example, the conservative apologists who argue that schools at all levels of instruction have a deep-seated responsibility to train certain students with "blue-collar virtues." James O'Toole writes:

> Because of the American school system's commitment to mobility and equality, there is now a shortage of working class people, individuals socialized for an environment of bureaucratic and hierarchical control and of strict discipline. Employers are correct in their observations that schools are failing to provide enough men and women who are passively compliant, who seek only extrinsic rewards for their labors, and who have the stamina and stoicism to cope with the work technologies and processes developed during the industrial revolution [O'Toole 1977].

The preceding analysis is not meant to suggest that we should throw up our hands and retreat into passive cynicism. Nor is it meant to suggest that there is a certain inevitability to the course of events in which educators and students currently find themselves. It is instructive to remember that the underlying instrumental logic that infuses educational theory and practice at the present time is not new. It has simply been recycled and repackaged to meet the needs of the existing political and economic crisis. For example, the technological and behaviorist models that have long exercised a powerful influence on the curriculum field were, in part, adapted from the scientific management movement of the 1920s, just as the roots of the competency-based education movement were developed in earlier research work adapted "from the systems engineering procedures of the defense industry" (Franklin 1976).

The issue here is that the current withdrawal of resources from the schools and the redefinition of the curriculum in watered-down pragmatic and instrumental terms cannot be viewed-as problems *solely* due to demographic shifts in the population and short-term recessional tendencies in the economy. Such a position not only abstracts the current crisis from its historical and political roots, it also uses the existing economic crisis to legitimate conservative modes of pedagogy and to silence potential critics. In fact, the ahistorical character of the current criticism represents a form of ideological shorthand that makes it a part of the very problem it claims to resolve. By divorcing itself from historical and political discourse, such criticism shapes the conditions under which it sustains itself.

I want to argue that a more viable approach for developing a theory of classroom practice will have to be based on a theoretical foundation that acknowledges the dialectical interplay of social interest, political power, and economic power on the one hand, and school knowledge and practices on the other. The starting point for such an approach is the tradition of educational critique that emerged around the issue of schooling and the hidden curriculum during the late 1960s and early 1970s. In essence, I want to try to take seriously Walter Benjamin's prophetic warning that "In every era the attempt must be made to wrest tradition away from a conformism that is about to overcome it" (Benjamin 1973).

I do not wish to suggest that a new mode of educational theorizing can be developed entirely from earlier debates surrounding the covert and overt role of schooling, but to argue instead that these debates generated only a number of partial insights, which now need to be abstracted from their original frameworks and developed into a more comprehensive analysis of the schooling process. The earlier debates performed the creditable task of undermining the mainstream assumptions that school curriculum was socially and politically neutral and reducible to the engineering of discrete behaviors. While these insights led to a variety of markedly different conclusions, the general significance of this mode of analysis was that schools were now seen as agencies of socialization. Moreover, it was generally agreed that education meant more than providing students with instructional goals and objectives, and that schools did more than teach students how "to read, write, compute, and master the content of such subjects as history, social studies, and science" (Mehan 1980). Schools came to be seen as social sites with a dual curriculum—one overt and formal, the other hidden and informal. The nature of school pedagogy was to be found not only in the stated purposes of school rationales and teacher-prepared objectives but also in the myriad beliefs and values transmitted tacitly through the social relations and routines that characterized day-to-day school experience.

As a whole, such concerns with the hidden curriculum provided a more productive starting point for grappling with the fundamental question of what schools actually do than either earlier mainstream modes of theorizing or many current technocratic educational perspectives. By developing a new attentiveness to the linkages between schools and the social, economic, and political landscape that make up the wider society, the hidden curriculum theorists provided a theoretical impetus for breaking out of the methodological quagmire in which schools were merely viewed as black boxes (Karabel & Halsey 1977). The black-box paradigm had allowed educational researchers to ignore the concrete experiences of both teachers and students in favor of larger structural analyses concerned primarily with school achievement and input-output studies of social distribution (Mehan 1979; Wexler 1977). A major benefit deriving from the work on the hidden curriculum was that schools were now seen as political institutions, inextricably linked to issues of power and control in the dominant society. Questions about efficiency and smoothness of operation were, in part, supplemented with inquiries about the way in which the schools mediate and legitimate the social and cultural reproduction of class, racial, and gender relations in the dominant society (Giroux & Penna 1979).

While there was and continues to be considerable disagreement over the function of schooling, earlier hidden curriculum theorists generally agreed that schools processed not only knowledge but people as well. Consequently, to extend a previous point, schools were now seen not only as social sites that controlled meanings, but also as cultural sites that contributed to the formation of personality needs. While it may strike some as commonplace to acknowledge that schools mediate between society and the consciousness of individuals, analyses regarding the purpose, nature, and consequence of such socialization are myriad and complex. Underlying these analyses is the fundamental theoretical task of unraveling the distinctions between what have been termed ideologies *about* schools and ideologies *in* schools. The first of these refers to particular expressed "versions of what schools are for, of how they work, and of what it is possible for them to achieve" (Whitty, 1981). The second refers to dispositions, structure and modes of knowledge, pedagogic relationships, and the informal culture that make up the daily character of the school itself.

Out of this concern over the inherent ideological tensions that mediate between the discourse about schooling and the reality of school practices, three important insights have emerged that are essential to a more comprehensive understanding of the schooling process:
1. Schools cannot be analyzed as institutions removed from the socioeconomic context in which they're situated.
2. Schools are political sites involved in the construction and control of discourse, meaning, and subjectivities.
3. The commonsense values and beliefs that guide and structure classroom practice are not *a priori* universals, but social constructions based on specific normative and political assumptions.

I will look at these insights from a number of theoretical perspectives and attempt to illuminate both their shortcomings and strengths, before assessing the implications we can draw from them regarding classroom practice. The main assumption guiding my own analysis is that the previous work on the hidden curriculum is either too functional or too pessimistic, and that such work needs to be critically engaged and re-defined.

Perspectives on the Hidden Curriculum

Though the concept of the hidden curriculum has received strikingly conflicting definitions and analyses in the last decade, the definitional thread that runs through all of these analyses defines the hidden curriculum as those unstated norms, values, and beliefs embedded in and transmitted to students through the underlying rules that structure the routines and social relationships in school and classroom life. Elizabeth Vallance expresses a representative definition when she writes, "I use the term to refer to those non-academic but educationally significant consequences of schooling that occur systematically but are not made explicit at any level of the public rationales for education. . . It refers broadly to the social control function of schooling" (Vallance 1973).

I want to argue that analyses of the hidden curriculum gain some theoretical mileage only when they move from description to critique. That is, rather than concern themselves merely with an investigation of the social meaning "behind schools being schools" (Apple 1977), they owe themselves the task of analyzing how the hidden curriculum functions not simply as a vehicle of socialization but also as an agency of social control, one that functions to provide differential forms of schooling to different classes of students. Unfortunately, descriptions of the hidden curriculum greatly outnumber concrete critical analyses of its mechanisms and consequences. This is not to suggest that the latter distinction can be merely reduced to either intellectual style or disagreement. What are at stake in the divergent styles and modes of analyses that make up the literature on the hidden curriculum are deep-seated philosophical and ideological perspectives that clash over the very meaning and nature of social reality. These perspectives represent divergent world views acting as historical and social facts. The usefulness of understanding these perspectives as philosophical systems derives not only from the obvious necessity of identifying them as specific "totalities of ways of thinking, feeling, and acting" (Goldman 1980), but also as belief systems to be examined critically against the reality they are trying to portray and explain. Consequently, before the concept of the hidden curriculum can be used as a theoretical tool for developing a critical pedagogy, it is important to understand and critique the ideological assumptions embedded in the perspectives under study.

I have distinguished three basic approaches that characterize the work dealing directly with the hidden curriculum. These approaches can be roughly construed under categories of traditional, liberal, and radical. These are, of course ideal-typical categories derived for the sake of clarity. And yet, while each of these approaches contains rather broad theoretical boundaries, their respective distinctiveness rests with what might be called their *problematic*. The problematic of any theoretical approach refers not only to the questions that govern its mode of social inquiry, but also to the questions *not* asked, and the relationship between them. My guiding assumption is that all of the approaches to be analyzed inevitably fail to provide the theoretical elements essential for a comprehensive critical pedagogy. In order to infuse the concept of hidden curriculum with a more critical spirit, I will interrogate these approaches to reveal the interests they represent and to come to a better understanding of their limitations and of the theoretical and practical insights they offer.

Traditional Approach

The traditional perspective on schooling and the hidden curriculum takes as one of its central concerns the question: what makes the existing society possible? The key assumption that governs its problematic is that education plays a fundamental role in maintaining the existing society. By organizing its approach to issues such as cultural transmission, role socialization, and value acquisition around a preoccupation with the principles of consensus, cohesion, and stability, the traditional approach accepts uncritically the existing relationship between schools and the larger society. In these accounts, the hidden curriculum is explored primarily through the social norms and moral beliefs tacitly transmitted through the socialization processes that structure classroom social relationships. Given their basic concern with consensus and stability, these approaches accept the dominant societal values and norms and are interested primarily in how they are actually taught in schools. The transmission and reproduction of dominant values and beliefs via the hidden curriculum is both acknowledged and accepted as a positive function of the schooling process. Nevertheless, while the content of what is actually transmitted through certain classroom practices is analyzed, and economic interests such beliefs and values legitimize are ta... granted.

The traditional perspective becomes particularly clear in the work of Talcott Parsons (1959), Robert Dreeben (1968a), and Philip Jackson (1968). All three offer relatively bland descriptions of how structural processes such as crowds, power, praise, and the homogeneity of classroom tasks reproduce in students the dispositions necessary to cope with achievement, hierarchical work roles, and the patience and discipline required to function in the existing society. Parsons and Dreeben view schools from a functionalist perspective, with an emphasis on the way students learn values required by the existing society. For both theorists, schools are places where students learn valuable societal norms and skills they could not learn within the confines of the family. Formal schooling, for instance, becomes for Dreeben an important social site that teaches the social norms of independence, achievement, universalism, and specificity. While Jackson appears at times somewhat critical of the docility and patience that students often must endure in classroom settings, he ultimately leaves little doubt about the importance of the hidden curriculum in preparing students for their adult roles in the wider society. For instance, the implicit critical tone in comments such as "people must learn to suffer in silence" or "because the oppressive use of power is antithetical to our democratic ideals it is difficult to discuss its normal occurrence in the classroom without arousing concern" is eventually reduced by Jackson to a cheery celebration of social conformity. He writes, ". . . [S]chool might be called a preparation for life, but not in the usual sense in which educators employ that slogan. Powers may be abused in school as elsewhere, but its existence is a fact of life to which we must adapt" (Jackson 1968).

In the end, the notions of conflict and ideology disappear from this perspective, and the question of the abuse or neglect of power both within and outside of schools evaporates behind a static and reified view of the larger society. Consequently, students get defined in reductionist behavioral terms, and learning is reduced to the transmission of predefined knowledge. Needless to say, schools, like other institutions, appear to exist in these accounts beyond the somewhat questionable imperatives of capital and its underlying logic of class, race, and gender discrimination.

The conservative nature of this position is summed up by Rachel Sharp in her critique of the work of Jackson and Dreeben. She writes:

Jackson regards the hidden curriculum as relatively benign, as does Dreeben. In their view it provides the necessary preconditions for effective learning in the classroom and is in no sense discontinuous with the norms and values of adult society on which social order ultimately depends. . . . Neither of them discuss the hidden curriculum in terms of its ideological and political significance in sustaining a class society [Sharp 1980].

Liberal Approach

Traditionalists provide a theoretical service in illuminating how certain necessary societal values get tacitly transmitted via the hidden curriculum. But in doing so they do not question the underlying logic that gives shape to the institutionalized relationship among power, knowledge, and classroom control. On the other hand, the liberal perspective on the hidden curriculum begins from an entirely different assessment of the relationship between power and social order in the classroom. The focus of this more critical perspective resembles Michael Young's claim in his earlier work that there is a "dialectical relationship between access to power and the opportunity to legitimize certain dominant categories, and the process by which the availability of such categories to some groups enable them to assert power and control over others" (Young 1971).

The liberal perspective rejects most top-to-bottom models of pedagogy, with their conservative view of knowledge as something to be learned rather than critically engaged, as well as their equally uncritical notion of socialization, in which students are viewed simply as passive role-bearers and recipients of knowledge. At the core of the liberal problematic is the question of how meaning gets produced in the classroom. By considering knowledge a social construction, liberal critics have focused their research on the variety of ways by which knowledge gets arbitrarily mediated and negotiated within classroom settings. A fair amount of empirical research has emerged around questions concerning (a) the actual and hidden content of schooling; (b) the principles that govern the form and content of teacher-student interaction; and (c) the importance of seeing educational knowledge as commonsense categories and typifications selected from the larger culture and society that teachers, students, and researchers use to give meanings to their actions.

In using this problematic to study schools, liberal theorists have provided a dual theoretical service. They have furnished new critical tools by illuminating how technocratic or positivistic models of pedagogy either hide or distort the normatively grounded categories and patterns of interaction that underlie the structure of daily school experience. Put another way, the liberal critique both exposes and rejects those aspects of the hidden curriculum in which the truth claims of particular forms of knowledge and social practices are based on appeals to external forms of authority that parade under the guise of objectivity (Whitty 1974).

On the other hand, liberal theorists have attempted to develop pedagogical models that consider the importance of intentionality, consciousness, and interpersonal relations in the construction of meaning and classroom experience, as well as revealing to teachers the socially constructed nature of the classroom categorizations and labels that they utilize (Rist 1977b). The concrete nature of these concerns becomes obvious when they are situated within specific conceptual and classroom studies.

For example, in Nell Keddie's (1971) work, one finds a classic example of the type of approach that reveals how the typifications and categories that teachers use function not only to define student success but more importantly to guarantee, in some cases, student failure. In this case, a number of high school teachers used their categorization of the concept of ability to teach the same course material differently to groups of students from divergent socio-economic backgrounds. These teachers believed that middle-class students approached classroom knowledge with expectations and interests different from those used by working-class students. What resulted were dissimilar modes of pedagogy for different groups of students. Working-class students were taught how to follow rules, which usually meant learning how not to ask questions or raise issues that challenged teacher-based assumptions. On the other hand, the middle-class students were offered more complex treatments of class material, and their personal involvement in the class was endorsed rather than discouraged. Ironically, what constituted success for these students seemed less to be a result of their superior intellectual skills than of their willingness, as Keddie puts it, "to take over the teacher's definition of the situation. . . . Appropriate pupil behaviour . . . is not necessarily a question of the ability to move from higher levels of generalization and abstraction so much as an ability to move into an alternative system of thought from that of his everyday knowledge. In practical terms this means being able to work within the framework which the teacher constructs" (Keddie 1971).

The most sustained focus that this type of liberal critique has exhibited has been in the area of gender studies. That is, the liberal focus on the social construction of meaning and its hidden implications within school settings can be seen in much of the work on gender that developed in the late 1960s and 1970s in the United States and England. This work took as its central concern the way in which the internal structures and processes of schooling function to promote sex-role socialization. What came under detailed scrutiny in this perspective was the way in which the school reproduced a gender code that either worked against the success of women in certain academic areas or limited their economic opportunities in the wider society (Arnot 1981). The hidden curriculum in this perspective was to be found in specific social practices, cultural images, or forms of discourse that reinforced gender discrimination while simultaneously promoting its ideological justification. Within this approach to gender studies, the development of a critical consciousness was seen as the most important pedagogical objective capable of resolving various forms of sex (and race) discrimination. As a result, it was assumed that by exposing the sex-based stereotypes inherent in school practices, the problems of gender discrimination would be solved. Consequently, much research focused on how the values inherent in the dominant society's notion of "femininity" got reproduced in schools (Frazier & Dadker 1973; Lobban 1978; Weitzman, et al. 1972). More specifically, the focus of this type of liberal research centered on the one hand around how girls came to "underachieve" in school settings; on the other hand, the level of discussion of such studies was characteristically steeped in detailed descriptions of the mechanisms of gender stereotyping and discriminatory modes of socialization. Thus, there developed extensive depictions of textbook bias, analyses of curricula differentiation and tracking, and presentations of task and activity separations that depicted girls as inferior to boys (Levy 1972; Macdonald, 1981; Arnot 1982).[1]

Unfortunately, the value of this type of liberal critique of the hidden curriculum is considerably diminished by its insistence that the source as well as the ultimate solution to the problem of gender discrimination resides in merely uncovering and eliminating those sexist typifications that inform various social practices and aspects of school life. Excluded from this perspective is the insight that gender discrimination may have a material power base outside the schools, and that the resolution of such discrimination may be more than an ideological problem. In other words, the issue of how the gender relations presented and legitimated in schools benefit *both men and the interests and needs of capital* is left unconsidered

(MacDonald 1981). Moreover, such perspectives also failed to provide any form of historical analysis that explains why gender relations under changing socio-historical conditions have taken different forms in different social sites, such as the family, workplace, and school. Finally, not only has the liberal perspective excluded the mediation of class from its analysis of the hidden curriculum of gender, it has also failed to analyze the ways in which sexism reaches into the deep structure of the personality itself, i.e. the way in which sexism gets sedimented in its various forms in the personality structures of boys and girls from different classes. In addition to studies that focus on the use of teacher categories, the liberal perspective has also generated classroom studies that analyze the question of what "students need to know in order to operate effectively in class" (Mehan 1979). The central concern of these studies is the way teachers and students influence each other through their mutual production of meanings and interactions. Rejecting the notion that the hidden curriculum is uniformly repressive, these critics attempt to provide a theoretical antidote to the assumption that classroom socialization flows only from the socially constructed world of the teacher. Instead, a number of liberal critics have developed conceptual frameworks and empirical analyses that go to great lengths to demonstrate how teachers and students set limits on each others' actions.

One such study sums up the theoretical essence of most of this work with the "insight" that "a teacher teaches a child, while the child teaches the teacher," or ". . . children structure and modify their environment just as they are structured and modified by it" (Mehan 1979).

Elizabeth Vallance's (1973, 1980) work on the hidden curriculum is in the same tradition. That is, Vallance uses the term to connote a number of definitions, and in the end it appears as a curiously empty concept, signifying no political commitment or critical perspective. For instance, in a paper in which she traces the history of the hidden curriculum, Vallance acknowledges that the idea of the hidden curriculum may be linked to unduly authoritarian and class-based forms of social control; however, she separates herself from that position by providing a definition of the concept that is as apolitical as it is theoretically underdeveloped: "I use the term to refer to those non-academic but educationally significant consequences of schooling that occur systematically but are not made explicit at any level of the public rationales for education" (Vallance 1973).

In a more recent statement on the issue, Vallance acknowledges that the hidden curriculum is a vague but valuable tool for educational inquiry, but how it might be useful becomes questionable because of her confusion over the difference between systematic theoretical inquiry and what she calls "arrogance." Carrying her anti-theoretical posture to its logical end, Vallance ultimately lapses into a non-committal stance that reduces the notion of the hidden curriculum to a concept that has little explanatory power, except to inform us that there is always more going on in the schools than we realize:

> But the real value of the hidden curriculum concept as a tool for educational dialogue is not that it allows us to acknowledge our current ignorance, but that it allows us to acknowledge that much of schooling may be too subtle to ever fully capture. It allows us to accept this degree of mystery and encourages us to find intelligent ways of working around it without needing to fully control it [Vallance 1980].

Another theoretical twist in the liberal problematic can be found in the work of critics such as Richard M. Merelman (1980). This group argues aggressively against more radical definitions of the hidden curriculum, especially those that claim that the hidden curriculum promotes docility and conformity in all social classes of students, and that the hidden curriculum has a direct effect on student attitudes towards the wider political system. After "discovering" that schools are social sites marked by both conflict and conformity, Merelman decides that the hidden curriculum is, in essence, a product of the school's contradictory allegiance to teaching democratic values while demanding social control. It is this division within the school that allegedly justifies certain forms of testing and age-grading, and particular forms of teacher authority and control over almost all aspects of student behavior. Curiously, Merelman does not seem bothered by the notion that the division to which he refers may have its roots in the dominant society. That is, the notion that such a division may be inherent in the very nature of capitalist society, with its restriction of democracy to the political realm and its concomitant support for inequality in the economic realm, is not considered. What Merelman ignores is well put by Clark and Gintis: "For democracy requires that the historical evolution of society be responsive to the popular will; while capitalism, as an essential determinant of social evolution, rests on fundamental inequalities in wealth, power, and participation" (Clark & Gintis 1978).

Since Merelman refuses to trace the political and economic determinants of the hidden curriculum, he ends up largely blaming teachers for its existence and influence. We are told for example that future teachers have grade-point averages far below the averages of their academic peers, that most of the elementary schools are filled with our least gifted minds (Merelman 1980). Under such circumstances, Merelman can only conclude that the hidden curriculum functions through the ignorance and political ineptitude of the very people who are in a position to alter its effects.

There is a certain logic in Merelman's remarks that characterizes the liberal perspective in general. There seems to be little or no understanding of how the social, political, and economic conditions of society create either directly or indirectly some of the oppressive features of schooling. More specifically, there is little or no concern with the ways in which powerful institutions and groups influence the knowledge, social relations, and modes of evaluation that characterize the ideological texture of school life. The lack of such an understanding appears to result in either a relativistic posture or a blaming-the-victim stance (Holly 1977). Questions of false consciousness or structural determinations fade away in such accounts. For example, the one-sided emphasis on consciousness and the production of classroom meanings in the liberal approach exists at the expense of developing criteria by which to judge the adequacy of contradictory knowledge claims. Moreover, the orientation towards description in some of these accounts provides no criteria for critically evaluating the competing interpretations of social and political reality. There seems to be an indifference in these accounts to "how and why reality comes to be constructed in particular ways and how and why particular constructions of reality seem to have the power to resist submission" (Whitty 1974:125).

Related to the failure of the liberal approach, and characteristic of critics like Merelman, is the theoretical disregard for the way in which ideological and structural constraints in the larger society are reproduced in the schools to mediate against the possibility of critical thinking or constructive dialogue. The notion that teachers and pupils may face ideological and structural constraints over which they have little control is ignored. In this view, powerlessness is confused with passivity, and pedagogical shortcomings are reduced to questions of mindlessness, ignorance, or individual failings (Silberman 1970). As might be expected, the hierarchical and often authoritarian relationships of school management, the conservative nature of school ideology, the material conditions of the classroom, the structural isolation teachers often face, and the fiscal and ideological constraints imposed by school boards on faculty appear to vanish as structural constraints in many liberal accounts of the workings of the hidden curriculum.

In the traditional approach to the study of the hidden curriculum, the focus is on how the system of schooling serves to reproduce stability and cohesion in the wider society. In the liberal approach, the study of social structures is put aside for analyses of how people produce and negotiate classroom meanings. In the radical approach, the traditional emphasis on consensus is replaced by a radical focus on conflict, and the liberal concern with the way teachers and students create meanings is replaced by a focus on social structures and the constriction of meaning. The question at the core of the radical problematic on the hidden curriculum is, how does the process of schooling function to reproduce and sustain the relations of dominance, exploitation, and inequality between classes? (Early representative examples of this position can be found in Bowles & Gintis 1976; Carnoy & Levin 1976).

Radical Perspectives

Radical perspectives on the hidden curriculum provide a number of valuable insights into the schooling process. First, they help to explain the political function of schooling in terms of the important concepts of class and domination. Second, they point to the existence of structural factors outside the immediate environment of the classroom as important forces in influencing both the day-to-day experiences and the outcomes of the schooling process.

In both the theoretical and empirical work that dominates this approach, the focus is on the political economy of schooling. The central thesis is that the social relations that characterize the production process represent the determining force in shaping the school environment. For example, Bowles and Gintis, in their celebrated *Schooling in Capitalist America,* establish a theoretical basis for this position and argue that the form of socialization, rather than the content of the formal curriculum, provides the chief vehicle for inculcating in different classes of students the dispositions and skills they will need to take their corresponding places in the work force (Bowles & Gintis 1976). At the heart of these accounts is what is called the "correspondence principle." In essence, it argues that the social relations of the school and classroom roughly mirror the social relations of the workplace, the final outcome being the reproduction of the social and class divisions needed for the production and legitimation of capital and its institutions.

The political-economy position on the hidden curriculum has had a major influence on radical theories of schooling. Its influence is derived, in part, from a theoretical perspective that focused on how schools functioned as major socializing influences in preparing students for different places in a hierarchically divided labor force. Sweeping aside the liberal discourse of meritocracy, theorists such as Carnoy and Levin (1976) illuminated how schools as class-specific enterprises functioned to provide students from different socioeconomic groups with qualitatively different forms of education. The logic of these arguments was compelling, and appeared to capture the reality of schooling in a way that traditionalist and liberal accounts had missed (or simply ignored). Occupational and educational stratification, whether based on gender, class or race, were quite visible beneath the cheery mainstream discourse of equal opportunity and individual achievement, and could be seen in the texture, social processes, and tensions that made up the reality of school life. New metaphors emerged from this perspective to describe school experience and its relation to the larger social and economic order. Schools became factories for the working class, and, it was alleged, performed an insidious but efficient job of reproducing the existing class structure and labor force. The model of schooling that emerged from the political-economy position has virtually dominated radical school criticism for the last decade, especially in the United States (e.g., Benet & Daniels 1980). While its more recent elaborations are more theoretically sophisticated than earlier versions, the logic that informs them remains the same. A more recent representation of the political economy position can be found in theorists such as Mickelson. What is significant about this work is that it has attempted to buttress its analyses with empirical research. Mickelson is worth quoting at length:

> The social relations of production reflect the social division of labor. The social relations of different tracks in school tend to conform to different behavioral norms. Thus vocational and general tracks, where most working-class adolescents are channeled, emphasize rule-following and close supervision, whereas college-bound tracks, where most upper-

and middle-class children, are channeled, tend toward a more open atmosphere emphasizing internalization of norms and standards of control.

The relations of dominance and subordination in education differ by level of school and by class of the community. The role orientation of the high school reflects the close supervision of low-level workers. The internalization of norms and freedom from continued supervision in middle-class suburban high schools and in colleges reflects the social relationships of upper-level white-collar work. It can easily be seen that the close correspondence between the social relations that govern personal interactions in the workplace and the social relations of authority between teachers and students and their work replicate the hierarchical division of labor in the workplace. Students in vocational and general tracks have a low level of control over their curriculum and daily activities in school, which is in turn comparable to that of industrial or service workers over the content of their jobs [Mickelson 1980].

Accounts such as Mickelson's, while important, end up providing a one-sided and theoretically underdeveloped perspective on the role of the hidden curriculum. One problem is that they misconstrue the relationship between schools and the economic order. That is, even though it may be difficult to contest that schools exist in a particular relationship to the industrial order, this insight is not quite the same as assuming that the relationship is simply one of correspondence or cause-and-effect. Furthermore, in many of these accounts there is not only little understanding of the contradictions and social spaces that promote oppositional tendencies and behavior in schools, there is also a one-dimensional view of socialization. Students and teacher do not simply comply with the oppressive features of schooling, as radical critics suggest. In some cases both groups resist; in some cases they modify school practices. In no sense do teachers and students uniformly function in schools as simply the passive reflex of the logic of capital. In other words, these radical accounts fail to understand that while schools serve the interests of capitalism, they also serve other interests as well, some of which are in opposition to the economic order and the needs of the dominant society.[4] At the same time, active agents disappear in these accounts, reduced to passive role bearers and products of wider social processes. The notion that there is no steadfast correlation between a predefined institutional role and how people both interpret and respond to that role goes unexamined in the radical perspective. Teachers and students do not simply receive information; they also produce and mediate it. By forgetting the latter, many supporters of the radical perspective fail to acknowledge or develop an adequate view of either consciousness, resistance, or culture. Also, this perspective has consistently ignored the existence of forms of domination other than those of class oppression (McRobbie 1980; MacDonald, in Deem 1980). Missing from these accounts are detailed studies of either racial oppression or gender discrimination. Finally, these perspectives are deeply pessimistic. By providing an 'air-tight' notion of domination and an equally reductionist notion of socialization, radical accounts provide little hope for either social change or the promise of oppositional teaching within the schools. Consequently, they help to provide a blue-print for cynicism and despair, one that serves to reproduce the very mode of domination they claim to be resisting.

In addition to the political economy position on the hidden curriculum, there developed, particularly in the United States, a lesser known but more dialectical and theoretically sophisticated analysis. Rejecting the one-sided structuralism and gloom-and-doom pessimism in the political-economy posture, neo-Marxist accounts of the hidden curriculum focused more specifically on how a variety of mechanisms in the schools tacitly worked in the interest of reproducing the ethos and structure of capitalist society. For instance, Apple (1971) analyzed the way in which schools promote a mode of rationality that both sustained and characterized capitalist social relations. By focusing on how schools select and present school knowledge, such as science and social studies, Apple revealed how notions of conflict and resistance are either ignored or assigned a negative value by both teachers and textbooks. Apple and King (1977) broadened that analysis by arguing that the hidden curriculum of schooling encompassed and reproduced a whole range of meanings that represent selections from the ideological and cultural resources of dominant interest groups. In this perspective, the hidden curriculum is located in a range of norms, decisions, and social practices that tacitly structure school experience in the interest of social and class control. The interconnection among power, economic resources, and social control is explored by Apple and King through the way in which knowledge is distributed to students in a specific kindergarten class. By examining teacher discourse and the meanings inherent in classroom socialization processes, these theorists illustrate how children at this grade level are taught quite quickly how to separate work from play, and how to treat the former as an activity that requires obedience, passivity, and teacher-dominated activities.

Giroux and Penna (1979) operate within a similar framework, with a dual focus. First, they attempt to identify those social processes in schools that constitute the matrix of a hidden curriculum. In addition, they attempt to illuminate those counter-hegemonic classroom practices that may function to minimize the impact of the hidden curriculum while simultaneously helping teachers and students develop radical classroom practices that work in the interest of emancipatory rather than dominating concerns.

In spite of the theoretical advances that the neo-Marxist work on the hidden curriculum displays over the political-economic perspective, it too is marked by serious flaws. The early work of Apple (1971), Apple and King, (1977), Giroux and Penna (1979), as well as the more recent work of Anyon (1980) say too little about the complex ways in which consciousness and culture interact, about how students operating out of the specificities of gender, race, and class offer resistance to the mechanisms of social control and domination in schools. This is not to suggest that such work on the hidden curriculum does not mention resistance or deal with the question of how subjectivities get constituted in schools. It does, but often in a manner that trivializes the importance and complexity of these issues. In other words, most of these accounts appear "trapped" in one-dimensional perspectives that lack adequate conceptions of consciousness and culture, and an adequate theory of ideology. Thus it is understandable that most of them stress social and cultural domination while almost completely ignoring theories of cultural production and political struggle (Willis 1981).

In summary, while many of these analyses of the hidden curriculum provide valuable insights into its day-to-day mechanisms and consequences, they ultimately present perspectives that are far too undialectical. As such, they are unable either to contribute significantly to a comprehensive understanding of the relationship between schooling and capitalism or to provide the theoretical elements necessary to develop a more critical mode of pedagogy. I want to conclude this chapter by pointing to some of the theoretical elements needed to reconceptualize the notion of the hidden curriculum and its use in the interest of a critical pedagogy.

The Hidden Curriculum: A Redefinition

If the notion of the hidden curriculum is to be rescued from its own intellectual heritage to claim value as an important theoretical element in the development of a critical pedagogy, it will have to be both redefined and resituated as a pedagogical concern. That is, the concept will have to occupy a central rather than a marginal place in the development of curriculum theory. Curriculum theory and practice will have to integrate into its problematic a notion of critique that is capable of questioning the normative assumptions underlying its logic and discourse. Furthermore, if the notion of the hidden curriculum is to become meaningful it will have to be used to analyze not only the social relations of the classroom and school, but also the structural "silences" and ideological messages that shape the form and content of school knowledge. Finally, a redefinition of the hidden curriculum requires that it be seen as something more than an interpretative tool buttressed with good intentions. While it is important to use the concept of the hidden curriculum as a heuristic tool to uncover the assumptions and interests that go unexamined in the discourse and materials that shape school experience, such a position does not go far enough. It is crucial that the notion of the hidden curriculum also be linked to a notion of liberation, grounded in the values of personal dignity and social justice. As such, the essence of the hidden curriculum would be established in the development of a theory of schooling concerned with *both* reproduction and transformation. At the core of such a theory would be the imperative to link approaches to human consciousness and action to forms of structural analysis that explore how they interpenetrate each other rather than appear as separate pedagogical concerns.

Implication for Classroom Practice: Outline of a Theoretical Model

One of the major shortcomings of the existing literature on schooling and the hidden curriculum is that it has failed to develop a dialectical conceptual framework for grasping education as a societal process. Caught between a watered-down functionalism and an unbounded focus on subjectivity, such literature has portrayed the modalities of structure and human agency as opposing forces rather than forces that, while somewhat distinct, affect each other. Amidst this dualism of action and structure, the contextuality of meaning often appears in either a historical or a structural vacuum. From the opposite perspective, structuralist literature on the hidden curriculum suggests not only a mistrust of consciousness, but a refusal to acknowledge human agents in both the production and transformation of meaning and history (Giroux 1981). What is needed is a theoretical model in which schools as institutions are viewed and evaluated, both in historical and contemporary terms, as social sites in which human actors are both constrained *and* mobilized. In other words, schooling must be analyzed as a societal process, one in which different social groups both accept and reject the complex mediations of culture, knowledge, and power that give form and meaning to the process of schooling.

In addition to schooling being viewed as a social process in which the elements of structure and agency come together as social practices taking place within ever-changing constraints, it is crucial that it also be viewed within a theory of totality. That is, school as both an institution and a set of social practices must be seen in its integral connections with the realities of other socio-economic and political institutions that control the production, distribution, and legitimation of economic and cultural capital in the dominant society. But a relational analysis of schools becomes meaningful only if it is accompanied by an understanding of how power and knowledge link schools to the inequalities produced in the large social order.

Equally important is the necessity for teachers and other educators to reject educational theories that reduce schooling either to the domain of learning theory or to forms of technocratic rationality that ignore the central concerns of social change, power relations, and conflicts both within and outside of schools. The hidden curriculum concept is important in this instance because it rejects the notion of immediacy that runs through both the discourse of traditional learning theory and the logic of technocratic rationality.

Rather than celebrating objectivity and consensus, teachers must place the notions of critique and conflict at the center of their pedagogical models. Within such a perspective, greater possibilities exist for developing an understanding of the role power plays in defining and distributing the knowledge and social relationships that mediate the school and classroom experience. Critique must become a vital pedagogical tool— not only because it breaks through the mystifications and distortions that "silently" work behind the labels and routines of school practice, but also because it models a form of resistance and oppositional pedagogy.

Finally, one of the most important theoretical elements missing from the hidden curriculum literature is a view of schools as sites of *both domination and contestation.* The incorporation of this perspective is crucial because it redefines the nature of domination as well as the notion of power. In other words, domination is never total in this perspective, nor is it simply imposed on people. Such an insight demands that teachers examine not only the mechanisms of domination as they exist in the schools, but also how such mechanisms are reproduced and resisted by students via their own lived experiences (Willis 1977). Similarly, power must be seen as a force that works both on people and through them. As Foucault continually reminds us, power is not a static phenomenon; it is a process that is always in play (Foucault 1980). Put another way, power must be viewed in part as a form of production inscribed in the discourse and capabilities that people use to make sense out of the world. Otherwise, the notion of power is subsumed under the category of domination, and the issue of human agency gets relegated to either a marginal or insignificant place in educational theorizing. This position will be taken up in more detail in Chapter 4.

While it is crucial to see schools as social sites in which the class, gender, and racial relationships that characterize the dominant society are roughly reproduced, it is equally important to make such an analysis function in the interest of developing alternative pedagogical practices. The first step in developing such practices would be to focus on the relationship between school culture and the overt and covert dimensions of the curriculum, as well as on the contradictory, lived experiences that teachers and students bring to the school on the other. It is in the relationship between school culture and contradictory lived experiences that teachers and students register the imprints and texture of domination and resistance. In particular, it is in this relationship that culture is divided into dominant and repressive forms, into categories that "silently" delineate the essential from the inessential, the legitimate from the illegitimate. It is around these categories or practices that conformity, tension, and resistance develop in the schools. Culture as contradictory, lived experience represents the shared principles that emerge among specific groups and classes under concrete socio-historical conditions. It is both the critical and the unexamined everyday practices that guide and constrain individual and social action. While school cultures may take complex and heterogeneous forms, the principle that remains constant is that they are situated within a network of power relations from which they cannot escape.

The practical implications of this analysis suggest that since the mechanisms of reproduction and transformation are located partly within the dominant school culture, teachers should critically consider questions of where such a culture comes from, whose culture is being implemented, whose interests it serves, and how it gets inscribed and sustained in school discourse and social practices. An understanding of the political nature of academic culture and of its relationship to the categories and processes that different classes of students bring to the school is required. Moreover, it is essential that teachers take seriously not only the beliefs and routines of the school, but also the underlying meanings and experiences that characterize students from different socio-economic groups, and which exist in various degrees of compatibility and resistance to the dominant school culture. What is needed to unravel the source, mechanisms, and elements that constitute the fabric of school culture is what I have labeled a theory of *dialectical critique.*

Drawing on Adorno's (1973) notion of negative dialectics, a theory of dialectical critique begins with a rejection of the "official" representation of reality. Its guiding assumption is that critical reflection is formed out of the principles of negativity, contradiction and mediation. In short, negativity refers to a thorough questioning of all universals, an interrogation of those "received" truths and social practices that go unquestioned in schools because they are dressed in the discourse of objectivity and neutrality. Negativity in this case represents a mode of critical engagement with the dominant culture, the purpose of which is to see through its ideological justifications and explode its reifications and myths. The significance of this notion of relentless negativity has been captured by Buck-Morss in her comment on Adorno's use of the concept: "The whole point of his relentless insistence on negativity was to resist repeating in thought the structures of domination and reification that existed in society, so that instead of reproducing reality, consciousness could be critical, so that reason would recognize its own nonidentity with social reality. . . ." (Buck-Morss 1977).

The principle of contradiction is informed by the assumption that the contradictory nature of social reality in the wider sense, and school life in particular, invalidates mainstream appeals to the imperatives of social harmony and the logic of consensus. Moreover, the very existence of such contradictions suggest that theory and critique comprise only one essential means of illuminating the conditions that maintain the existing society, and that ultimately such conditions cannot be altered through a change in consciousness but through the force of collective action. Lastly, the principle of mediation points to the importance of the active intervention of men and women in the production and reception of meaning. As a critical concept, mediation contains two important dimensions. First, it is essential that radical theories of the hidden curriculum generate as well as rescue the critical categories of class and ideology from their treatment by both Marxist and liberal educators. These categories need to be re-fashioned not only to illuminate the contradictory character of working-class discourse, consciousness, and experience, but also to illuminate the strengths and weaknesses these contain, and to use this information as a basis for developing a radical pedagogy. For instance, by drawing upon the "texts" and codes that mediate and construct working-class culture (in its varied forms), it becomes possible to develop a critical discourse to present the latter in terms that reveal the contradictions they conceal. Thus, the first moment in a theory of mediation highlights the ideological interests and contradictions inherent in cultural texts and social processes. It does so by subjecting them to a mode of critical reflection that exposes the social function of those meanings and ideas legitimated by the dominant culture. Critique in this instance becomes a form of refusal, a probing of those aspects of school life that appear to "speak" for themselves, that are presented in such a way that they can be judged only in their immediacy.

The second important dimension of the principle of mediation does more than reveal the social function of dominant ideas and practices; instead, it points to the need for a theory of critique that focuses on the nature and construction of thought itself. It examines self-critically how thought is constructed and produced, and looks at both its intentional and unintentional consequences. This point is of crucial importance because it provides the ground work for reappropriating and restructuring those aspects of dominant and subordinate cultures that enhance the possibilities for critique and self-determination.

Thus a theory of dialectical critique speaks to a dual concern: on the one hand, it attempts to link social experiences with the development of modes of criticism that can interrogate such experiences and reveal both their strengths and weaknesses. On the other hand, it points to a mode of praxis fashioned in new modes of critical thought aimed at reclaiming the conditions of a self-determined existence. Although the issues of culture and ideology will be dealt with in a detailed manner in Chapter

4, the importance of these concepts for developing a more radical pedagogy that stresses the centrality of the hidden curriculum will be touched on briefly here.

Underlying the logic of the hidden curriculum and schooling is a structured silence about the relationship between class and culture. Though schools are cultural sites marked by complex relations of dominance and resistance, the official discourse of schooling depoliticizes the notion of culture and dismisses resistance, or at least the political significance of resistance. By presenting schools as institutions designed to benefit all students, the dominant culture, its knowledge and social practices, misrepresent the nature or effects of social and cultural processes weighted against the interest of students from subordinate cultures. Domination and power represent a "silent" motif of school life; this can be seen in the way they mediate the instances of class and culture to reproduce in approximate form the social relations of domination that characterize the larger society. The imprint of the dominant society and culture is inscribed in a whole range of school practices, i.e., the official language, school rules, classroom social relations, the selection and presentation of school knowledge, the exclusion of specific cultural capital, etc. Needless to say, it is not simply inscribed or imposed in the consciousness or ideologies of the oppressed. It is always mediated—sometimes rejected, sometimes confirmed. More often than not it is partly accepted and partly rejected. The issue here is that class and power intersect within the relations of domination and resistance in the form of lived experiences that accommodate and contest the dominant school culture in a complex way. What is crucial to recognize is that schools represent contested terrains in the formation of subjectivities, but that the terrain is heavily weighted in favor of the dominant culture. While the gaps and tensions in schools need to be used and unraveled to extend their radical potential, it must be remembered that economic and political constraints also exert a force in these institutions, and these must be acknowledged as well. Clearly, under certain conditions, whether they stem from an authoritarian principal, a homogeneous right-wing community, a conservative school board, or an unreceptive faculty, it may be nearly impossible to exert any influence pedagogically, regardless of how insightful one may be in the theoretical sense.

It is at this point that a critical notion of ideology becomes important. Ideology, as used here, refers to the production, interpretation, and effectivity of meaning. It contains both a positive and negative moment, each of which is determined, in part, by the degree to which it promotes or distorts reflexive thought and action. As a distortion ideology becomes hegemonic; as an illumination it contains elements of reflexivity and the grounds for social action. It is the positive moment in the dialectic of ideology that has been ignored by educational critics. My attempt to reintroduce the positive dimension of ideology into the discourse of educational theorizing takes its cue from Gramsci and Aronowitz. Both point out that ideologies mobilize human subjects as well as create the "terrain on which men move and acquire consciousness of their position" (Aronowitz 1980; Gramsci 1971). One important clarification to this definition is that as a form of reflexivity ideology is not synonymous with liberation, particularly since it is exercized within economic and political conditions that ultimately determine its influence or effect.

The notion of ideology becomes a critical pedagogical tool when it is used to interrogate the relationship between the dominant school culture and the contradictory, lived experiences that mediate the texture of school life. I want to argue that three important distinctions provide the foundation for developing a theory of ideology and classroom practice. First, a distinction must be made between theoretical and practical ideologies. (Sharp 1980; Whitty 1981). Theoretical ideologies refer to the beliefs and values embedded in the categories that teachers and students use to shape and interpret the pedagogical process, while practical ideologies refer to the messages and norms embedded in classroom social relations and practices. Second, a distinction must be made between discourse and lived experience as instances of ideology and as the material grounding of ideologies as they are embodied in school "texts," films, and other cultural artifacts that make up visual and aural media. Third, these ideological elements gain part of their significance only as they are viewed in their articulation with the broader relations of society.

One implication for classroom practice to be drawn from a theory of ideology is that it presents teachers with a heuristic tool to examine critically how their own views about knowledge, human nature, values, and society are mediated through the commonsense assumptions they use to structure classroom experiences. In other words, the concept of ideology provides a starting point for raising questions about the social and political interests that underlie many of the pedagogical assumptions taken for granted by teachers. Assumptions about learning, achievement, teacher-student relations, objectivity, school authority, and so on, all need to be evaluated critically by educators. As Michael Apple points out, such an approach demands a critical style: "The curriculum field has been much too accepting of forms of thought that do not do justice to the complexity of inquiry and thus it has not really changed its basic perspective for decades" (Apple 1979).

Needless to say, ideology as critique must also be used to examine classroom social relations that "freeze" the spirit of critical inquiry among students. These pedagogical practices must also be decoded and measured against their potential to foster rather than hamper intellectual growth and social inquiry. This becomes particularly important for those students who experience daily the pain of humiliation and powerlessness because their own lived experiences and sedimented histories are at odds with the dominant school culture. These students need to be placed in classroom social relationships that affirm their own histories and cultures while at the same time providing them with the critical discourse they need to develop a self-managed existence. Relevance here means that teachers must structure classroom experiences that give students the opportunities not only to affirm their own experiences but also to examine critically the ways in which they have become part of the system of social reproduction. Thus, if teachers are to move beyond the role of being agents of cultural reproduction to that of being agents of cultural mobilization, they will have to critically engage the nature of their own self-formation and participation in the dominant society, including their role as intellectuals and mediators of the dominant culture (Greene 1978).

The contradictory nature of school life provides a site for teachers to explore how the knowledge and meanings of subordinate groups are experienced and interpreted both within and outside of discourse. For it is within and between the spoken and unspoken experiences of subordinate cultures that an immanent critique of the dominant society may be found. Moreover, by examining the immanent logic that underlies forms of subordinate cultural accommodation and resistance, it may be possible to develop a theory of working-class representation, i.e., an understanding of how working-class groups in their complexity mediate the overt and hidden messages that constitute the ongoing dynamics of school experience (Willis & Corrigan 1980). The real issue here is that it is necessary to critically decode those elements in the hidden curriculum of schooling that speak to working-class needs and desires but that in so doing limit their radical potential. These elements must be uncovered and linked to their location in the parent culture, i.e., family, workplace, etc., so they can be reclaimed and used as part of a radical pedagogy. Thus, ideology as critique can be used by teachers not only to understand how the dominant culture becomes embedded in the hidden curriculum, it can also be used for developing a mode of knowledge that would allow teachers and students to understand and negotiate the world of meanings that relegate schools to a particular relationship with the dominant society. The production of self-awareness is also linked to understanding how curriculum materials and other cultural artifacts produce meanings. That is, teachers must learn how to decode the messages inscribed in both the form and content of such artifacts and materials. This becomes all the more imperative in light both of recent studies about teacher attitudes toward classroom materials and of a number of content-analysis studies on the messages embedded in school curriculum materials. For example, a major National Science Foundation study on social-studies teaching concluded that the "dominant instructional mode is the conventional textbook, . . . the knowing expected of students is largely information-oriented, . . . [and] teachers tend not only to rely on, but to believe in the textbook as the source of knowledge" (Shaver, Davis, Helburn 1979). Recent content-analysis studies of current social studies books used in the public schools paint the same bleak picture. For instance, Jean Anyon's extensive studies conclude that such books are dominated by themes such as (1) an over-valuing of social harmony, social compromise and political consensus, with very little said about social struggle or class conflict; (2) an intense nationalism and chauvinism; (3) an almost total exclusion of labor history; and (4) a number of myths regarding the nature of political, economic, and social life [Anyon 1979, 1980]. Similarly, Popkewitz (1978) found in his study of the discipline-centered curriculum in the social studies that they express a conservative bias toward social-political institutions.

The production of self-awareness also requires an ability to decode and critique the ideologies inscribed in the form or structuring principles behind the presentation of images in curriculum materials: the significant "silences" of a classroom text also have to be uncovered. For instance, teachers must learn to identify the ideological messages implicit in "texts" that focus on individuals to the exclusion of collective action, that juxtapose high-quality art next to descriptions of poverty and exploitation, or use forms of discourse that do not promote critical engagement by students. Recently, a number of curricular theorists have pointed to the production of curriculum packages that promote what has been called *teacher de-skilling* (Apple 1981; Buswell 1980). Rather than promote conceptual understanding on the part of the classroom teacher, these curriculum 'kits' separate conception from execution. In other words, objectives, knowledge skills, pedagogical practices, and modes of evaluation are built into and predefined by the curriculum program itself. The teacher's role is reduced to merely following the rules. Assembly-line control, in this case, parades as the newest insight in curriculum development.

Finally, I think that if teachers are going to make the concept of the hidden curriculum a central part of their educational theorizing and practice, they will have to turn their attention to the labor process of schooling. More specifically, teachers must collectively challenge the often-hidden message of powerlessness that characterizes the division of labor in most schools. The separation of content, pedagogy, and evaluation to different groups of specialists not only limits teacher autonomy, it also promotes the division between mental and manual labor, albeit at a higher level. Regardless of the form it takes, the message that emerges from such a division is generally the same: "Don't think, simply follow the rules." Consequently, there are political elements within the labor process itself that work both ideologically and structurally against teachers, and on a more visible level against students as well. As Apple and Feinberg point out:

> The removal of the teacher from participating in the complex issues surrounding the process of producing instructional material can reinforce an image in which the teacher is viewed as only a conduit between the homogenized curriculum and the child. And this image reinforces the impression that teachers need only to know about the techniques of management. In the process, our ability to make reasoned choices and to explain these to the public is diminished [Apple & Feinberg, forthcoming].

Conclusion

In conclusion, I have argued that the notion of the hidden curriculum as it currently exists in the literature fails to provide the theoretical elements necessary to develop a critical pedagogy based on a concern with cultural struggles in the schools. Most of the approaches that characterize this literature ultimately dissolve the notion of politics in, among other things, a false celebration of subjectivity or an equally false treatment of students and teachers as social props passively carrying out the requirements of larger social structures. What is needed to move beyond these positions is a view of the hidden curriculum that encompasses all the ideological instances of the schooling process that "silently" structure and reproduce hegemonic assumptions and practices. Such a focus is important because it shifts the emphasis away from a one-sided preoccupation with cultural reproduction to a primary concern with cultural intervention and social action. While such an approach in and of itself will not change the larger society, it will provide the foundation for using the schools as important sites to wage counter-hegemonic practices.

3

Reproduction, Resistance, & Accommodation in the Schooling Process

In the previous chapters I argued that the foundation for a radical theory of schooling can, in part, be developed from the work of the Frankfurt School and the more recent literature on the hidden curriculum. Whereas the Frankfurt School provides a discourse and mode of critique for deepening our understanding of the nature and function of schooling, critiques of the hidden curriculum have provided modes of analysis that uncover the ideologies and interests embedded in the message systems, codes, and routines that characterize daily classroom life. But as important as these two modes of analysis are, they do not provide a systematic account of how power and human agency interconnect to promote social practices in schools that represent both the condition and the outcome of domination and contestation. Fortunately, within the last decade a body of theoretical work has developed which provides a structural and interactional analysis of the process of schooling. It is to this work that I will now turn in order to assess not only the strengths and weaknesses of the theoretical perspectives that characterize its major accounts, but also to indicate the potential these may have for developing an ideological foundation essential for a reconstructed theory of radical pedagogy.

As I indicated in Chapter 2, the specificities of culture, ideology, and power have never figured prominently in the dominant language of educational theory and practice. In the long history of educational theory, extending from Bobbitt (1918) and Charters (1923) to the more recent work of Tyler (1950), Popham (1969), and Mager (1975), there has been a powerful and deep-seated commitment to viewing schools and classroom pedagogy in terms that separate power from knowledge while simultaneously abstracting culture from politics.

In both its conservative and liberal versions, educational theory has been firmly entrenched in the logic of necessity and efficiency and has been mediated through the political discourse of integration and consensus. This becomes clear if it is recognized that notions such as conflict and struggle are either downplayed or ignored in the discourse of traditional educational theory and practice. More specifically, the Parsonian (1959) view of schooling, which argues for a view of schools as neutral institutions designed to provide students with the knowledge and skills they will need to perform successfully in the wider society, laid the basis for a sociology of education that refused to interrogate the relationship between schools and the industrial order. One consequence of this view was that the structure and ideology of the dominant society was rendered unproblematic. Similarly, a disquieting silence emerged regarding how schools might be influenced, bent, and molded by interest groups that both sustained and benefited from the deep-seated political, economic, racial, and gender inequalities that characterize American society (Feinberg 1975).

On the other hand, traditional educational theory offered no real basis for understanding the relationship among issues such as ideology, knowledge, and power. That is, bleached from this perspective was any attempt to reflect on the historical development, selection, use, and legitimation of what schools defined as "real" knowledge. The crucial question ignored here is the way in which the power distributed in a society functions in the interests of specific ideologies and forms of knowledge to sustain the economic and political concerns of particular groups and classes (Young & Whitty 1977). The failure to develop this type of analysis is evident in traditional educational theory's long standing emphasis on the management and administration of knowledge, as opposed to a critical concern with the historical and social determinants that govern the selection of such knowledge forms and attendant practices (Apple 1979). What we are presented with and often victimized by in this perspective is an epistemology, a mode of thinking that has been flattened out and largely reduced to the celebration of methodological refinement, i.e., a preoccupation with control, production, and observation (Aronowitz 1980). Lost from this calculus of social engineering are the basic rudiments of critical thought—that is, behind traditional theory's insistence on a definition of truth, one that appears to be synonomous with objective methodological inquiry and empirical verification, there is a structured silence around how normative interests provide the grounding for theory and social inquiry. Less abstractly, beneath the seemingly serious commitment to objectivity and value-freedom stands a reductionist logic that not only displays little critical attentiveness to the grounding of knowledge, but also suppresses notions of ethics and the value of history (Jacoby 1975; Giroux 1981). Dancing on the surface of reality, traditional educational theory ignores not only the latent principles that shape the deep grammar of the existing social order, but also those principles underlying the genesis and nature of its own logic.

Within this framework are a number of practices worth mentioning: first, ideology is dissolved within the concept of objective knowledge; second, the relationship between the hidden curriculum and social control are discarded for a preoccupation with designing objectives; and finally, the relationship between socialization and the reproduction of class, gender, and racial inequalities are ignored for an overriding concern with finding ways to teach knowledge that is largely predefined (e.g., see Harty, 1979). It is important to stress here that schools are viewed within this perspective merely as instructional sites. That schools are also cultural sites is ignored, as is the notion that schools represent arenas of contestation and struggle among differentially empowered cultural and economic groups. The latter becomes evident in the dominant role that the discourse of learning psychology and structural-functionalism have played in defining traditional theory's view of schooling. Excluding the mediations of class and power, traditional educational theory either reduces culture to so-called standards of excellence, or simply treats it as a neutral social science category. Missing from the traditional view is the notion that culture refers to specific processes that involve lived antagonistic relations among different socio-economic groups with unequal access to the means of power and a resulting unequal ability to produce, distribute, and legitimize their shared principles and lived experiences (Gramsci 1971; Hall & Jefferson 1976). Thus one derives little sense from the traditional view of how schools function in the interest of the dominant culture to reproduce the logic and values of the existing society.

It is at this point that one can trace the beginnings of what has been loosely called the "new sociology of education." At the core of this approach, even in its earliest stages, was an attempt to understand how schools constituted subjectivities and produced meaning, and how they were linked to the issues of power and control (Young 1971; Young & Whitty 1977). Instead of separating knowledge from power, proponents of the new theory argued that what counts as knowledge in any given society, school, or social site presupposes and constitutes specific power relations. The critical sociology that developed out of this theoretical interest in the connection between power and knowledge was important because it called into question how meaning was produced in schools, and argued strongly for a mode of theorizing that questioned taken-for-granted school categories and practices (Bates 1981; Musgrave 1980).

Eventually, the phenomenological variant of the new sociology of education was challenged by critical analyses that argued that the real determinants of social control and change lay not inside the typifications and consciousness of teachers but in the political and economic structures of the larger society. In other words, the concern for human agency and transformative consciousness gave way to analyses of how schools function as institutions designed to reproduce the logic of domination and inequality. Thus the new sociology of education, while still focusing on the relationship among power, domination, and schooling, found itself torn between perspectives that stressed a one-sided structuralism or a limited focus on culture and the social construction of knowledge. On the one hand, the emphasis was on locating power relations outside of schools, and in attempting to unravel how these penetrated and shaped the organization of the school and the day-to-day classroom social relations (Baron, et al. 1981). On the other hand, phenomenological and interactional-based approaches focused on the processes at work in the production and construction of school knowledge.

As useful as each of these positions is, each approach has failed to develop a theory of schooling that dialectically links structure and human agency. Consequently, they have either distorted or undertheorized those complex and contradictory moments that tie schools to the state and economic sphere. Unknowingly, these perspectives not only helped reproduce the very mechanisms of domination they attacked, they have also ignored those ideological and cultural spaces that speak to resistance and the promise of a transformative critical pedagogy.

The current impasse in the new sociology of education is revealed in its inability to move beyond what I have labeled *theories of reproduction.* That is, in spite of the attempts to build on earlier structuralist and culturalist positions, the theoretical parameters of the new sociology have remained restricted to one-sided notions of power and human agency that need to be reconstructed if the ground work for a critical pedagogy is to emerge. It is to an analysis of these positions that I will now turn.

Theories of Reproduction

In the most general sense, theories of reproduction take as their central concern the issue of how schools function in the interest of the dominant society. But unlike liberal and structural-functionalist accounts, they reject the assumption that schools are democratic institutions that promote cultural excellence, value-free knowledge, and objective modes of instruction. Instead, reproduction theories focus on how power is used to mediate between schools and the interests of capital. By moving outside of the official view of schooling, such theories focus on how schools utilize their material and ideological resources to reproduce the social relations and attitudes needed to sustain the social divisions of labor necessary for the existing relations of production. The overwhelming concern of such theories is with the politics and mechanisms of domination, more specifically with the way in which these leave their imprint on the pattern of relations that tie schools to the industrial order and the character of daily classroom life. Theories of reproduction also share fundamentally different perceptions of how power and control function in the interest of the dominant society both in and out of schools.

In stressing the determinate nature and primacy of either the state or political economy in educational theory and practice, reproductive approaches have played a significant role in exposing the ideological assumptions and processes behind the rhetoric of neutrality and social mobility characteristic of conservative as well as liberal views of schooling. Yet while such approaches represent an important theoretical break from idealist and functionalist paradigms in educational theory, they still remain situated within a problematic that ultimately supports rather than challenges the logic of the existing order. The point here is that there are some serious deficiencies in existing theories of reproduction, the most important of which is the refusal to posit a form of critique that demonstrates the theoretical and practical importance of counter-hegemonic struggles.

By failing either to acknowledge the degree to which the oppressed are *not* constituted by capital or to recognize those aspects of daily life to which capitalist ideology is indifferent, reproductive theories have been trapped in a reductive logic that appears at odds with the aim or even the possibility of developing a radical theory of education. In other words, neither the promise of oppositional teaching nor the more encompassing task of radical social change represents an important moment in these perspectives. The implications that these approaches have for a model of radical pedagogy seems obvious, for between the fact of class, race, and gender domination, and the promise of counter-ideologies embedded in the contradictions and tensions of classroom experiences, reproductive theories posit models of domination that appear so stark that even references to resistance or social change sound like a weak utterance inscribed in madness. In the end, abstract negation gives way to unrelieved despair, and the rhetoric of radical reproductive approaches points to a mode of theorizing that belongs to the rationality of the existing administered system of corporate domination.

The shortcomings of such approaches to radical pedagogy are not new. Earlier criticisms of theories of reproduction have pointed to their one-sided determinism, their somewhat simplistic view of social and cultural reproduction, and their often-ahistorical mode of theorizing (Young & Whitty 1977; Giroux 1981). What is disconcerting is that radical educational critics, especially in the United States,[1] have failed to abstract and develop partially articulated and potentially valuable elements within existing theories of reproduction. Some of these offer concrete possibilities for developing a theory of radical pedagogy—in this case, a theory of pedagogy that both accounts for the connection between structure and intentionality, and points to the need for a connection between critical theory and social action. It is imperative that such a pedagogy be informed by a political project that speaks not only to the interest of individual freedom and social reconstruction, but also has immediate relevance for educators as a mode of viable praxis.

There are two major positions that emerge from the broad range of reproductive approaches presently relying on macro-sociological models to analyze the relationship between schooling and the capitalist societies

of the advanced industrial countries of the West. But before identifying
and examining these positions, I want to stress that the categories under
use in this essay represent ideal-typical terms that have been hardened
and compressed for the sake of analytical clarity. The two positions are
(a) theories of social reproduction, which take as representative examples
the seminal work of Althusser (1969, 1971) and Bowles and Gintis (1976,
1980); and (b) theories of cultural production, with a primary focus on
the work of Pierre Bourdieu and his cohorts (1977a, 1977b), and on the
work of Basil Bernstein (1977, 1981).

Theories of Social Reproduction and the Problematic of Ideology and Power

Theories of social reproduction take as a central issue the notion that
schools occupy a major, if not critical, role in the reproduction of the
social formations needed to sustain capitalist relations of production. Put
simply, schools have emerged historically as social sites that have integrated the traditionally separate tasks of reproducing work skills and
producing attitudes that legitimize the social relations in which these
skills are located. In other words, workers historically have trained for
their work skills on the job under apprenticeship programs (Aronowitz
1973). Similarly, the production of a consciousness compatible with the
interest of the dominant society was initially accorded to the family and
the developing apparatus of the culture industry (Adorno & Horkheimer
1972). Schools, in this view, have now integrated these two tasks, and
while not being the only agency to do so, are the most important one.
In short, schooling represents a major social site for the construction of
subjectivities and dispositions, a place where students from different social
classes learn the necessary skills to occupy their class-specific locations in
the occupational division of labor. While Althusser (1971) and Bowles
and Gintis (1976) stress different aspects of the reproduction process, they
both believe that the economy-school nexus represents the major set of
relations in the maintenance and reproduction of the advanced industrial
countries of the West. Moreover, they exhibit a strong structuralist preoccupation in their concern with the way in which social systems position
or structure human subjects. In analyzing these positions, I will examine
the work of Althusser (1969, 1971) before I look at the work of Bowles

and Gintis (1976, 1980) and the implications that these two perspectives have for a radical theory of pedagogy.

LOUIS ALTHUSSER

Broadly speaking, Althusser attempts to tackle the difficult question of how a labor force can be constituted to fulfill the important material and ideological functions necessary for reproducing the capitalist mode of production. For Althusser (1971), this involves not only training workers with the skills and competencies necessary for working within the process of production, but also ensuring that workers will embody the attitudes, values, and norms that provide the required discipline and respect essential for the maintenance of the existing relations of production. Like Gramsci (1971), Althusser believes that the maintenance of the existing system of production and power arrangements depends on both the use of force and the use of ideology. Thus, for him, the reproduction of the "conditions of production" (Althusser 1971) rests upon three important interrelated moments in the process of production, capital accumulation, and reproduction of social formations characteristic of industrialized societies. These are: 1) the production of values that support the relations of production; 2) the use of force and ideology to support the dominant classes in all important spheres of control; and 3) the production of knowledge and skills relevant to specific forms of work.

Since this position has been treated extensively by others (Hirst 1979; Erben & Gleeson 1977; Callinicos 1977; Aronowitz 1981a), I will focus my analysis primarily on the conception of power and ideology that emerges from Althusser's position.

Jettisoning more vulgar interpretations of the base-superstructure issue in Marxist theory, Althusser (1971) argues that the relation of the economic base to the institutions of civil society cannot be reduced to a simple cause-and-effect determination. Instead, he claims that the legitimizing principles of capitalist industrialized societies are rooted in the self-regulating practices of the state, which consist of the *repressive state apparatus,* which rules by force and is represented by the army, police, courts, and prisons; and the *ideological state apparatus,* which rules primarily through consent and consists of schools, the family, the legal structure, the mass media, and other agencies. Though Althusser (1971) insists that in the final analysis the economic realm is the most important mode of determination, he manages to escape from an orthodox reading of this issue. He does this by claiming that within particular historically located societies there is a displacement of the logic of determination and domination from its primary contradiction in the economic sphere to other levels of determination within the social totality. For instance, he argues that at the present moment the primary determination in reproducing capitalist societies rests with institutions in the Ideological State Apparatus. More to the point, Althusser claims that schools in advanced capitalist societies have become *the* dominant institution in the ideological subjugation of the work force, for it is the schools that teach both the skills and the know-how that constitute the subjectivity of future generations of workers. He goes on to assert that ". . . one ideological state apparatus certainly has the dominant role, although hardly anyone lends an ear to its music; it is so silent! This is the School" (Althusser 1971). Althusser's theory of the state and reproduction is clearly an important advance over traditional and liberal accounts. For it argues that the meaning of schools can only be understood within the context of the ideological state apparatus; moreover, it dispels Marxist theories of schooling that argue that schools are simply the ethereal reflection of the economic order. Schools, in Althusser's view, are relatively autonomous institutions that exist in a particular relation with the economic base, but that at the same time have their own specific constraints and practices. For him, schools operate within a social structure defined by capitalist social relations and ideology; but the social relations and ideologies that mediate between schools and the economic base—not to mention the state—represent constraints that are modified, altered, and in some cases contradicted by a variety of political and social forces. What schools *don't do* as a set of collective agencies is challenge the structural basis of capitalism, though there are individuals within these institutions that may offer sharp criticisms and modes of oppositional teaching. As the major ideological state apparatus, schools, according to Althusser, generally serve their political function quite well and provide students with the appropriate attitudes for work and citizenship. These attitudes include "respect for the socio-technical division of labor and ultimately the rules of the order established by class domination" (Althusser 1971).

For our purposes, there are two questions in the Althusserian scheme: on the one hand, there is the question of the actual role that schools play in the reproduction of the existing order; on the other hand, there is the crucial issue of how the mechanisms of reproduction actually work themselves out within such institutions. Althusser's (1971) response to the first question is clear, but underdeveloped theoretically and empirically. He claims that schools teach students both the skills that are necessary for different jobs in the work force and the rules of behavior appropriate to the existing social relations of production. Althusser (1969, 1971) attempts to explain the nature of these functions through his notion of ideology.

In the Althusserian analysis of schooling, ideology contains two crucial elements. First, it has a material existence in the rituals, practices, and social processes that structure the day-to-day workings of schools. For example, ideological practices can be found in the very materiality of the architecture of the school building i.e., in the categorization of the separate academic subjects as they are exhibited concretely in different departments, often housed in separate buildings or situated on separate floors; in the hierarchical relations between teachers and students inscribed in the lecture hall where ". . . the seating arrangements—benches rising in tiers before a raised lectern—dictate the flow of information, and serve to neutralize professorial authority" (Hebdige 1979). Second, ideology neither produces consciousness nor a willing passive compliance. Instead, it functions as a system of representations, carrying meanings and ideas that structure the unconsciousness of students. The effect is to induce in them an "imaginary relationship . . . to their real conditions of existence" (Althusser 1971). Althusser writes at length on this issue:

> It is customary to suggest that ideology belongs to the region of "consciousness." . . . In truth, ideology has very little to do with "consciousness." . . . It is profoundly unconscious, even when it presents itself in a reflected form. Ideology is indeed a system of representations, but in the majority of cases these representations have nothing to do with "consciousness": they are usually images and occasionally concepts, but it is above all as structures that they impose on the vast majority of men, not via their "consciousness." They are perceived-accepted-suffered cultural objects and they act functionally on men in a process that escapes them. Men "live" their ideologies as the Cartesians "saw" the moon at two hundred paces away: not at all as a form of consciousness, but as an object of their "world"—as their world itself [Althusser 1969].

Althusser's (1969, 1971) view of ideology occupies a central position in his view of power and domination. The interplay between power and domination in this perspective is visible at two important levels. At the macro-level, the notion of the materiality of ideology highlights not only the "political" nature of space, time, routine, and rituals as they function within determinant institutional settings, it also illuminates the relation between capital and the dominant classes in the appropriation and use of apparatuses deemed essential to the production of ideologies and lived experiences. The notion that ideas are free-floating, or the equally reductionist notion of culture as mere excellence, are dealt an effective blow in this critique, which is amplified in the work of Foucault (1977). On another level, Althusser's (1969) more focused discussion of the effects of ideology, specifically his claim that it is a structuring feature of the unconscious, points to a relation between depth psychology and domination that itself raises a number of important issues, particularly in modes of educational theory where a one-sided concern with the cognitive aspects of schooling appears unquestioned. Unfortunately, Althusser (1969, 1971) situates these insights in a theoretical framework that is based on a reductionist notion of power and a one-dimensional view of human agency.

As a number of critics have pointed out (Erbeen & Gleeson 1977; Aronowitz 1981a; Willis 1981), Althusser has fashioned a theory of domination in which the needs of capital become indistinct from the effects of capitalist social relations. In fact, Althusser's (1971) notion of domination is so one-sided that it is impossible to deduce from his perspective the possibility of ideologies which are oppositional in nature (Hall 1981). This is no small point, because it suggests that schools are *not* to be viewed as social sites marked by the interplay of domination, accommodation, and struggle, but rather as sites that function smoothly to reproduce a docile labor force.

Ideology, in this perspective, is treated undialectically in a number of instances. First, ideology collapses into a theory of domination that restricts its meaning to such a degree that it appears as a "force" able to invalidate or diffuse any type of resistance. Ideology is in this case not simply a negative moment in the lived experience of human beings; its locus of operation at the level of the unconscious appears to make it immune to reflexive self criticism. In a second undialectical treatment of the concept, ideology becomes an institutional medium of oppression that appears to function so efficiently that the state and its ideological state apparatus are presented as part of a static and administrative fantasy. In this view, schools and other social sites seem free from even the slightest vestige of conflict, contradiction, and struggle. Finally, Althusser has developed a notion of power that appears to eliminate human agency. The notion that human beings are neither homogeneously constituted subjects nor passive role bearers is lost in Althusser's (1971) analysis. In effect, there is no theory of mediation in this perspective; nor is there any conception of how people appropriate, select, accommodate, or simply generate meaning. Instead, in Althusser's reductionist schema human beings are relegated to static role-bearers, carriers of predefined meanings, agents of hegemonic ideologies inscribed in their psyche like irremovable scars. Consequently, it is impossible to explain from this perspective what mechanisms are at work to allow or characterize schools as relatively autonomous institutions.

Althusser's (1971) work is in marked contrast to the work of Bowles and Gintis (1976), who do point to some of the specific mechanisms of schooling that serve the logic of capital. If the working class is to be judged as dumb and inert, we at least deserve a glimpse of how the machinery of oppression makes them "hop and jump" for their appointed slots in the labor process. Exaggerations aside, one reason for Althusser's failure is that he has fashioned a theory of reproduction and domination at a level of abstraction that appears uninformed by the concrete interplay of power relations. As Willis and Corrigan point out, "If pure dominance has any meaning at all it can only be in formal sets of possibilities and abstract relations. It is in profane material struggles that opposition takes on meaning through practice" (Willis & Corrigan 1980). The point here is that in the end Althusser falls prey to an abstract system of power and domination that appears to suffer from the very reification it analyzes. Instead of providing a dialectical understanding of the logic of domination, he has enshrined it in a formalistic system that is as insular as it is theoretically demeaning to the notions of struggle and human agency.

BOWLES & GINTIS

Bowles and Gintis (1976) share Althusser's basic notion of the role of schooling in capitalist society. That is, like Althusser, Bowles and Gintis believe that schools serve two functions in capitalist society. One essential function is the reproduction of the labor power necessary for capital accumulation. This is provided for in schools through differential selecting and training along class and gender lines of students with the "technical and cognitive skills required for adequate job performance" (Bowles & Gintis 1976) in the hierarchical social division of labor. The second essential function requires the reproduction of those forms of consciousness, dispositions, and values necessary for the maintenance of "institutions and social relationships which facilitate the translation of labor into profit" (ibid).

Althusser (1971) used the concept of ideology to direct us to the role that schools play in securing the domination of the working class. Bowles and Gintis (1976) take us along a similar route but employ a different theoretical vehicle. Instead of the overbearing weight of the ideological state apparatus, we are given the notion of the *correspondence principle.* Broadly speaking, the correspondence principle posits that the hierarchically structured patterns of values, norms, and skills that characterize the work force and the dynamics of class interaction under capitalism are mirrored in the social dynamics of the daily classroom encounter. Classroom social relations inculcate students with the attitudes and dispositions necessary for acceptance of the social and economic imperatives of a capitalist economy. Bowles and Gintis clearly specify the nature of their structural analysis:

> The educational system helps integrate youth into the economic system, we believe, through a structural correspondence between its social relations and those of production. The structure of social relations in education not only inures the student to the discipline of the workplace, but develops the types of personal demeanor, modes of self-preservation, self-image, and social identifications which are crucial ingredients of job adequacy. Specifically, the social relationships of education—the relationships between administrators and teachers, teachers and students, students and their work—replicate the hierarchical division of labor [Bowles & Gintis 1976].

While Bowles and Gintis are helpful in pointing to specific classroom social relations as social processes that link schools to determinate forces in the workplace, they eventually end up with a theory of social reproduction that is much too simplified and overdetermined. Not only does their argument point to a spurious "constant fit" between schools and the workplace, it does so by ignoring important issues regarding the role of consciousness, ideology, and resistance in the schooling process. In other words, dominant control in this view is characterized by a mode of analysis that overlooks the fact that social structures like the school and workplace represent ". . . both the medium and the outcome of reproduction practices" (Giddens 1979). The notion that human action and structure presuppose one another is ignored by Bowles and Gintis in favor of a model of correspondence in which the subject gets dissolved

under the weight of structural constraints that appear to
personality and the workplace (Best & Connolly 1979).

What is disregarded in the notion of "correspondence" is
issue of resistance, but also any attempt to delineate the co
in which working-class subjectivities are constituted. Instead o\
of the way in which various sites with their complex of ideologies and
different levels of structural constraints function to produce a working
class marked by a variety of distinctions, we are presented with a homogeneous image of working-class life fashioned solely by the logic of
domination. The impetus toward self-creation appears to be generated
for them by the dominant, who are presented here under the rubric of
a spurious harmony.

Lacking a considered theory of consciousness or ideology, Bowles and
Gintis grossly ignore what is taught in schools as well as how classroom
knowledge is either mediated through school culture or given meaning
by the teachers and students under study. The authors provide no conceptual tools to unravel the problem of how knowledge is both consumed
and produced in the school setting. What we are left with is a theoretical
position that reinforces the idea that there is little that educators can do
to change their circumstances or plight. In short, not only do contradictions and tensions disappear in this account, but also the promise of
critical pedagogy and social change.

In fairness to Bowles and Gintis, it must be stressed that their work
has made a number of positive contributions to educational theory. Since
I have examined these in detail elsewhere (Giroux, 1981), I will simply
mention some of the more saliant contributions. First, the earlier work
improved our knowledge of how the mechanisms of the hidden curriculum
worked through the social relations of the classroom. Secondly, their work
was invaluable in articulating the relationship between class- and gender-
specific modes of schooling with social processes in the workplace.
Moreover, Bowles and Gintis helped to illuminate the non-cognitive
dimensions of domination by focusing on the role the schools played in
the production of certain types of personality traits. Furthermore, in their
most recent work, these authors have argued for the importance of contradictions in the process of social reproduction as well as for the importance of social sites such as the family (Bowles & Gintis 1981). But
even this work, in spite of its theoretical gains, says very little about
either consciousness or how schools produce subjectivities that are not
subsumed within the imperatives of reproduction.

SUMMARY

In summary, both Althusser (1971) and Bowles and Gintis (1976) fail either to define hegemony in terms that posit a dialectical relationship among power, ideology, and resistance, or to provide a framework for developing a viable mode of radical pedagogy. Both views relegate human agency to a passive model of socialization and overemphasize domination while ignoring contradictions and forms of resistance that also characterize social sites like schools and the workplace. Moreover, both views stress the notion of social reproduction at the expense of cultural reproduction, and in spite of Althusser's insistence on the role of ideology as a mechanism of domination, the concept ultimately functions to mystify rather than explain how people resist, escape, or change the "crushing" weight of the existing social order.

It is also important to note that in these perspectives not only are the mechanisms of power and domination either underdeveloped or ignored, there is also a failure to consider that domination is never total or that power itself is something other than a negative force reducible to the economic sphere or state apparatus. Lost from the social reproductive perspective is any serious consideration of schools as social sites that produce and reproduce ideologies and cultural forms that stand in opposition to dominant values and practices. By ignoring the notion that dominant ideologies and social processes have to be mediated rather than simply reproduced by the cultural field of the school, social-reproduction theorists exempt themselves from one of the central questions in any theory of reproduction, i.e., the question of explaining both the nature and existence of contradictions and patterns of opposition in schools. The existence of such patterns suggests that dominant educational values and practices have to be viewed in such a way that their determinate effects can neither be guaranteed nor taken-for-granted (Moore 1978, 1979).

A more viable approach to understanding the role that schools play in the process of social reproduction of class and gender relationships should focus on the role that the cultural field of the school plays as a *mediating* force within the complex interplay of reproduction and resistance. At this juncture, we may turn to theories of cultural reproduction.

Theories of Cultural Reproduction

Theories of cultural reproduction begin precisely at the point where social reproduction theories end. That is, the work of Althusser (1971) and

Bowles and Gintis (1976) is characterized by a singular failure to develop a theory of consciousness and culture, whereas theories of cultural reproduction have made a sustained effort to develop a sociology of curriculum that links culture, class, and domination with the logic and imperatives of schooling. In other words, theories of cultural reproduction are concerned with the question of how capitalist societies are able to repeat and reproduce themselves, but the focus of their concern with issues of social control centers around either an analysis of the principles underlying the structure and transmission of the cultural field of the school or questions of how school culture is produced, selected, and legitimated. In other words, the mediating role of culture in reproducing class societies is given priority over the study of related issues such as the source and consequences of economic inequality. The work of Pierre Bourdieu and his cohorts (1977a, 1977b) in France and the work of Basil Bernstein (1977) in England represent two instrumental perspectives for studying the cultural reproduction position.

PIERRE BOURDIEU

Pierre Bourdieu and Jean-Claude Passeron (1977a) have made a sustained effort to develop a sociology of curriculum that links culture, class, and domination, on the one hand, and schooling, knowledge, and biography on the other. Bourdieu and Passeron reject reproductive accounts that view the school as simply a mirror of society, and argue that schools are relatively autonomous institutions only indirectly influenced by more powerful economic and political institutions. Rather than being directly linked to the power of an economic elite, schools are seen as part of a larger universe of symbolic institutions that, rather than impose docility and oppression, reproduce existing power relations subtly via the production and distribution of a dominant culture that tacitly confirms what it means to be educated.

Bourdieu's theory of cultural reproduction begins with the assumption that class-divided societies and the ideological and material configurations on which they rest are mediated and reproduced, in part, through what he calls "symbolic violence" (1979). That is, class control is not simply the crude reflex of economic power imposing itself in the form of overt force and restraint. Instead, it is constituted through the more subtle exercise of symbolic power waged by a ruling class in order "to impose a definition of the social world that is consistent with its interests" (Bourdieu 1979). Culture in this perspective becomes the mediating link between ruling-class interests and everyday life. It presents the economic and political interests of the dominant classes, not as arbitrary and historically contingent, but as necessary and natural elements of the social order.

Education is seen as an important social and political force in the process of class reproduction, for by appearing to be an impartial and neutral "transmitter" of the benefits of a valued culture, schools are able to promote inequality in the name of fairness and objectivity. This is an important point in Bourdieu's (1977a, 1977b) analysis, because through this argument he rejects both the idealist position, which views schools as independent of external forces, and orthodox radical critiques in which schools merely mirror the needs of the economic system. In contrast to these positions, Bourdieu argues that it is precisely the relative autonomy of the educational system that "enables it to serve external demands under the guise of independence and neutrality, i.e., to conceal the social function it performs and so to perform them more effectively (Bourdieu 1977a). Moreover, it is in analyzing how the school actually performs the functions of cultural reproduction that we begin to benefit most from this analysis.

The concepts of cultural capital and habitus are central to understanding Bourdieu's (1977a, 1977b) analysis of how the mechanisms of cultural reproduction function concretely within schools. The first concept, cultural capital, refers on the one hand to the different sets of linguistic and cultural competencies that individuals inherit by way of the class-located boundaries of their families. In more specific terms, a child inherits from his or her family sets of meanings, qualities of style, modes of thinking, and types of dispositions that are accorded a certain social value and status as a result of what the dominant class or classes label as the most valued cultural capital. Schools play a particularly important role in both legitimating and reproducing the dominant culture, for schools, especially at the level of higher education, embody class interests and ideologies that capitalize on a kind of familiarity and set of skills that only specific students have received by means of their family backgrounds and class relations. For example, students whose families have a tenuous connection to forms of cultural capital highly valued by the dominant society are at a decided disadvantage. Bourdieu sums up the process well when he argues that the educational system:

. . . offers information and training which can be received and acquired only by subjects endowed with the system of predispositions that is the condition for the success of the transmission and of the inculcation of the culture. By doing away with giving explicitly to everyone what it implicitly demands of everyone, the educational system demands of everyone alike that they have what they do not give. This consists mainly of linguistic and cultural competence and that relationship of familiarity with culture which can only be produced by family upbringing when it transmits the dominant culture [Bourdieu 1977c].

Within the logic of this analysis, the dynamics of cultural reproduction function in two important ways. First, the dominant classes exert their power by defining what counts as meaning, and in doing so they disguise this "cultural arbitrariness" in the name of a neutrality that masks its ideological grounding. This is an important point because Bourdieu and Passeron (1977a) use it to illustrate convincingly the "illusory nature of all discourses which assume the student milieu to be homogeneous" (Baudelot & Establet 1971). What is argued here is that the effects of class reach deep into the university student body and are replicated in the various ways in which different student groups relate to the culture, ideology, and politics of the school. Second, class and power connect with dominant cultural production not only in the structure and evaluation of the school curriculum, but also in the dispositions of the oppressed themselves, who actively participate in their own subjugation. This becomes more clear if we examine Bourdieu's notion of *habitus*.

According to Bourdieu, the habitus refers to the subjective dispositions which reflect a class-based social grammar of taste, knowledge, and behavior inscribed permanently in the "body schema and the schemes of thought" (Bourdieu 1977b) of each developing person. The habitus, or internalized competencies and sets of structured needs, represents the mediating link between structures, social practice, and reproduction. That is, the system of "symbolic violence" does not mechanically impose itself on the oppressed; it is at least in part reproduced by them, since the habitus governs practices that assign limits to its "operations of invention" (ibid). In other words, objective structures—language, schools, families—tend to produce dispositions, which in turn structure social experiences that reproduce the same objective structures.

The value of Bourdieu's educational theory centers around his political analysis of culture, his examination of how the dominant culture is produced in schools, and his attempt at developing a notion of depth psychology that partially unravels the question of why the dominated take part in their own oppression. Yet as important as Bourdieu's theoretical advances are, especially over liberal and structural-functionalist models of schooling, they remain trapped in a notion of power and domination that is one-sided and over-determined. For instance, as important as the notion of habitus is in linking the concept of domination to the structure of personality needs, its definition and use constitute a conceptual strait-jacket that provides no room for modification or escape. Thus the notion of habitus smothers the possibility for social change and collapses into a mode of management ideology. More specifically, Bourdieu (1979b) disregards the assumption that reflexive thought may result in social practices that qualitatively restructure one's disposition or structure of needs, one's habitus (Heller 1974). Consequently, Bourdieu (1977b) ends up with a theory of hegemony irreversibly rooted in the personality structure; in doing so, he appears to short-circuit the hope for individual and social transformation.

Equally important is the fact that culture, in Bourdieu's view, represents a one-way process of domination. As a result, it suggests falsely that working-class cultural forms and knowledge are both homogeneous and merely a pale reflection of dominant cultural capital. Working-class cultural production and its link to cultural reproduction through the processes of resistance, incorporation, or accommodation is not acknowledged by Bourdieu. The collapse of culture and class into the dynamics of dominant cultural reproduction raises a number of significant problems. First, such a portrayal eliminates conflict both within and between different classes. Thus notions such as struggle, diversity, and human agency get lost in a reductionist view of human nature and history. Second, by reducing classes to homogeneous entities whose only differences are based on whether or not they exercise or respond to power, Bourdieu (1977a) provides no theoretical opportunity to unravel the way in which cultural domination *and* resistance are mediated through the complex interface of race, gender, and class (Arnot 1981). This point is important because it indicates not only that there are elements in society that structure important distinctions within and between classes, but that there are forms of cultural production that are not class-specific, just as there are modes of behavior and ideologies to which capital is relatively indifferent. What is missing from Bourdieu's analysis is the notion that culture is *both* a structuring and transforming process. Davies captures this dynamic in his comment, "Culture refers paradoxically to conservative adaptation and lived subordination of classes to other classes and to opposition, resistance, and creative struggle for change" (Davies 1981).

Bourdieu's (1977a, 1979) analyses also suffer from a one-sided treatment of ideology. In this case, ruling class values, meanings, and codes appear to exist outside of a theory of struggle and imposition. Ideology as a construct that links relations of meaning with relations of power in a dialectical fashion is lost in this perspective. That is, while it is useful to argue, as Bourdieu does, that dominant ideologies are transmitted by schools and actively incorporated by students, it is equally important to remember that ideologies are also *imposed* on students who occasionally view them as contrary to their own interests and who either resist openly or conform only under pressure from school authorities. The point here is that dominant ideologies are not simply transmitted in schools, nor are they practiced in a void. On the contrary, they are often met with resistance by teachers, students, or parents, and must therefore, to be successful, repress the production of counter-ideologies. Moreover, schools are not simply static institutions that reproduce the dominant ideology, they are active agents in its construction as well. As Connell, et al, point out in one of their ethnographic studies of a ruling class school:

> The school generates practices by which the class is renewed, integrated, and re-constituted in the face of changes in its own composition and in the general social circumstances in which it tries to survive and prosper. (This is an embracing practice, ranging from the school fete, Saturday sport, and week-night dinners with parents, to the organization of a marriage market—e.g., interschool dances—and informal networks in business and the professions, to the regulation of class membership, updating of ideology, and subordination of particular interests to those of class as a whole.) The ruling-class school is no mere agent of the class; it is an important and active part of it. In short, it is organic to its class. Bourdieu wrote a famous essay about the school as conserver; we would suggest an equal stress should be laid on the school as constructor [Connell, et al 1981].

By failing to develop a theory of ideology that speaks to the way human beings dialectically create, resist, and accommodate themselves to dominant ideologies, Bourdieu excludes both the active nature of domination as well as the active nature of resistance. Consequently, by reducing the dynamics of ideological domination and construction to a transmission process, the notion of ideology is reified, and reduced to a static structural category.

Of course, Bourdieu (1977a) provides a theoretical service in linking the family and school in his theory of cultural reproduction; but his refusal to examine how contradictions arise either through the internal divisions of age, sex, and race or between the different classes themselves raises the question of why one should bother to study the issue of working-class domination in the first place, particularly since the latter appears as part of an Orwellian nightmare that is as irreversible as it is unjust. It is important to argue, in spite of Bourdieu, that schools do not simply usurp the cultural capital of working-class homes and communities. Complex relations develop in the context of the school, and these need to be analyzed (Clarke, et al. 1979; Hakken 1980). This point is worth pursuing. R. Timothy Sieber (1982) argues that Bourdieu's notion of academic success, which links class-based and linguistic a priori cultural competencies and experiences to the privileged position of middle-class students in universities, contains some important theoretical insights into how the process of social and cultural reproduction works in higher education. But he qualifies his praise by arguing that Bourdieu's model of analysis reifies the way in which mechanisms of social and cultural reproduction work in urban elementary schools. For example, Sieber's (1982) ethnographic study of a public elementary school in New York not only revealed that middle-class students, because of their cultural competencies and experiences, were accorded specific academic privileges and freedoms denied to working-class and Puerto Rican students in the school. Also, this "privileged standing" and educational benefits provided to middle-class students were the outcome of a long struggle that had pitted the middle-class segment of the community against its predominantly working-class residents. The predominance of middle-class culture in this school was the outcome of a political struggle, and, contrary to Bourdieu's position, was actively and systematically developed "both inside and outside the school" by middle-class parents (Sieber 1982). Sieber recounts:

> [M]y conjoint research in the wider school and community revealed something that might have remained hidden had I confined my investigation to classrooms alone. The privileged standing of the middle-class children in the school was not simply the result of the cultural advantage afforded by their upbringing; in fact, their "middle-class" culture conflicted on many points with the culture of the school and its staff. The middle-class children's success at P. S. 4 had been, rather, achieved only through a history of ongoing political conflict that had pitted their parents against the school staff, as well as against the school's other parents. Indeed, the classroom events I was witnessing were the end product of a much broader process of gentrification the school's middle-class parents had brought to Chestnut Heights over the

previous decade. . . . In the case of urban elementary schools such as P. S. 4, however, Bourdieu's model seems to reify the process by which schools enhance the cultural capital of elites, underestimating the hand that parent and community forces have in this process. The present consideration of community history, school-community relations, and middle-class parent involvement indicates that intense political struggles were key factors in the establishment of elite education at P. S. 4 [Sieber 1982].

Angela McRobbie (1980) presents a similar critique. She argues that educators need to take both the social and sexual divisions of labor into account in cultural studies, and that Marxist analyses in general have ignored the latter when looking at the family-school relationship. She indicates that the complexity of such relationships raises questions not only about domination but also about the determinant forces that unwittingly promote resistance. For example, schools may set children against their family cultures, they may provide more progressive models of gender relations than exist in the family, or they may highlight modes of domination that allow students to understand the limits of both the school and family structure within the wider society. One wonders how Bourdieu's theory of domination would explain the following behavior of a group of fifth grade students in Toronto, as chronicled by their teacher;

Let's have art this afternoon, Mr. McLaren!

Yah. We want art!

Well, we've got some math to do this afternoon, perhaps after we're finished with that. . . .

We wanna naked model . . . one with really big tits that stick out to here!

. . . and lots of fuzzy hair down here!

You guys are sick! Is that all you think about?

Shut up Sandra! All you think about is naked boys!

Barry's a fag. He thinks about naked boys too! . . .

Sir! Let's have floor hockey instead!

I hates floor hockey!

We don't want you girls! Hey, sir! Let the girls play skippin or somethin, but let us play floor hockey!

There will be no playing anything until we finish our math.

Kids should be allowed to choose sometimes. You said so!

Yah! You never let us have fun—real fun!

Okay, okay. What does "real fun" mean?

If we wanna go somewheres, the creek or somethin, they say you should let us . . . .

. . . Open your books to the math review on page fifty-one.

Wait a minute! I ain't gots no pencil!

That's because you used it to jab that little kid at recess and the teacher took it off you!

Get lost. . . .

Here, you can use my pencil.

Thanks, sir! Hey look! I stole the teacher's pencil!

Can I turn on the radio during art?

Quietly, yes . . . quietly. But first, our math!

Hey Sandra, get up on the desk and take off your shirt!

Anybody who doesn't finish this test gets a note to take home and get signed!

Sir! Can I have a note, please! I love notes!

Me too! I wanna note saying I'm bad!

Everybody line up for bad notes!

. . . Hey! Gimme back my math book!

Cut the crap!

This is boring . . . . {McLaren 1980}.

McLaren's account suggests that schools are much less successful in producing docile working-class students than Bourdieu (1977a 1977c) would have us believe. More importantly, Bourdieu (1977a 1977c) offers no theoretical insights into either the nature of such resistance or what its value might be in pedagogical terms, i.e., what opportunities it provides for seeing beyond its phenomenal forms and unraveling the possibilities that might be gleaned from understanding its strengths and weaknesses for critical thought.

Finally, there is a serious failure in Bourdieu's work regarding his unwillingness to link the notion of domination with the materiality of economic forces. There is no sense in Bourdieu's (1977a 1977c) work of how the economic system, with its asymmetrical relations of power, produces concrete constraints on working-class students. Foucault's (1980) notion that power works on the body, in the family, on sexuality and on knowledge, is worth acknowledging because it serves to remind us that the relations of power weigh down more than just the mind. The constraints of power are not exhausted in the concept of symbolic violence. Domination as an objective, concrete instance cannot be ignored in any discussion of schooling. For instance, the privileged have a relationship to time which enables them to make long-term plans for their futures, whereas the children of the working class, especially those in higher-education, are often burdened by economic constraints that lock them into the present and limit their goals to short-term plans. Time is a privation, not a possession, for most working-class students (Bisseret 1979). It is the economic issue that often plays the crucial role in the decision over whether a working-class student can go to school full- or part-time, or in some cases, at all. Likewise, the economic issue is often the determining factor in whether a student will have to work part-time while attending school. Bourdieu and Passeron (1977a) appear to have forgotten that domination has to be grounded in something other than ideology, that it also has material conditions. This is no small matter, because it points to a major gap in Bourdieu's (1977a) reasoning regarding working-class failure. That is, the internalization of dominant ideology is not the only force that motivates the working-class student or secures his or her failure. The behavior, failures, and choices of these students are also grounded in material conditions.

As a result of Bourdieu's (1977a, 1977b) one-sided emphasis on ruling-class domination and its attendant cultural practices, it becomes clear that both the concept of capital as well as the notion of class are static categories. Class involves a notion of social relations in opposition to each other. It refers to shifting relations of domination and resistance, to capital and its institutions as they constantly regroup and attempt to resituate the logic of domination and incorporation (Gramsci 1971). These oppositions are missing from Bourdieu's analyses, and what we are left with is a theory of reproduction that displays no faith in subordinate classes and groups, no hope for their ability or willingness to reinvent and reconstruct the conditions under which they live, work, and learn. As a result, reproduction theories informed by logic of Bourdieu's notion of domination say too little about how to construct the theoretical basis for a radical pedagogy.

BASIL BERNSTEIN

At the core of Bernstein's (1977) analysis of education and the role it plays in the cultural reproduction of class relationships is a theory of cultural transmission. Bernstein points to the problematic at the center of this theory: "How a society selects, classifies, distributes, transmits, and evaluates the educational knowledge it considers to be public, reflects both the distribution of power and the power and the principles of social control. From this point of view, differences within, and change in, the organization, transmission, and evaluation of educational knowledge should be a major area of sociological interest" (Bernstein 1977).

Arguing that education is a major force in the structuring of experience, Bernstein attempts to illuminate how curriculum, pedagogy, and evaluation constitute message systems whose underlying structural principles represent modes of social control rooted in the wider society. In investigating the question of how the structure of education shapes both identity and experience, he develops a theoretical framework in which he claims that schools embody an educational code. Such a code is important because it organizes the ways in which authority and power are to be mediated in all aspects of school experience.

The dominant educational code in Bernstein's typology is either a collection code or an integrated code, the meanings of which are directly connected to concepts of classification and framing. Classification refers "not to what is classified, but to the relationship between contents" (Bernstein 1977); in other words, to the strength or weakness in the construction and maintenance of the boundaries that exist between different categories, contents, and the like. Boundary strength in Bernstein's perspective is a critical feature that underlies the division of labor at the heart of the educational experience and wider society. Framing, on the other hand, refers to the pedagogical relationship itself and the issue of how power and control are invested and mediated between teachers and students. Or as Bernstein puts it, framing refers "to the degree of control teacher and pupil possess over the selection, organization, pacing and timing of the knowledge transmitted and received in the pedagogical relationship" (Bernstein 1977). Either or both concepts may be strong or weak in different combinations; thus they constitute the dominant educational code. For example, the collection code refers to strong classification and framing and could take the form of a traditional curriculum characterized by rigid subject boundaries and strong hierarchical teacher-student relationships. By contrast, an integrated code, characterized by weak classification and weak framing, represents a curriculum in which subjects and categories become more integrated and teacher-student authority relationships more negotiable and open to modification. What is important to understand is that both codes are tied to modes of social reproduction, although Bernstein believes that the integrated code contains more possibilities for a progressive pedagogy.

By using this typology, Bernstein has attempted to conceptualize the structural features that link schools and the mode of production as they reproduce class relationships. Power and control in this perspective are embedded in the structuring devices that shape the experiences and consciousness of human beings passing through social sites such as the family, the school, and the workplace. While Bernstein rejects any form of mechanical correspondence among these different social sites, he nevertheless tends to assume that regardless of the *form* of social control they perpetuate, all of these social spheres share in the reproduction of class control and the maldistribution of power that underlies the existing mode of production. Thus, in the end, educational reforms that call for a change in the *form* of social control pose little threat to the class basis of power and will do just as little to effect social change.

Bernstein's (1977) work is particularly useful in identifying how the principles of social control are coded in the structuring devices that shape the messages embedded in schools and other social institutions. In the final analysis, however, Bernstein's work does not go far enough as a theory of radical pedagogy. While he points to the importance of a semiotic reading of the structural features that shape knowledge, classroom social relationships, and organizational structures in the day-to-day functioning of schools, he does so at the expense of analyzing the lived-experiences of the actors themselves. That is, Bernstein ignores how different classes of students, teachers, and other educational workers give meaning to the codes that influence their daily experiences. By disregarding the production of meaning and the content of school cultures, he provides a weak and one-sided notion of consciousness and human action, and needless to say, whether in the self-constituted acts of discourse, social practices, or in the school materials themselves, he thus escapes the tricky question of how the state and other powerful capitalist institutions such as the corporate conglomerates influence school policy and curriculum making through the production of specific ideologies and cultural materials.

In conclusion, both Bourdieu and Bernstein surrender to a version of domination in which the cycle of reproduction appears unbreakable. In spite of insightful comments on the form and substance of cultural re-production, social actors as possible agents of change disappear in these accounts, as do instances of conflict and contradiction. Though both theorists provide illuminating analyses of the relative autonomy of schools and the political nature of culture as a reproductive force, Bourdieu and Bernstein end up either ignoring or playing-down the notions of resistance and counter-hegemonic struggle. As a result, their insights are limited and incomplete.

Beyond Theories of Social and Cultural Reproduction

Within the last few years, a number of educational studies have emerged that attempt to move beyond the important but limited theoretical ad-vances that characterize social and cultural reproduction theories. Taking the concepts of conflict and resistance as starting points for their analyses, these accounts have sought to redefine the importance of power, ideology, and culture as central constructs for understanding the complex relations between schooling and the dominant society. Consequently, the work of Willis (1977), Hebdige (1979), and Corrigan (1979) has been instru-mental in providing a rich body of detailed literature that integrates neo-Marxist social theory with ethnographic studies in order to illuminate the dynamics of accommodation and resistance as they work through oppos-sitional youth cultures both inside and outside of schools.

In contrast to the vast amount of ethnographic literature on schooling both in the United States (Jackson, 1968; Becker, 1961; Stinchombe, 1964; Mehan, 1979) and England (Lacy, 1970; Hargreaves, 1967; Woods, 1979), neo-Marxist accounts have not sacrificed theoretical depth for methodological refinement. That is, more recent Marxist studies have not followed the generally bland method of merely providing exhaustive de-scriptive analyses of the internal workings of the school. Instead, these perspectives—especially Willis (1977)—have attempted to analyze how determinant socio-economic structures embedded in the dominant society work through the mediations of class and culture in shaping the lived antagonistic experiences of students at the level of everyday life. Rejecting the functionalism inherent in both conservative and radical versions of educational theory, neo-Marxist accounts have analyzed curriculum as a complex discourse that not only serves in the interests of the relations of domination, but which also contains interests that speak to emancipatory possibilities.

The importance of the neo-Marxist work on resistance and reproduction cannot be overstressed. Its attempts to link social structures and human agency to explore the way they interact in a dialectical manner represent a significant theoretical advance over functional-structuralist and inter-actional accounts. Of course, neo-Marxist resistance theories are also beset with problems, and I will mention some of the more outstanding ones here. Their singular achievement is the a priori status allotted to critical theory and emancipatory interests as the basic elements upon which to assess the problem under study, the political nature of the researcher's views, and the centrality of concepts such as class, power, ideology, and culture in analyzing the relationship between schooling and capitalism. One qualification should be made regarding the a priori importance given to theory in neo-Marxist resistance studies. To celebrate theory as the central mediating category in research is not to argue simultaneously that practice or empirical work is either unimportant or irrelevant to theory. On the contrary, it is meant to argue that theory and practice, while interconnected at the point of experience, represent distinct analytical moments and should not collapse into each other (Horkheimer 1972). Theory serves the function of establishing the problematic that governs the nature of social inquiry; it also illuminates the interests embodied in the rationality that governs its dominant and subordinate assumptions. A specific constellation of assumptions and values provides the reflexivity that gives a theoretical framework its value. Put another way, theory must be celebrated for its truth content, not for the methodological refinements it employs. Needless to say, theory is informed by practice; but its real value lies in its ability to provide the reflexivity needed to interpret the concrete experience that is the object of research. Theory can never be reduced to practice, because the specificity of practice has its own center of theoretical gravity, and cannot be reduced to a predefined formula. That is, the specificity of practice cannot be abstracted from the complex of forces, struggles, and mediations that give each situation a unique defining quality. Theory can help us understand this quality, but cannot reduce it to the logic of a mathematical formula. Furthermore, it must be remembered that experience and concrete studies do not speak for themselves, and that they will tell us very little if the theoretical framework we use to interpret them lacks depth and critical rigor. This point appears to be lost on a whole range of recent critics currently responding to work that comes out of the neo-Marxist tradition (Lacey 1982; Hargreaves 1982). These critics belabor neo-Marxist studies for not drawing on or conducting empirical studies grounded in the problematic of liberal social theory. The point, of course, is that in redefining the nature of educational theory, the struggle will not be over the use of data or types of studies conducted. The real battle will be over the theoretical frameworks in use, for it is on the contested terrain of theory that the debate needs to be conducted (Laclau 1977). By forgetting this issue, such critics either have little sense of the irrelevancy of their work or they have an over-inflated view of it. In short, neo-Marxist studies on resistance have performed an important theoretical service by reinserting empirical work into the framework of critical theory.

What is significant about this work is that in pointing to the gaps and tensions that exist in social sites such as schools, it successfully undermines theories of reproduction that support a "constant fit" between the school and the workplace. Moreover, it further undermines over socialized and over determined models of schooling, so fashionable among leftist ped- agogues. Thus, one major contribution that has emerged from neo-Marxist studies is that, in part, they demonstrate that the mechanisms of social and cultural reproduction are never complete and are always faced with partially realized elements of opposition. Moreover, this work points to a dialectical model of domination that offers valuable alternatives to many pessimistic models of schooling that reduce the logic of domination to external forces that appear impossible to challenge or modify. Instead of seeing domination as simply the reflex of external forces—capital, the state, etc.—Willis (1977), Apple (1982), Olson (1981), and others have developed a notion of reproduction in which working-class domi- nation is viewed not only as a result of the structural and ideological constraints embedded in capitalist social relationships, but also as part of the process of self-formation within the working class itself. Central to this perspective is a notion of culture in which the production and consumption of meaning are connected to specific social spheres and traced to their sources in historical and class-located parent cultures. Put simply, culture is not reduced to an overly-determined, static analysis of dominant cultural capital like language, cultural taste, and manners. Instead, culture is viewed as a system of practices, a way of life that constitutes and is constituted by a dialectical interplay between the class-specific behavior and circumstances of a particular social group and the powerful ideological and structural determinants in the wider society. Hall and Jefferson express this clearly:

> Culture is the distinctive shapes in which the material and social organization of life expresses itself. A culture includes the "maps of meaning" which make things intelligible to its members. These "maps of meaning" are not simply carried around in the head: they are objectivated in the patterns of social organizations and relationships through which the individual becomes a social individual. Culture is the way the social relations of a group are structured and shaped, but it is also the way those shapes are experienced, understood, and interpreted [Hall & Jefferson 1976].

Theories of resistance provide a study of the way in which class and culture combine to offer outlines for a cultural politics. Central to such a politics is a semiotic reading of the style, rituals, language, and systems of meaning that constitute the cultural field of the oppressed. Through this process, it becomes possible to analyze what counter-hegemonic elements such cultural fields contain, and how they tend to get incorporated into the dominant culture to be stripped of their political possibilities. Implicit in such an analysis is the need to develop strategies in schools in which oppositional cultures might provide the basis for a viable political force. Willis sums up this position when he writes:

> We must interrogate cultures, ask what are the missing questions they answer; probe the invisible grid of context, inquire what unsaid propositions are assumed in the invisible and surprising external forms of cultural life. If we can supply the premises, dynamics, logical relations of responses which look quite untheoretical and lived out "merely" as cultures, we will uncover a cultural politics [Willis 1978].

Theories of resistance perform a theoretical service in their call for forms of political analyses that study and transform the radical themes and social practices that make up the class-based cultural fields and details of everyday life. Willis is stunningly accurate in his perception that if radical social theory is to investigate how "the detailed, informed, and lived can enjoy its victory in a larger failure" (Willis 1978), it will have to develop strategies that link a politics of the concrete, not just with questions of reproduction, but also with the issue of social transformation. Moreover, rather than seeing culture simply as the reflex of hegemony and defeat, Willis (1977) and others have illuminated it as a social process that both embodies and reproduces lived antagonistic social relationships (Bennet 1980a; Giroux 1981). This points to the importance of studying schools as social sites that contain levels of determination of unique specificity, social sites that do not reflect the wider society but only have a particular relationship to it.

Finally, resistance theories deepen our understanding of the notion of relative autonomy, a greatly needed corrective in light of the long history of orthodox Marxist readings of the base-superstructure issue in which institutions like schools were reduced to the reflex or shadow of the mode of production. The notion of relative autonomy is developed through a number of analyses that point to those non-reproductive "moments" that constitute and support the critical notion of human agency. For example, there is the active role assigned to human agency and experience as key mediating links between structural determinants and lived effects. Furthermore, there is the recognition that different spheres or cultural sites, e.g., schools, families, trade unions, mass media, etc., are governed by complex ideological properties that often generate contradictions both within and between them. At the same time, the notion of ideological domination as all-encompassing and unitary in its form and content is rejected. As such, it is rightly argued that dominant ideologies themselves are often contradictory, as are different factions of the ruling classes, the institutions that serve them, and the subordinate groups under their control.

I want to conclude this chapter by pointing to the weaknesses in theories of resistance, and may I suggest as well that the criticisms presented here represent starting points for further development of a critical theory of schooling.

First, though studies of resistance point to the social sites and "spaces" in which the dominant culture is encountered and challenged by subordinate groups, such studies have not adequately conceptualized the genesis of the conditions that promote and reinforce contradictory modes of resistance and struggle. In other words, what is lost in this perspective are analyses of those historically and culturally mediated determinants that produce a *range* of oppositional behaviors, not to mention the diverse ways in which they are experienced by subordinant groups. Put simply, not all oppositional behavior has "radical significance," nor is all oppositional behavior rooted in a reaction to authority and domination. The point here is that there have been too few attempts by educational theorists to understand how subordinate groups embody and express a combination of reactionary and progressive ideologies, ideologies that both underlie the structure of social domination and contain the logic necessary to overcome it. Above and beyond the questionable interests and ideologies that fuel various forms of resistance there is also the point that oppositional behavior may not be simply a reaction to powerlessness, but instead it might be an expression of power that is fueled by and reproduces the most powerful grammar of domination. Thus resistance may on one level be the simple appropriation and display of power, and as such it may manifest itself through the interests and discourse of the worst aspects of capitalist rationality.[1]

Oppositional behaviors, like the subjectivities that constitute them, are produced amidst contradictory discourses and values. The logic that informs a given act of resistance may on the one hand be linked to interests that are class-, gender-, or race-specific; but, on the other hand, such resistance may represent and express the repressive moments inscribed by the dominant culture rather than a message of protest against their existence. The dynamics of resistance may not only be informed by a reactionary as well as a radical set of interests, it may also get sustained most strongly outside of the school—in the workplace, the home, or the neighborhood. To understand the nature of such resistance necessitates placing it within a wider context in order to see how it is mediated and articulated amidst the everyday institutions and lived experiences that constitute the culture of the oppositional groups under analyses. The message here is that because of a failure to understand the dialectical nature of resistance, the concept has been treated superficially in both theoretical and ideological terms in most theories of education. For instance, where domination and resistance are stressed in such studies, the portrayals provided of schools, of working-class students, and of classroom pedagogy often appear too homogeneous and static to be taken seriously. Where resistance is analyzed, its contradictory nature is not analyzed seriously, nor is the contradictory consciousness of the students and teachers under analysis treated dialectically. Of course, there are exceptions to this trend, and the work of Willis (1981), Popkewitz, et al (1981, 1982), and Arnot (1981) should be mentioned; but such work is marginal to the field and to the theoretical perspective under analysis. A representative example of the work I am criticizing can be found, for instance, in some of the early studies done by Anyon (1980, 1981a, 1981b). While Anyon's work is interesting and important, she has a tendency to present the mechanisms of domination as they work in schools as a relatively coherent and homogeneous set of practices. The educators who appear in her studies seem as if they have been pressed out of some hegemonic fantasy, and as such demonstrate a uniformity of behavior—especially toward working-class students—that is not only overdrawn, but borders on being demeaning. We are told that the teachers of working-class students care little for them and teach simply to enforce routine and discipline. Throughout her studies the same theme appears: "Work is following the steps of a procedure. The procedure is usually mechanical, involving rote behavior and very little decision-making or choice. The teachers rarely explain why the work is being assigned, how it might connect to other assignments, or what the idea is that lies behind the procedure or gives it coherence and perhaps meaning or significance" (Anyon 1980). The notion that different styles of work, diverse community pressures, and conflicting professional ideological perspectives may generate a diversity of administrative and teaching approaches is downplayed in Anyon's studies. More significantly, there is no attempt to provide a theoretical understanding of what resistance as a construct actually means. When the concept is employed, it is reduced to descriptive categories such as passive and active resistance (1981b). It is no wonder that where resistance does appear in her work, it lacks the theoretical depth and grounding to appear very useful, and as such emerges like the unexpected exclamation point tacked on to the end of the sentence to emphasize a point that should have been developed more fully.

A second weakness in theories of resistance is the inadequate number of attempts to take into account the issues of gender and race. As Arnot (1981), McRobbie (1980), Walkerdine (1981), and others have pointed out, resistance studies generally ignore women and gender issues to focus instead primarily on males and class when analyzing domination, struggle, and schooling. This has meant that women are either disregarded altogether or that when they are included in such studies it is only in terms that echo the sentiments of the male countercultural groups being portrayed. This raises a number of significant problems that future analyses will have to face. On the one hand, such studies have failed to come to grips with the notion of patriarchy as a mode of domination that cuts across various social sites as well as a mode of domination that mediates between men and women within and between different social-class formations. The point here, of course, is that domination is not singularly informed or exhausted by the logic of class oppression; nor does domination take a form that affects men and women in similar ways. Women, though in different degrees, experience dual forms of domination in both the home and the workplace. How the dynamics of these get interconnected, reproduced, and mediated in schools represents an important area of continuing research. On the other hand, these studies contain no theoretical room for exploring forms of resistance that are race- and gender-specific, particularly as these mediate the sexual and social divisions of labor in various social sites such as schools. The failure to include women and minorities of color in such studies has resulted in a rather uncritical theoretical tendency to romanticize modes of resistance even when they contain reactionary views about women. The irony here is that a large amount of neo-Marxist work, while allegedly committed to emancipatory concerns, ends up contributing to the reproduction of sexist attitudes and practices, albeit unknowingly (Arnot 1981; McRobbie 1980; Walkerdine 1981).

Third, neo-Marxist studies of schooling seem to have an uncanny attachment to a definition of resistance celebrating it as a mode of apolitical style. As a result, there are very few attempts within the literature on schooling and countercultural movements to situate the notion of resistance within specifically political movements, movements that display resistance in the arts and/or in concrete political action. Surely, as E.P. Thompson (1966), David Hakken (1980), and Willis and Corrigan (1980) have pointed out, working-class resistance is rooted in a variety of forms and does not move solely on an ideological and cultural terrain that rejects intellectual analyses and overt political struggle in favor of symbolic resistance.

Fourth, theories of resistance have under-theorized the point that schools not only repress subjectivities but are also actively involved in their production. Thus, as I mentioned previously, there have been too few attempts to understand how different discourses and classroom practices function to promote in a wide variety of students contradictory forms of consciousness and behavior, some of which may be exhibited in resistance, in accommodation, or in outright self-indulgence. It must be remembered that students from all classes and groups bear the logic of domination and control in different degrees, and that this logic is a constituting as well as a repressive force in their lives. More to the point, not only has the question of how subjectivities get produced been played-down, so has the crucial issue of trying to distinguish politically viable forms of resistance, whether latent or overt,[2] from acts of behavior that are either one-sidedly self-indulgent or are linked to the dynamics of domination. It must be understood that it is theoretically incorrect to view working-class cultural capital as a single entity, just as it is important to remember that while the diversity within the working classes is marked, it is formed within economic, political, and ideological contexts that limit the capacity for self-determination. To forget this allows one to run the risk of both romanticizing the culture of subordinate groups and mystifying the dynamics of hegemonic ideologies and structure. The crucial issue is that educators need to acknowledge the contradictions in working-class culture and learn how to discard the elements that are repressive, while simultaneously reappropriating those features that are progressive and enlightening.

Fifth, theories of resistance have not given enough attention to the issue of how domination reaches into the structure of the personality itself. That is, there is little concern with the often contradictory relation between understanding and action, and why one does not always lead to the other. Part of the answer may lie in uncovering the genesis and operation of those socially constructed needs that tie people to larger structures of domination. Radical educators have shown a lamentable tendency to occlude the question of needs and desires in favor of issues that center around ideology and consciousness. What is needed is a notion of alienation that points to the way in which un-freedom reproduces itself in the psyche of human beings. We need to understand how dominating ideologies limit the development of many-sided needs to particular groups, as well as how the transformation of radical needs into the egoistic, calculable greed of capitalist interest relations can be prevented. Alienating need structures represent one of the most crucial areas from which to address a radical pedagogy. The question of the historical genesis and transformation of needs constitutes, in my mind, the most important basis for radical educational praxis. Until educators can point to the possibilities for the development "of radical needs that both challenge the existing system of interest and production and point to an emancipated society" (Cohen 1977), it may be exceptionally difficult to understand how schools function to incorporate people or what that might mean to the establishment of a basis for critical thinking and responsible action.

Put another way, without a theory of radical needs and depth psychology, educators have no way of understanding the grip and force of alienating social structures as they manifest themselves in the lived but often non-discursive aspects of everyday life.

Toward a Theory of Resistance

Resistance is a valuable theoretical and ideological construct that provides an important focus for analyzing the relationship between school and the wider society. More importantly, it provides new theoretical leverage for understanding the complex ways in which subordinate groups experience educational failure, and directs attention to new ways of thinking about and restructuring modes of critical pedagogy. Unfortunately, the way the concept is used currently by radical educators suggests a lack of intellectual rigor and an overdose of theoretical sloppiness. It is clear that a rationale for employing the concept needs to be considered more fully. Similarly, it is imperative that educators be more precise about what resistance actually is and what it is not. Furthermore, there is a need to be more specific about how the concept can be used in the service of developing a critical pedagogy. I want to turn to these issues and briefly outline some basic theoretical concerns for developing a more intellectually rigorous and politically useful foundation for developing such a task.

In the most general sense, resistance has to be grounded in a theoretical rationale that points to a new framework and problematic for examining schools as social sites, particularly the experience of subordinate groups. That is, the concept of resistance represents more than a new heuristic catchword in the language of radical pedagogy,—it represents a mode of discourse that rejects traditional explanations of school failure and oppositional behavior. In other words, the concept of resistance represents a problematic governed by assumptions that shift the analysis of oppositional behavior from the thoeretical terrains of functionalism and mainstream educational psychology to those of political analysis. Resistance in this case redefines the causes and meaning of oppositional behavior by arguing that it has little to do with the logic of deviance, individual pathology, learned helplessness (and, of course, genetic explanations), and a great deal to do, though not exhaustively, with the logic of moral and political indignation.

Aside from shifting the theoretical ground from which to analyze oppositional behavior, the construct of resistance points to a number of assumptions and concerns about schooling that are generally neglected in both traditional views of school and social and cultural theories of reproduction. First, it celebrates a dialectical notion of human agency that rightly portrays domination as neither a static process nor one that is ever complete. Concommitantly, the oppressed are not viewed as being simply passive in the face of domination. The notion of resistance points to the need to understand more thoroughly the complex ways in which people mediate and respond to the interface between their own lived experiences and structures of domination and constraint. Central categories that emerge in the problematic of resistance are intentionality, consciousness, the meaning of common sense, and the nature and value of non-discursive behavior. Secondly, resistance adds new theoretical depth to Foucault's (1977) notion that power works so as to be exercised on and by people within different contexts that structure interacting relations of dominance and autonomy. What is highlighted here is that power is never uni dimensional; it is exercised not only as a mode of domination, but also as an act of resistance or even as an expression of a creative mode of cultural and social production outside the immediate force of domination. This point is important in that the behavior expressed by subordinate groups cannot be reduced to a study in domination or resistance. Clearly, in the behavior of subordinate groups there are moments of cultural and creative expression that are informed by a different logic, whether it be existential, religious, or otherwise. It is in these modes of behavior as well as in creative acts of resistance that the fleeting images of freedom are to be found. Finally, inherent in a radical notion of resistance is an expressed hope, an element of transcendence, for radical transformation—a notion that appears to be missing from a number of radical theories of education that appear trapped in the theoretical cemetery of Orwellian pessimism.

In addition to developing a rationale for the notion of resistance, there is a concrete need to lay out the criteria against which the term can be defined as a central category of analysis in theories of schooling. In the most general sense, I think resistance has to be situated in a perspective or rationality that takes the notion of emancipation as its guiding interest. That is, the nature and meaning of an act of resistance has to be defined next to the degree to which it contains the possibilities to develop what Marcuse termed "a commitment to an emancipation of sensibility, imagination, and reason in all spheres of subjectivity and objectivity" (Marcuse 1977). Thus, central to analyzing any act of resistance would be a concern with uncovering the degree to which it speaks to a form of refusal that highlights, either implicitly or explicitly, the need to struggle against the social nexus of domination and submission. In other words, resistance must have a revealing function, one that contains a critique of domination and provides theoretical opportunities for self-reflection and for struggle in the interest of self-emancipation and social emancipation. To the degree that oppositional behavior suppresses social contradictions while simultaneously merging with, rather than challenging, the logic of ideological domination, it falls not under the category of resistance but under its opposite, i.e., accommodation and conformism. The value of the resistance construct lies in its critical function, in its potential to speak to the radical possibilities embedded in its own logic and to the interests contained in the object of its expression. Of course, this is a rather general set of standards by which to ground the notion of resistance, but it does provide a notion of interest and a theoretical scaffold upon which to make a distinction between forms of oppositional behavior that can be used for either the amelioration of human life or the destruction or denigration of basic human values.

Some acts of resistance reveal quite visibly their radical potential, while others are rather ambiguous; still others may reveal nothing more than an affinity to the logic of domination and destruction. It is this ambiguous area that I want to analyze briefly, since the other two areas are fairly self-explanatory. Recently, I heard a "radical" educator argue that teachers who rushed home early after school were, in fact, commiting acts of resistance. She also claimed that teachers who do not adequately prepare for their classroom lessons were participating in a form of resistance as well. Of course, it is equally debatable that the teachers in question are simply lazy or care very little about teaching, that what is in fact being displayed is not resistance but inexcusable unprofessional and unethical behavior. In these cases, there is no logical, convincing response to either argument. The behaviors displayed do not speak for themselves; to call them resistance is to turn the concept into a term that has no analytical preciseness. In cases like these, one has to either link the behavior under analyses with an interpretation provided by the subjects who display it or dig deeply into the specifical historical and relational conditions out of which the behavior develops. Only then will the conditions possibly reveal the interest embedded in such behavior.

It follows from the argument I have advanced that the interests underlying a specific form of behavior may become clear once the nature of that behavior is interpreted by the person who exhibits it. But I do not mean to imply that such interests will automatically be revealed. It is conceivable that the person interviewed may not be able to explain why he or she displayed such behavior, or the interpretation may be distorted. In this case, the underlying interest in such behavior may be illuminated against the backdrop of social practices and values out of which the behavior emerges. Such a referent might be found in the historical conditions that prompted the behavior, the collective values of a peer group, or the practices embedded in other social sites such as the family, the workplace, or the church. What must be urged is that the concept of resistance not be allowed to become a category indiscriminately hung over every expression of "oppositional behavior." On the contrary, it must become an analytical construct and mode of inquiry that contains a moment of critique and a potential sensitivity to its own interests, i.e., an interest in radical consciousness-raising and collective critical action.

Let us now return to the question of how we define resistance and view oppositional behavior, and what the implications are for making such a distinction. On one level, it is important to be theoretically precise about what form of oppositional behavior constitutes resistance and what does not. On another level, it is equally important to argue that all forms of oppositional behavior represent a focal point and a basis for dialogue and critical analysis. Put another way, oppositional behavior needs to be analyzed to see if it constitutes a form of resistance, which, as I have mentioned, means uncovering its emancipatory interests. This is a matter of theoretical preciseness and definition. On the other hand, as a matter of radical strategy *all* forms of oppositional behavior, whether they can be judged as forms of resistance or not, need to be examined in the interests being used as a basis for critical analysis and dialogue. Thus oppositional behavior becomes the object of theoretical clarification as well as the basis for possible radical strategy considerations.

On a more philosophical level, it must be stressed that resistance as a theoretical construct rejects the positivistic notion that the categorization and meaning of behavior is synonomous with an observation of a literal reading based on the immediacy of expression. Instead, resistance needs to be viewed from a very different theoretical starting point, one that links the display of behavior to the interest it embodies. As such, the emphasis is on going beyond the immediacy of behavior to the notion of interest that underlies its often hidden logic, a logic that also has to be interpreted through the historical and cultural mediations that shape it.

Finally, it must be strongly emphasized that the ultimate value of the notion of resistance has to be measured against the degree to which it not only prompts critical thinking and reflective action, but, more importantly, against the degree to which it contains the possibility of galvanizing collective political struggle around the issues of power and social determination.

I now want to speak briefly to the value of resistance as an educational principle. The pedagogical value of resistance rests, in part, in its situating the notions of structure and human agency, and the concepts of culture and self-formation, in a new problematic for understanding the process of schooling. It rejects the notion that schools are simply instructional sites, and in doing so it not only politicizes the notion of culture, but also points to the need to analyze school culture within the shifting terrain of struggle and contestation. Educational knowledge, values, and social relations are now placed within the context of lived antagonistic relations, and need to be examined as they are played out within the dominant and subordinate cultures that characterize school life.[3] Elements of resistance now become the focal point for the construction of different sets of lived experiences, experiences in which students can find a voice and maintain and extend the positive dimensions of their own cultures and histories. Resistance also calls attention to modes of pedagogy that need to unravel the ideological interests embedded in the various message systems of the school, particularly in the curriculum, modes of instruction, and evaluation procedures (Bernstein 1977). Moreover, the concept of resistance highlights the need for classroom teachers to decipher how the modes of cultural production displayed by subordinate groups can be analyzed to reveal both their limits and their possibilities for enabling critical thinking, analytical discourse, and new modes of intellectual appropriation. In the most profound sense, the concept of resistance points to the imperative of developing a theory of signification, a semiotic reading of behavior that not only takes discourse seriously, but also attempts to unravel how oppositional moments are embedded and displayed in nondiscursive behavior (Giddens 1979). Put more theoretically, what is being called for here is the need to reformulate the relationship among ideology, culture, and hegemony to make clear the ways in which these categories can enhance our understanding of resistance as well as how such concepts can form the theoretical basis for a radical pedagogy that takes human agency seriously.

SECTION TWO

Resistance
& Critical Pedagogy

Education has fundamental connections with the idea of human eman-cipation, though it is constantly in danger of being captured for other interests. In a society disfigured by class exploitation, sexual and racial oppression, and in chronic danger of war and environmental destruction, the only education worth the name is one that forms people capable of taking part in their own liberation. The business of the school is not propaganda. It is equipping people with the knowledge and skills and concepts relevant to remaking a dangerous and disordered world. In the most basic sense, the process of education and the process of liberation are the same. They are aspects of the painful growth of the human species' collective wisdom and self-control. At the beginning of the 1980s it is plain that the forces opposed to that growth here and on the world scale are not only powerful but have become increasingly militant. In such circumstances, education becomes a risky enterprise. Teachers too have to decide whose side they are on {Connell, et al, 1982}.

THIS QUOTATION CONTAINS A NUMBER OF IMPORTANT INSIGHTS OFTEN either missing or suppressed in educational discourse. It makes a con-nection between schooling and emancipation suggesting that schools have a responsibility to equip students with the knowledge and skills they will need to develop a critical understanding of themselves as well as what it means to live in a democratic society. Furthermore, the quotation points to education as both an activity and a region of social life that contribute to the legitimation and reproduction of a society steeped in domination and class, gender, and racial inequalities. The "risky" nature of education is rooted in the tension that characterizes the difference between the 114 promise and the reality of schooling. It finds concrete expression in the antagonistic relations and practices in most schools, and in the choices that educators have to make to conform or attempt to transform such relations. The reality of this tension, the possibilities that it offers, and the necessity to develop a theoretical framework and discourse that reveal the different educational experiences, needs, and interests in the landscape of schooling, are the central topics discussed in this section.

I want to address, in part, the fundamental question of what must be done in order to understand schools not only as sites of sociocultural reproduction, but also as sites involved in contestation and struggle. The task is no less than finding a new discourse and a new way of thinking about the nature, meaning, and possibilities for working in and outside of schools. The goal here is to establish the conditions for "increasing the understanding which social actors have of their sociohistorical situation, of themselves and, ultimately, [for] illuminating the existence of hypostatized and reified social forces which may impinge upon autonomous action" (Stewart 1980). What is at stake is the goal of developing an understanding of the immanent possibilities for a radical critique and a mode of social action based on the creation of a culture of critical discourse. The aim of such a discourse is to create the ideological and material conditions for a radical public sphere (Gouldner 1979).

In this view, the importance of schools and radical pedagogy is illuminated by a number of crucial assumptions. First is the requirement of a mode of analysis that captures the dialectical relation between collective agents and the particular historical and local conditions in which they find themselves. In other words, a critical discourse is needed that shows human beings from different social classes reacting to limitations to either change or maintain them. Social classes, in this analysis, are both the agents and the products of the larger society. A second requirement is that schools have to be viewed as contradictory social sites, marked by struggle and accommodation, which cannot be viewed as totally negative in terms of their effects on the politically dispossessed. That is, while there is little doubt that schools are tied to educational policies, interests, and resources that bear the weight of the logic and institutions of capitalism, they also provide room for emancipatory teaching, knowledge, and social practices. Schools produce social formations around class, gender, and racial exploitation, but at the same time they contain contradictory pluralities that generate possibilities for both mediation and the contestation of dominant ideologies and practices. In effect, the school is neither an all-encompassing foothold of domination nor a locus of revolution; thus, it contains ideological and material spaces for the development of radical pedagogies. Of course, the school is only one place where radical educators can battle for emancipatory interests. However, it is a sphere that must be seriously considered as a site for creating a critical discourse around the forms a democratic society might take and the socio-economic forces that prevent such forms from emerging.

Radical pedagogy must be defined here as an entry point in the contradictory nature of schooling, a chance to force it toward creating the conditions for a new public sphere. A third assumption is that the purpose of schooling and critical pedagogy must be linked to the issue of developing a new public sphere. That is, the task of radical educators must be organized around establishing the ideological and material conditions that would enable men and women from oppressed classes to claim their own voices. This would enable the development of a critical discourse that would allow the insertion of a collective interest in the reconstitution of the wider society. In effect, the concept of the public sphere (Habermas 1974) represents a theoretical grounding for developing a new view of both citizenship and literacy. That is, the public sphere represents a critical category that redefines literacy and citizenship as central elements in the struggle for self and social emancipation. More specifically, this concept becomes the theoretical lens for analyzing the depoliticization of the masses in contemporary society as well as their possible self-transformation toward a conscious and active citizenry. Within this perspective, the notion of the public sphere points to the need for an active public engagement in the struggle to define and create counter-public spheres embodied in institutions and representing values and practices that promote what Heller (1976) has called civic courage. Civic courage is a central concept here and it represents a form of behavior in which one thinks and acts as if one lived in a real democracy. It is a form of bravery aimed at exploding reifications, myths, and prejudices. At the same time, civic courage is the organizing principle that informs and defines a notion of literacy grounded in the grammar of self-determination and transforming praxis. The public sphere becomes both a rallying point and a theoretical referent for understanding the nature of the existing society and the need to create a critically informed citizenry that can fight for fundamentally new structures in the public organization of experience. The public sphere represents, in part, the ideological mediations and institutions that oppressed groups must struggle to develop in order to reclaim their own experiences and the possibilities of social change. Knodler-Bunte's analysis of the concept of the proletarian public sphere captures this notion:

> . . . the public sphere can be understood as organizing human experience, and not merely as this or that historically institutionalized manifestation—as a historically developing form of mediation between the cultural organization of human qualities and senses on the one hand and developing capitalist production on the other. . . . In this context the public sphere can best be understood as a necessary form of mediation, as the center of a production process in the course of which the varied and fragmented experiences of social contradictions and social interests can be combined into a theoretically mediated consciousness and life-style directed toward transforming praxis [Knodler-Bunte 1975].

This section develops the theoretical groundwork for a more viable and radical view of the dialectical relation between agency and structure. In this case, the concepts of ideology and culture are rescued from the theoretical traditions that dissolve them in either a one-sided notion of idealism or an equally deterministic view of structuralism. A new problematic, while raising new questions and demonstrating a mode of critique, attempts to answer the question of how we can create a conception of radical literacy that informs the way in which people critically and politically embrace the concept of citizenship and the task of demonstrating civic courage. Literacy in this case not only provides the tools for "reading" oneself and the world critically, it also becomes the vehicle for demonstrating that education has broader implications than creating an educated and skilled labor force. In other words, this concept of literacy radicalizes the notion of citizenship education and creates new opportunities for positive action. Such struggles for ideological and material conditions are necessary for the development of a public sphere informed by the critical mediations of social groups that examine and act on the nature of their existence, "rather than just enjoy or suffer it" (Gouldner, 1979).

4

Ideology, Culture, & Schooling

Educational theory and practice stands at an impasse. In spite of the recent gains analyzed in previous chapters, it remains caught in a theoretical legacy that has plagued social theory in general, and Marxism in particular, for decades. This legacy constitutes a strongly embedded dualism which separates human agency and structural analyses and finds expression in not only the conservative theories of Parsons (1951), Merton (1957), and Durkheim (1969) but also in orthodox and revisionist versions of Marxism. Both the nature and the persistence of this dualism have presented something of a paradox for radical educational theorists. On the one hand, traditional versions of socialization and power have been rejected in favor of a Marxist problematic that takes the notions of class, power, and domination as its theoretical starting point. On the other hand, what radical educators have ignored are exactly those theoretical moments that reproduce in both traditional and Marxist perspectives a dualism that either suppresses the significance of human agency and questions of subjectivity, or ignores the structural determinants that lie outside of the immediate experience of human actors. In other words, both traditional and radical Marxian perspectives are informed by a dual- 119 ism that in effect severs the dialectic between consciousness and structure, and as such they fail to offer the theoretical insights necessary to develop a more critical theory of schooling.

I am not suggesting that the legacy of Marxist thought that informs radical theories of schooling should be discarded. On the contrary, I want to argue that if Marxism, in its various forms, is to offer any insight into developing a critical theory of schooling, it will have to be critically interrogated to reveal the logic embedded in its failure to provide a dialectical treatment of subjectivity and structure. What this means is that some of the most crucial assumptions of both orthodox and revisionist Marxism will have to be examined and revised in order to reconsider and reformulate how human beings come together within specific social practices and historical contexts to make and reproduce the conditions of their existence. In more specific terms, I want to argue in this chapter that we can develop a more dialectical treatment of agency and structure by restructuring the ideas of ideology and culture. It will be my argument that these terms can be situated in a theoretical perspective that illuminates how structure and agency presuppose each other, and that the value of such an assumption for developing a radical theory of schooling is enormous. But before redefining and examining these concepts for their pedagogical value, I want to provide a brief critique of those versions of orthodox and revisionist Marxism which have failed to escape an undialectical treatment of agency and structure. I will then point to the ways this dualism repeated itself in debates around ideology and culture that emerged in the 1950s and 1960s in Western Europe. A critique of these debates is particularly important since the arguments that framed them had a significant effect on the emergence of the new sociology of education in 1970 and on the diverse traditions that grew out of it in the 1970s and 1980s.

Radical theories of schooling have continually patterned themselves after positivist versions of Marxism which have frozen the dialectical moment of uncertainty in human behavior and have opted for that part of the classic Marxian formulation which stresses that history is made "behind the backs" of members of society. The notion that people do make history, including its constraints, appears to have gone unheeded in this formulation. That is, underlying the legacy of orthodox Marxism is a positivist historicism and a one-sided emphasis on the determining force of the productive process. It is a legacy animated by a refusal to develop analyses of everyday life in which subjectivity and culture are treated as more than a reflex of the needs of capital and its institutions. Moreover, in orthodox Marxism the critical ideas of self-reflexivity and social transformation are subsumed under the overbearing "weight" of capitalist domination. In those versions of radical schooling in which orthodox Marxist assumptions were accepted, critique seemed to give way to descriptions of the mechanisms of domination as they operated in schools and other social sites. The power of capital and the weakness of human beings to either struggle or resist is a familiar theme in the discourse of theorists like Bowles and Gintis (1976), and has been detailed in the previous chapter. What is often missed in examining radical theories of schooling that draw on one-sided theories of determination and power derived from orthodox Marxism is the extent of the debt incurred in the form of theoretical problems inherited from the Marxist legacy.

While it may be argued that this picture is overdrawn and simplified, the logic that underlies it remains. Its presence permeates even those strands of Marxism that have challenged some of the basic assumptions of orthodox Marxist thought. For example, as important as the Frankfurt School has been in politicizing culture and in stressing its importance as a tool of class and social reproduction in advanced Western countries, it never entirely escaped from orthodox Marxism's crushing logic, a logic which believes in the power of capital to control all aspects of human behavior. For example, in his criticism of the Marxist theories that focus on the state and everyday life, Aronowitz (1978) reveals the one-sided belief in the power of capital, with its underlying disdain of human agency, from which Frankfurt School members such as Adorno and Marcuse never entirely liberated themselves. Aronowitz writes:

> It may also be shown that the darkest analysis of the theorists of everyday life and cultural production, particularly the representatives of the so-called Frankfurt school, were also animated by their belief in the absolute power of capital over all social relations. For Theodore Adorno and Herbert Marcuse, the advent of mass culture could only be understood as a function of the accumulation and expansion of capital into the farthest reaches of ordinary existence, of the invasion of the private sphere by the marketplace. In the felicitous phrase of Hans Magnus Enzensberger, the tendency of late capitalism is to "industrialize the mind," just as capitalism industrialized the production of goods during its rise. Human thinking becomes mechanized and the mind corresponds to the machine—a technicized, segmented, and degraded instrument that has lost its capacity for critical thought, especially its ability to imagine another way of life [Aronowitz 1978].

If the contours of orthodox Marxism reveal a disdain for subjectivity and consciousness, its conceptual center of gravity appears rent by an inconsistency that offers no theoretical challenge. The inconsistency is rooted in a paradoxical denunciation of capitalism, on the one hand, and a self-proclaimed demoralization on the other. Critique exists, but in this case without the benefit of hope, and as such without the benefit of human agents who can use it to transform social reality. Russell Jacoby is on target when he claims, "Not the least of the ills of orthodox Marxism is the wake it leaves of demoralization and cynicism. Hopes perpetually raised and dashed take their toll" (Jacoby 1981). In effect, orthodox Marxism has passed onto history more than dashed hopes—its theoretical cemeteries abound, and can be found in a number of radical educational theories that have failed to discard its theoretical baggage. The point here is that the failure of orthodox Marxism to bridge the dualism between structure and agency has had dire consequences for those engaged in developing a radical theory of schooling. Faced with a version of Marxism characterized by a marked puritanism regarding the notions of romanticism, utopianism, and desire, many radical educators turned away from the notions of subjectivity and consciousness. The logic underlying such a choice is rooted in a Marxian legacy that fears the unstructured, a fear that finds its counterpart in a disdain for subjectivity and a love of structures. Even where subjectivity and consciousness do appear in perspectives based on this logic, particularly in some Marxist versions of schooling, its surfaces within the context of a paralyzing pessimism that consigns it to a mere instance of active participation in its own defeat.

Culture and Ideology: The Legacy of Conflicting Paradigms

Within the last two decades a number of important developments in Marxist theory have pointed to a way out of the legacy of determinism and pessimism that has "crippled" orthodox Marxism and the host of radical social theories informed by its basic presuppositions. At the core of these critical theoretical developments was an attempt to break from the restraints of the base-and-superstructure metaphor and to redefine it and re-evaluate its practicality. There emerged a number of Marxist theoreticians who rejected the classical Marxian notion that "the economic infrastructure determined in a kind of one-to-one correspondence all aspects of the so-called superstructure—law, religion, and . . . art" (Aronowitz 1981a). Within these theoretical shifts, economics no longer represented the privileged force in structuring social relations. Those institutions that had been previously viewed as being mere reflections of the mode of production were now defined as having a "specificity and effectivity, a constitutive primacy, which pushed them beyond the terms of reference of 'base' and 'superstructure'." (Hall 1981). Culture now became a terrain inhabited by lived struggles and conflicting levels of determinancy. Moreover, ideology was rescued from the reductionist notion of false consciousness and redefined in terms of its effects on both the realm of the unconscious and the social relations and material practices that characterized a wide range of institutions.

One of the most significant debates that developed out of this universe of alternative Marxist paradigms centered around the starkly counterposed issues of culture and ideology. While a number of divergent and contrasting arguments emerged in these debates, the two most significant tendencies centered around the work of the culturalist paradigm represented by Raymond Williams (1963, 1965, 1977) and E.P. Thompson (1966), on the one hand, and a variety of structuralisms that ranged from the early work of Barth (1957, 1975, 1977) and Poulantzas (1973) to the highly influential work of Louis Althusser (1969, 1971), on the other hand.

The concrete work that has emerged from these differing perspectives speaks to two significant issues regarding the study of ideology and culture. First, the culturalist paradigm focused on the moment of self-creation and lived experience within the class-specific conditions of everyday life. On the other hand, the structuralists forcefully interrogated the question of how subjectivities get formed within the material practices of society so as to sustain capitalist social relations.

The significance of analyzing the basic assumptions and shortcomings of these two traditions is also twofold. In the first place, both of these traditions have had to and continue to exercise a significant influence upon the forms of educational theorizing that have developed around the issues of cultural studies, reproduction, and resistance. Furthermore, while neither 'structuralism' nor "culturalism" have fulfilled the task of constructing an adequate problematic for developing a theory of either culture or ideology, there are in the selectively combined insights of the two traditions the necessary theoretical elements to reconstruct a more precise understanding of culture and ideology and to begin to see the full extent of their usefulness for a radical pedagogy. It is also worth noting that while each of these traditions speaks to the issues of agency and structure in ways that constitute a theoretical advance over the positions previously mentioned, each eventually falls prey to a dualism that limits its theoretical offerings.

At the outset, it must be stipulated that it is impossible to provide a detailed analyses of the many themes that run through the paradigms of the 'culturalists' and 'structuralists'. This has been done quite well by other theorists and need not be repeated here (Hall 1981; Johnson 1979a, 1979b; Bennett 1981). But I will attempt to look first at the basic assumptions that characterize the 'culturalists' position as characterized particularly in the work of Raymond Williams (1963, 1965, 1977) and E.P. Thompson (1966, 1975, 1978). I shall then turn to a general treatment of the 'structuralists' paradigm, focusing primarily on the work of Louis Althusser (1969, 1971).

The Culturalist Tradition: Recovering the Subject

In the late 1950s and early 1960s, Richard Hoggart (1958), Raymond Williams (1963) and E.P. Thompson (1966) published seminal works that marked a theoretical turning-point in the conceptualization and critical reconstruction of the relations between class and culture. All three theorists posited a major challenge to both Marxist and conservative perspectives on the meaning and significance of culture. According to Williams and others within the culturalist tradition, Marxism had done more than merely display a theoretical and historical sensitivity to the problems of culture. In effect, it had misconceived the very meaning and nature of culture, and as such had failed to develop adequate notions of consciousness, experience, or human agency. This was no small mistake, for its ultimate consequence was a theoretical and political perspective that placed the working class, and Marxism in general, to the rear rather than to the forefront of radical social change. The culturalists launched their attack on two fronts. First, they argued that orthodox Marxism had posited a model of base-and-superstructure relations that had turned history into an automatic process and culture into a domain of ideas and meanings that were merely a reflex of the economic structure of society. In othodox Marxism, culture was reduced to epiphenomena, and the tensions, mediations, and lived experiences of real human beings were reduced to irrelevancy. Second, Williams and Thompson criticized conservative and Marxist traditions that argued for the relative autonomy of culture in a context that reduced it to either a celebration of high culture or a celebration of bourgeois art and social values. That is, they attacked conservative, elitist versions of high culture that equated bourgeois art and values with the essence of civilization itself. However, the culturalists raised penetrating criticisms of Marxist revisionists who had abstracted culture from everyday life and assigned it to the olympian heights of high culture. The relevance of this critique becomes particularly clear, for instance, in the work of the Frankfurt School discussed in the first chapter of this book. For in spite of the Frankfurt School's singular achievement in politicizing the realm of culture and extending its definition as a mode of life rooted in the resources and activities of a class-specific society, its members were never able to escape from the preeminently conservative position that qualitatively separated high culture from mass culture. This was an important failure, for underlying it was a celebration of the distinction between art and mass culture—a distinction that often served to denigrate working-class cultural experience as well as the possibility for working-class praxis.

In short, any analysis of the culturalist tradition has to begin with its major achievement of breaking with reductionist accounts of culture provided by orthodox Marxism. Equally important is its refusal to reduce the privileges of cultural production, creation, and resistance to the realm of high culture. Underlying these theoretical starting-points are a number of important assumptions that loosely characterize the culturalist tradition.

First, the centrality of the concept of culture is based on the assumption that it is a set of ideas and practices in which specific ways of life are integrated. In this context, culture becomes democratized and socialized through patterns of organization and practice that underlie all social life. The stress here is on the complex of indissoluble practices that pervade the social totality and on the importance of constitutive activity as the organizing principle of such practices. This suggests, particularly in Williams's early work, a theory of culture that took as its most pressing concern "a study of relationships between elements in a whole way of life" (Williams 1965). Equally important to this theory is the notion that culture cannot be abstracted into analytically discrete instances removed from the general and characteristic activity and social intercourse of everyday life. A radical interactionism is at the core of this perspective and can be seen in one of Williams's later formulations regarding his critique of traditional Marxism's view of culture:

> I came to believe that I had to give up or at least leave aside what I knew as the Marxist tradition: to attempt to develop a theory of totality, to see the study of culture as the study of relations between elements in a whole way of life; to find ways of studying structure . . . which could stay in touch with and illuminate particular art works and forms, but also forms and relations of more general social life; to replace the formula of base and superstructure with the more active idea of a field of mutually if also unevenly determining forces [Williams 1971].

E.P. Thompson's concern with culture and experience is no less marked but has been formulated from a more rigorous Marxist perspective. This perspective insisted on a distinction between culture and non-culture on the one hand, and a modification of Williams's theory of culture as a study of "relations between elements in a whole way of life" (Thompson 1961) on the other. Thompson resists Williams's generalizing perspective to focus instead on classes in relations of struggle, particularly as they develop within the context of historically specific conflicts and transformations.

In spite of their differences, Williams and Thompson both attempted to recover the historical subject and analyzed history and culture from the experiential side of human agency. This points to the second major assumption underlying the culturalist perspective, that is, their strong emphasis on the importance of human agency and experience as the fundamental theoretical cornerstone of social and class analysis. Thompson made this clear in one of his earliest formulations of the issue: "It is the active process . . . which is . . . the process through which men make their history" (Thompson 1961). It is in this intersection of class and conflict that the culturalist notion of human agency becomes clear.

In the culturalist tradition, the concept of class is viewed not as an abstract set of external determinations structured around economic relations. It is not from the vantage point of how they objectively structure a person's class membership, but rather from the vantage point of how they are understood as experienced by varying classes and social groups, that economic relations are viewed here. As Richard Johnson points out, in the culturalist perspective "it is the quality of human relationships rather than the structuring of these through relations that is the key concern. One symptom of this is the massive overloading of the term 'experience' " (Johnson 1979a). Class is viewed less as a structural than an interpersonal medium through which people define experience and respond to the conditions under which they live. Class divisions and struggle are both registered and fought within sets of dominant and subordinate relations that make up society and its collective field. For Williams (1965, 1977), classes exhibit different patterns of regularities, different patterns of thought and ways of feeling, and each registers the effects of class divisions differently through sets of relations unevenly and unequally structured by the ruling class and its dominant culture. Thus class, culture, and experience are viewed in the context of the differing experiences and "structures of feeling" that different groups produce.

The relationship among domination, class, and culture points to another major assumption inherent in the culturalist position. The nature of class domination is viewed not as a static, one-dimensional imposition of power by ruling classes. Instead, ruling-class domination is seen as an exercise of power that takes place within an arena of struggle—a continuous and shifting element of contestation rooted in historically specific tensions and conflicts. Put another way, the culturalist perspective argues that struggles between dominant and subordinate classes, while taking place within conditions that favor ruling-class interests, are never tied to the logic of predetermined consequences. The central message here is that domination subsumes neither human agency nor resistance, since the constituting subject simply cannot be reduced to the dictates of the mode of production of material life or to the logic of domination inherent in agencies of social reproduction such as the school, family, etc. While ruling-class determinations establish the constraints and conditions within which subordinate groups respond to, live out, and make history, it is a history always marked by horizons that remain open rather than closed. Thus, closely tied to the culturalist emphasis on struggle and human agency is the attendant notion that the realm of culture has its own specificity and a unique orientation toward the various interrelated instances and forces that characterize a given social reality.

Another major assumption in the culturalist tradition is that theory becomes important only if it moves beyond abstract typologies and returns to the concrete. That is, theory becomes critical and valuable to the degree that it interrogates its own a priori assumptions by examining and recovering the ways human meaning is produced in lived experiences and in the historical artifacts produced by such experiences. On the one hand, this suggests a mode of inquiry that allows the oppressed to speak for themselves; that is, it provides a theoretical framework that gives a subordinate group a privileged opportunity to display how it produces and reproduces itself within the dominant society. On the other hand, it points to treating cultural artifacts "as sedimented forms of lived culture, documentary forms . . . to be analyzed with a view to rediscovering, as closely as possible, the structure of feelings—be it of a class, or a social group, or of a whole period—informing the lived culture which served as their support" (Bennett 1981). What is important here is that the consciousness and experience of the human subject is the point of reference from which to explain the origins of events as well as the cultural forms such subjects leave behind. Consequently, what we end up with in the culturalist paradigm is an approach that wishes to reduce theoretical categories to their living context, to subsume the abstract into the concrete and make the return to the lived experiences of subordinate classes the dominant motif in Marxist theory.

The Structuralist Tradition: Situating the Subject

Beginning in the mid-1960s, and continuing into the 1980s, a wide-ranging body of theories loosely labeled "structuralism" launched a major theoretical challenge against both orthodox Marxism and various versions of Western Marxism. Deriving its inspiration, in part, from the work of Ferdinand de Saussure (1974), structuralism registered an impact in a number of diverse fields and included among its followers both Marxists and non-Marxists. Its diverse tendencies and key figures could be found in the areas of film and literary criticism (Barth 1957, 1977), in French structuralist anthropology (Levi-Strauss 1972), in revisionist approaches to Freudian theories of psychoanalysis (Lacan 1977), in Marxist theories of the state (Poulantzas 1978), and especially in Althusser's (1969, 1971) reformulation of the Marxist theory of ideology. In spite of the differences separating these theorists, they all draw from a problematic that emphasizes the "force" of underlying structures or patterned material practices that "generate the surface appearances of cultural forms" (Bennett 1981). Since the range of structuralist writings is so immense, it is impossible to do anything more in this section than to summarize and analyze some of the major assumptions of structuralism and to compare the structuralist and culturalist problematics and to analyze the relevance each might have for developing a reconstructed theory of ideology and culture.

I want to argue that structuralist accounts are important in two respects. First, they have pointed to a number of significant, though incomplete, theoretical concerns necessary to reconstruct a critical Marxism. Their greatest value, however, lies in the critical analysis that they have brought to bear on both orthodox and culturalist versions of Marxism. At the core of the structuralist method is a rejection of the primacy of the human subject and the importance of consciousness and experience as the primary determinants in shaping history. The preference in this case is for more abstracted modes of analyses, particularly as these make visible the relations of structures that place, locate, and determine individual and group behavior. That is, the force of the structuralist argument rests in its rejection of consciousness, culture, and experience as adequate starting-points to understand how a society functions and reproduces itself. Instead, it argues that consciousness and experience are only secondary in the unfolding of history and social relations and that the primary sources are to be found in the materiality of practices as they are represented in the political and economic structures of society. This becomes clearer if we analyze the structuralist view of determinations, totality, and the relations between class and ideology.

A major assumption underlying structuralist Marxism rests on a rejection of the anthropological notion that human beings are the subjects or agents of history. Power, in this view, is not an attribute of theoretically informed individuals or groups acting within prescribed conditions to make history. On the contrary, power is a characteristic of structures that not only constitute and position human behavior, but that deny the very efficacy of human agency. Put another way, it is the force of material practices and the constituting social relations they produce that, in this case, reduce human beings to props or supports of structurally determined roles. Moreover, the totality of complex structural determinations can neither be perceived, explained, or transformed by making an appeal to the "ground" of human experience or subjectivity. That is, consciousness is an effect, not a cause, of such determinations, and as such renders the notion of human agency to a second-hand construct skating across the surface of reality. Even where intentionality emerges, it is the victim of an "ideology that deceives us into thinking we are subjects" (Appelbaum 1979). History is abstracted from the notion of praxis, in the structuralist perspective, and emerges as a process without subjects. Althusser is quite clear on this issue:

> The structure of the relations of production determine the places and functions occupied and adopted by the agents of production, who are never anything more than the occupants of these places, insofar as they are the supports (*Träger*) of these functions. The true subjects (in the sense of constitutive subjects of the process) are therefore not these occupants or functionaries . . . but the relations of production (and political and ideological social relations). But since these are "relations," they cannot be thought within the category subject [Althusser 1970].

Second, in opposition to culturalist approaches that argue that the social totality is characterized by a relatively autonomous culture secured primarily through the active mediations of human agents, structuralist analyses posit a notion of totality and relative autonomy tied to the irreducibility of specific levels of society. In this view, the unity of society comprises a complex structure of separate and specific "instances"—economic, political, and ideological. Moreover, each of these "instances" is viewed as being relatively autonomous from the others and is held as having a uniquely specific effect on historical outcomes. The concept of relative autonomy is the theoretical cornerstone of the structuralist arguments against the economic reductionism of orthodox Marxism. Relative autonomy attempts to bridge what at first appears to be a contradictory position: on the one hand, it posits the specificity of the economic, political, and ideological structures of society; on the other hand, it refuses to abandon the classical Marxian notion that the economic instance is central in the structuring of society. It resolves this internal contradiction by arguing that the economic level still represents the primary determination and contradiction in capitalist society, but that within the context of advanced capitalist societies it is reduced to a determination in the last instance. Consequently, a hierarchy of determinations develop of which the economic is only one—though implicitly the most powerful. Thus we are left with a unity structured within differences expressed through the distinctive levels and practices that make up society. The question of whether the economic, political, or ideological instance will embody the dominant contradiction between the ruling and subordinate classes, thus becoming the major force in shaping the relations of domination, will always be determined by the historically specific circumstances that prevail at a given time and place.

Two points can be used to illustrate the logic of this assumption. First, as I mentioned in Chapter 3, it is worth remembering that for Althusser (1971) the ideological state apparatus and particularly the schools represent the most important institutions currently securing the consent of the masses to the logic of capitalist rule. That is, the intervention of any one level—such as the ideological and its most powerful structural embodiment, the school—gains force to the degree it can set limits to the relative autonomy of other institutions. Second, the relative autonomy and specificity of different levels of society can be seen in Poulantzas's (1973 1978) theory of the state. For Poulantzas the state cannot be reduced to the vulgar Marxist notion of a "mere" instrument of monopoly capital exercising control over society. Instead, Poulantzas argues for the irreducible specificity of the state and points to its objective position as a mediating force that embodies the contradiction and struggles inherent in the ruling class itself. The state's role in the formation of dominant class relations is crucial, but it cannot be understood in merely instrumental terms. Its real character is revealed in its regulatory function and in the contradictions and tensions inherent therein. Its determining power depends on its ability at any one moment to limit the autonomy of other institutions.

The third major focus of structuralist thought centers around the concepts of class and ideology. Class, in the structuralist perspective, is conceptualized primarily as an objective position established by one's place in the network of ownership relations. In this view, the class-*in*-itself distinction supercedes that of the class-*for*-itself distinction emphasized by the culturalists. Rejecting the notion of class as an intersubjective mode of experience, structuralists replace the concept of class subjects being agents of history, or even *possible* agents of history, with the notion of class struggle. But the construct of struggle is used in this perspective to refer to the conflicts that emerge between and among social processes that exist in objectively antagonistic relations which constitute the social division of labor. The expulsion of the interpersonal dimensions of class relations as well as of the related notion that classes are potentially self-consciously organized agents making history is thoroughly rejected. On one level, the structuralist position represents an attack on culturalists such as Williams (1965) and Thompson (1966), who sometimes appear to reduce class to "merely" political and cultural categories, that is, to forms of consciousness and modes of collective action. On another level, the structuralist position is thoroughly compatible not only with the assumption that social classes are objectively determined, but also with the idea that the very nature of human subjectivity is an expression of political and ideological determinants. This takes us once again to Althusser's notion of ideology.

As I mentioned in Chapter 3, Althusser (1969, 1970, 1971) begins with a rejection of the idea that ideology can be conceptualized as false or distorted consciousness. Ideologies are not ideas. According to the structuralist perspective, ideology has a material existence and is deeply embedded in social practices that constitute such fields as schooling, law, history, and sociology. In some respects, this is a great advance over previous theories of ideology because it illuminates the structural basis of human oppression while simultaneously pointing to the need to struggle for something other than a change of consciousness, i.e., the transformation of specific social practices in concrete institutions such as schools. Of course, ideology in this case does more than shift the emphasis from consciousness to material practices; it also locates ideology as a structured feature of the unconscious, and in so doing obliterates the constitutive nature of consciousness itself. For Althusser (1970), ideologies are a fundamental part of every society and are as a source of cohesion and unity among men and women in that society. In essence, ideology has two functional requirements in Althusser's work. On the one hand, it is both the medium and product of material practices that constitute the famous ideological state apparatus (agencies which maintain control primarily through consent). On the other hand, individuals not only "live" in ideology via the practices in which they participate in various ideological apparatuses, they are also constituted by ideology. Ideology in this sense refers to a specific form of relation that human subjects have to the world, the source of which is in structured representations either lodged in the unconscious (Althusser, 1969, 1971) or situated in what Poulantzas (1975) describes as lived experience. What both of these formulations have in common is that ideology is described in terms of its function, which is to insert individuals into social relations for which they merely serve as props. The nature of the relationship between individuals and these social relations is best captured in Althusser's now famous thesis that "Ideology represents the imaginary relationship of individuals to their real conditions of existence" (Althusser 1971). Ideology, then, constitutes "subjects" in the structuralist view, but such subjects are human without either the benefit of reflexivity or the possibility of individual or collective struggle. Finally, class struggle in these accounts appears to be an estranged construct that raises more questions than it solves, since in the structuralist problematic there are no self-constituting agents to conduct it (Hirst 1979).

I want to conclude this descriptive analysis of culturalist and structuralist accounts by providing a critique of both positions while indicating how theoretical elements from each may be combined in a reasoned way to establish the groundwork for the analysis of ideology, culture, and power that is to follow.

The culturalist position suffers from a number of theoretical flaws. First, there is an overemphasis in culturalist accounts on the primacy of consciousness and experience. While these are clearly crucial in any social theory that attempts to be dialectical, it must also be acknowledged that there are determinants that work 'outside' the sphere of consciousness. While these do not show up in the most immediate experiences of men and women, they exercise a powerful force in shaping their lives. Marx (1969a) captured this point in his famous statement in "The Eighteenth Brumaire of Louis Bonaparte" that "Men make their own history, but they do not make it just as they please; they do not make it under circumstances chosen by themselves, but under circumstances directly encountered, given and transmitted from the past. The tradition of all the dead generations weighs like a nightmare on the brain of the living" (Marx 1969).

It is the dark side of this dialectic to which Marx refers, and which the culturalists deemphasize. By focusing on culture and experiences as the most prominent dimensions of class, culturalists seem to disregard the ways in which history works behind the backs of human agents. This leads to a second major criticism. Powerful determining structures such as work, family, and the state often ignored in these accounts, and the crucial question of what classes fight over or what gives one class more power than another is devalued in relation to the value and the authenticity of working-class experience. Classes involve conflicts over relations of power and not simply relations of meaning; culturalists seem to forget this. Of course, the processes of the category of class formation imply a notion of power, but the culturalists do not generally stress how power becomes useful as a part of a class strategy for appropriating the material conditions that underlie emancipatory activity. Third, there is a tendency among culturalists to equate the relation between class and culture and to treat the two as homogeneous. It is one thing to stress recovering the histories, meanings, and experiences of subordinate groups, but quite another thing to base the value of such an enterprise on the notion that the dignity of a class is synonomous with its grounding in a class-specific culture and set of experiences. Contradictions abound in the economic sphere and in dominant and subordinate culture as well. Clearly, one can find among working-class groups a selective affinity that speaks to certain values, practices, and concerns, but one also finds a whole range of differences expressed culturally and manifested in a variety of lived experiences. As Davies points out, ". . . classes are not undifferentiated masses but complex structures made up of different groups with different histories and cultural traditions. Differences may be expressed culturally and lived through a vast repertoire of specific working-class cultural traits—such as those pertaining to sex, regional and local dialects, clothes, sports, racial and ethnic differences and respectable and rough working-class allegiance" (Davies 1981).

What is important here is that once it becomes clear that classes embody a variety of contradictions and tensions we can begin to understand the notion of contradictory consciousness, the complex way in which subjectivities get constituted, and how it is that people may act against their own class interests. This leads to another major criticism of the culturalist perspective. By elevating the notion of experience to almost ethereal heights, we are left with an inadequate sense of how to judge such experiences, since it is assumed that they speak for themselves. Moreover, culturalist accounts provide few theoretical tools for understanding how material practices, particularly economic ones, weigh down and shape individual and collective experience. This is not meant to suggest a notion of determination with predefined outcomes as much as it is meant to bring into view those very real material constraints that limit the options people have. The link between lack of capital and powerlessness is quite real and determines whether the bills can be paid, food can be provided, cars can be fixed, hopes can be supported, health care can be acquired, etc. This is not to suggest that Williams (1977), Thompson (1966), Hebdige (1979), and others altogether ignore the economic or other material determinations. Such determinations are included in their work, but only as a theoretical convenience; they lack the gripping force they deserve. Johnson's critique of culturalism is provocative:

> Any analysis of "working class culture" must be able to grasp the relation between economic classes and the forms in which they do (or do not) become active in conscious politics. If the two aspects of class analysis are conflated, this is not possible. If class is understood only

as a cultural and political formation, a whole theoretical legacy is impoverished and materialist accounts are indistinguishable from a form of idealism. It may indeed be that the relation between what culturalism calls "experience" and the marshalling of political forces, or, more correctly, between economic classes and political organizations, is never or rarely as simple as "transitive" or "expressive" models imply. Economic classes rarely appear as political forces [Johnson 1979a].

In the end, culturalism recycles rather than bridges the dualism between agency and structure. Of course, culturalist accounts develop a view of culture as lived experience that attempts to recover human agency. But it does so at the cost of devaluing the importance of material practices and the different levels of specificity they exhibit within the social totality. In effect, as I have indicated, many of culturalism's weaknesses are structuralism's strengths. What is important to stress is that the culturalist approach contains a number of theoretical elements that are invaluable for developing a radical theory of pedagogy, and specifically a more viable understanding of the meaning and significance of the relation between ideology and culture. Put another way, culturalism begins at the right place but does not go far enough theoretically—it does not dig into subjectivity in order to find its objective elements.

Before providing a brief critique of the structuralist tradition, I want to reemphasize that in spite of its flaws culturalism has provided a major theoretical service in rescuing critical Marxism from an orthodoxy that threatens to strip it of all radical potential and possibilities. Moreover, it has made a major theoretical leap beyond all forms of structuralism in its insistence on what E.P. Thompson (1977) has called the "education of desire." That is, culturalism has refused to surrender to the tenets of a cosmic pseudo-science the utopian impulse and legacy, with its underlying faith in the dream, fantasy, and transcendent possibility. It is this impulse that summons so-called radical critiques of *what is* for *what could be;* it is also this impulse that speaks to human beings as more than simply consumers of economic goods. Put another way, culturalist accounts keep alive needs and desires that cannot be exhausted within the logic of certainty and rational calculation. This leads to a final qualification in favor of culturalism. Its stress on historical consciousness and critical intentionality as the most important terrains on which to begin the struggle to break through rigid and burdensome structures of oppression cannot be overemphasized. For example, Thompson's (1966) attempt to reconstruct the lived experiences of labor and the subordinate classes stands as a historical testimony, in spite of its flaws, to the power of human beings to struggle constantly against the forces of oppression. Capital has not constructed its ideological and material edifices without resistance on the part of those victimized by them. This is not meant to give support to the logic of bourgeois romanticism as much as it is meant to register the significance and facts of historical struggle and human agency. In short, the culturalist tradition, though deeply flawed, has provided a major contribution to the development of a critical Marxism insofar that its central assumptions have resonated with Nietzsche's claim that "man can only become man . . . by his power of transforming events into history" (Nietzsche 1949).

I want to furnish a brief critique of some of the structuralist assumptions discussed thus far. Since critical analyses of structuralism abound (Giddens 1979; Appelbaum 1979; Aronowitz 1981; Hirst 1979), it is unnecessary to repeat in detail the criticisms presented in such literature. Instead, I will focus on the structuralist treatment of such concepts as determination, human agency, mediation, and historical consciousness—all of which deserve some commentary.

First, in the structuralist problematic the human subject appears to be conceptualized in terms that are transhistorical in nature and universal in character. That is, human subjects appear to be dissolved in a theory of domination and determination that bears a strange resemblance to the positivist de-centering of the subject (Giddens 1979). In positivist rationality, the subject is subsumed within a quantifiable logic of certainty that leaves no room for the moment of self-creation and mediation; whereas, in the structuralist perspective human agents are registered simply as the effects of structural determinants that appear to work with the certainty of biological processes. In this grimly mechanistic approach, human subjects simply act as role-bearers, constrained by the mediations of structures like schools and responding primarily to an ideology that functions without the benefit of reflexivity or change. The notion that determinations and the incorporative powers of ideology may also produce resistance, struggle and contestation is lost from this perspective. More specifically, there is no sense of the significance of the historical conjuncture at which human beings living in determinate social relations not only reproduce but challenge the conditions under which they live. Moreover, there is no sense of how human agency, culture, and experience emerge historically under different socio-economic conditions so as to reveal that the logic of praxis is relatively autonomous, i.e., its outcome cannot be guaranteed. Furthermore, structuralist notions of human agency have glossed over the insight that theories of reproduction and determination are, as Aronowitz has reminded us, "only part of the algebra of revolution" (Aronowitz 1978). By repressing the importance of human reflexivity, structuralism provides the rationale and necessity for *not* looking at human beings in concrete settings in order to examine whether there is a substantial difference between the existence of structural determinants and their actual unfolding and effects. Best and Connolly raise this question in their criticism of Althusser's notion of ideology and its alleged iron grip on human agents. They argue quite rightly that the very need for ideology by an operative structure raises questions that are anthropological in nature and cannot be ignored. Best and Connolly are worth quoting at length on this issue:

> The function of ideology is clear enough. It constrains the political reflection of those who see themselves entering into reflexive relations and expressing reflexive attitudes in daily life. The structuralist theorist must tacitly acknowledge this; otherwise there is no need, according to the theory, for an ideology first to interpret the prevailing order in terms of standards acceptable to the participants, and second, to debunk alternatives standards whose application would threaten the legitimacy of the system. Ideology plays a function in the system, but why do the agents internalize it? If system *x,* given the characteristics of its role bearers, requires ideology to operate smoothly, the requirement does not explain why it is met. The ideology appropriate to role performance and the actual ideology of the role-bearers could fly apart, undermining the willingness of workers to bear these roles [Best & Connolly 1979].

Related to the critique of the structuralist view of human agency is the failure of structuralism to provide an adequate account of domination, mediation, and resistance. Structuralist analyses have provided a theoretical service in examining the complex ways in which dominant institutions and practices function in the interest of ruling-class formations. But the view of domination that underlies these analyses threatens to strip it of its critical possibilities. In other words, domination appears in structuralist accounts as an all embracing, one-dimensional construct that exhausts the possibility of struggle, resistance, and transformation. The moments of self-reflection, active participation in the structure of domination, or conscious refusal are not only played down, they are virtually ignored. For instance, in Althusser (1969, 1970, 1971) human agents remain locked in the ideological forms and practices of ideological state apparatus whose effects are indistinguishable from the dominating logic that informs them. In Foucault (1977) a dialectical view of power and determination is invoked only to collapse in a method that stays firmly within the internal discourse of the dominant classes. The dominated appear, but only as recipients of oppression, trapped within discourses that structure their every position. In the works of many structuralist literary critics, human agency fares no better. Relations of meaning and the logic of multiple interpretations not only decenter the subject, they also eliminate it. For example, Derrida (1977) indicates that the subject is as important as a plastic throw-away container next to the "real" task of developing a science of ideological formations. Power, in this view of domination, is limited to institutional and structural phenomena, and as a result the notion that power may also relate to the self-constituting acts and accomplishments of human actors is ignored. In the end, structuralism constructs a notion of domination that shares theoretical ground with the logic of management ideology. That is, it supports an oversocialized and mechanistic model of human development, a model that reduces the formation of subjectivities to an imprint of the logic of capital and its institutions.

Related to the structuralist view of domination is its view of mediation and conflict. The starting point for structuralism's theory of mediation is its denial of the efficacy of human intervention, i.e., the possibility that between the moment of determination and effect lies the sphere of consciousness and reflexivity. Althusser (1969, 1971), in particular, displays this position in his attempt to retain the notion of mediation while dropping the need for human agency. He does this by arguing that mediations are inscribed in the material practices that make up the ideological state apparatus. Aronowitz sums up his position well:

> [Althusser's] notion of ideology as a set of material practices through which people live their experience of capitalist social relations enables us to understand the concept of mediation as a material force and to remove it from its ideal form. Mediations are inscribed in institutions which are the scenes of the social reproduction of capital, that is, in the ways in which labor is reproduced in the family, school, religion, and bourgeois trade unions [Aronowitz 1981a].

Experience as a mode of behavior that is constituted at the interplay of structures and consciousness disappears in this notion of mediation.

Rather than being the primary moments in the mediating process, agency and experience become its product. What structuralist accounts have managed to ignore in this view of mediation and experience has been succinctly articulated by Adorno: "What is true in the concept of experience is the protest against a condition of society and scientific thought that would expel unregimented experience—a condition that would expel the subject as moment of cognition" (Adorno 1973).

Finally, another problem in the structuralist perspective is the failure to theorize the notions of conflict and resistance as examples of conscious struggle and action. Instead, in the absence of an anthropological notion of mediation and agency, contradictions and struggle are lodged either at the level of structures, in social practices, around the interpretations of "texts," or at the level of unconscious psychoanalytical processes (Hall 1981). Within this perspective, resistance is subsumed within the logic of domination; neither is there a theoretical starting-point from which to begin to understand how men and women feel and consider practices that alienate them, how they might accommodate or subvert such practices, or more significantly how they might transform their hopes and dreams into viable forms of social action. In essence, lived antagonistic relations disappear in these accounts, as do the possibilities for both understanding and acting to transform them.

In conclusion, I think it can be argued that structuralism makes a series of theoretical advances that eventually collapse under the failure to become reconciled with the most progressive assumptions in the culturalist tradition. Needless to say, the converse can be applied to culturalist accounts. Both positions have recycled the dualism between agency and structure, albeit in a more theoretically sophisticated form than in the past. Unfortunately, the underlying logic remains, and consequently both structure and agency get uprooted from their dialectical relation and are eventually placed in reductionist categories that strip them of their truly critical potential. What is needed is a more radical engagement with both traditions, an engagement marked by a disciplined abstraction and appropriation that rectifies and transcends the mistakes inherent in each position. The possibility exists to bridge the agency-structure dualism; but it must be pursued through a reworking of the notions of ideology and culture within a problematic that takes seriously the notions of agency, struggle, and critique. It is to an exploration of such a problematic that I will now turn.

Ideology and Educational Theory and Practice

The relationship between ideology and schooling is a problematic one. In part, this is the result of the powerful influence that positivist rationality has exercised historically on the development of educational theory and practice. Within this legacy the notion of ideology was ignored along with the assumption that schools were both ideological and instructional sites. Wedded to the celebration of facts and the management of the "visible", positivist rationality excluded from its perspective those categories and questions that pointed to the terrain of ideology. Fixated on the logic of immediacy, it found refuge in the world of appearances, and as such refused to interrogate the internal logic of the curriculum in order to reveal its hidden meanings, structured silences, or unintentional truths. Notions such as "essence", false consciousness, and immanent critique were safely tucked away in favor of the discourse of administration, management, and efficiency. Consequently, there was little room within the logic of dominant educational theory and practice to deconstruct the established meanings and practices that characterized the day-to-day workings of schools.

From a radically different perspective, Marxism has had a long and extensive tradition in which ideology has played a significant role as a critical concept in the ongoing critique of capitalism and its institutions. However, within that tradition the meaning and applicability of the notion of ideology has remained elusive and equivocal (Sumner 1979; Larrain 1979). The result has been that Marxist thought, with few exceptions, has failed to develop a systematic treatment of the concept; consequently, the value and applicability of the concept of ideology as a heuristic and critical theoretical tool has not played a role consistent with its potential in radical theory and practice.

The Marxist tradition is not informed by a unitary concept of ideology; instead one finds a plethora of interpretations and analyses of the meaning value of the concept. Amidst these wide-ranging interpretations there are hints and fleeting images of what the theoretical terrain of ideology might look like. If the relation between schooling and ideology is to be understood, the most important of these theoretical insights need to be identified and integrated into a more comprehensive theoretical framework. Thus, it is important to interrogate the dominant Marxist versions of ideology in order to see what is missing from them. This in turn demands a brief critical analysis of some of the assumptions that underlie the often contradictory and complex treatment of ideology in current Marxist social theory.

I think it is accurate and fitting to begin by arguing that ideology in the most traditional and orthodox Marxist sense has been primarily concerned with relations of domination rather than with the relations of struggle and resistance. One consequence has been a host of interpretations that define ideology in largely pejorative terms, i.e., as false consciousness (Marx 1972), as non-scientific beliefs (Althusser 1969), or as a set of beliefs that function to legitimize domination (Habermas 1975). In these interpretations, ideology has operated at such a high level of abstraction that it provides few clues as to how subjectivities are constituted in schools. Or, it has functioned to flatten the complexity and contradictory nature of human consciousness and behavior, and thus has dissolved important concerns regarding mediation and resistance in rigid theories of domination. Ideology has also been treated by a smaller number of Marxist theorists in the positive sense as a set of beliefs and modes of discourse constructed to satisfy the needs and interests of specific groups. For example, Lenin (1971) viewed ideology as a positive force to the degree that it provided the working class with the attitudes and skills necessary for self-determination. Similarly, Gouldner (1976) has made one of the most compelling attempts to rescue ideology from its pejorative status by arguing that all ideologies contain the possibility for developing a critical view of the world. However, in addition to the question of whether ideology is to be viewed in a positive or pejorative light, there is a related question as to whether ideology should be viewed primarily in objective or subjective terms. For instance, both Althusser (1969, 1971) and Volosinov (1973) view ideology as having a materiality rooted, respectively, either in practices produced in ideological state apparatus such as schools, or in the materiality of language, representations, and "signs". For both Althusser and Volosinov, ideologies address and constitute the human subject. But the human subject is the missing referent here, as are relations of battle conducted either outside the "text" or between real human beings who bleed, cry, despair, and think. On the other hand, the subjective and psychological character of ideology can be found in the work of critical theorists such as Marcuse (1964), or in the work of culturalists such as Williams (1977) and E.P. Thompson (1966). In these perspectives, ideology is either situated within the psychic structure of the oppressed or it is the central, active force constituted through shared experiences and common interests.

In the Marxist tradition, then, there is a central tension between a view of ideology as an all-encompassing mode of domination and a view of ideology as an active force in the construction of human agency and critique. Similarly, there is a tension between the notion of ideology as a material force and ideology as a mode of meaning. Each of these positions is by itself theoretically flawed, and each alone is only partially useful in providing a critical theory of ideology for radical educators. In order to constitute a theory of ideology as the basis for a critical theory of schooling it will be necessary to situate it within a theoretical perspective that takes seriously the notion of human agency, struggle, and critique. Moreover, it will be necessary to define the limits of the concept to retain its analytical value and particular field of application.

Ideology: Definition, Locations and Features

Any definition of ideology has to wrestle not only with the question of what it is but also with the question of what it is not. I want to begin with this point. One view of ideology in particular that must be abandoned before the concept can be rescued from its own history is the Althusserian notion that ideology exists in material apparatuses and has a material existence. As Johnson (1979b) points out, Althusser's argument transforms a "genuine insight" into a "reckless hyperbole" (Johnson 1978). To argue that ideologies are located in concrete social practices and have specific effects on such practices is an important insight, but to stretch the meaning of ideology to make it synonymous with the material world so generalizes the concept as to render it meaningless as an analytical tool. Moreover, this definition of ideology falsely collapses the distinction between ideological struggle and material struggle. That is, it confuses struggle at the ideological level meanings, discourse, and representation, with struggles over the concrete appropriation and control of capital, territory, and other such resources. Of course, both forms of struggle are related, but they cannot be fused. For example, schools are cultural apparatuses involved in the production and transmission of ideologies. It is one thing to talk about the school as a site where conflicting ideologies are fought over, and another issue altogether to view schools as political and economic institutions, as material embodiments of lived experience and historically sedimented antagonistic relations that need to be seized and controlled by subordinate groups for their own ends.

The distinction between ideology and the materiality of culture is an important one; it cannot be reduced to a simple dualism of ideas counterposed to material reality. The relation of ideology to material culture is more complex than this. On the one hand, ideology can be viewed as a set of representations produced and inscribed in human consciousness and behavior, in discourse, and in lived experiences. On the other hand, ideology affects, and is concretized in, various "texts", material practices, and material forms. Hence the character of ideology is mental, but its effectivity is both psychological and behavioral; its effects are not only rooted in human action but also inscribed in material culture. Ideology as a construct includes a notion of mediation that does not limit it to an ideal form (Aronowitz 1981a).

The distinction between ideology and the materiality of culture provides the basis for analyzing the meaning of ideology within a specific range of usefulness and applicability. I want to argue that ideology has a certain specificity that links it to the production, consumption, and representation of meaning and behavior. That is, ideology is located in the category of meaning and has an active quality to it, the character of which is defined by those processes "by which meaning is produced, challenged, reproduced and transformed" (Barrett 1980). Within this perspective, ideology refers to the production, consumption, and representation of ideas and behavior, which can either distort or illuminate the nature of reality. As a set of meanings and ideas, ideologies can be either coherent or contradictory; they can function within the spheres of both consciousness and unconsciousness; and, finally, they can exist at the level of critical discourse as well as within the sphere of taken-for-granted lived experience and practical behavior (Giddens 1979; Bourdieu 1977a, 1977b; Marcuse 1955). The complexity of the concept is captured in the notion that while ideology is an active process involving the production, consumption, and representation of meaning and behavior, it cannot be reduced to either consciousness or a system of practices, or to a mode of intelligibility or a mode of mystification. Its character is dialectical, and its theoretical strength stems both from the way it shuns reductionism, and from the way it bridges the seemingly contradictory moments mentioned above.

But a number of qualifications must be made if the definition of ideology developed thusfar is to be prevented from collapsing into the kind of sociology of knowledge that, as Adorno remarks, suffers from the weakness of calling "everything into question and criticizing nothing" (Adorno 1967a). To repeat, the characteristic feature of ideology is its location in the category of meaning and thought production, its critical potential only becomes fully clear when it is linked to the concepts of struggle and critique. When linked to the notion of struggle, ideology illuminates the important relationships among power, meaning, and interest. This suggests Marx's (1969b) important insight that ideologies constitute the medium of struggle among classes at the level of ideas, as well as the corollary insight provided by Gramsci in his comment that ideologies "organize masses . . . and create the terrain on which men move, acquire consciousness of their position, struggle, etc." (Gramsci 1971).

Both Marx and Gramsci are indicating that any theory of ideology has to take into account the concept of power and its corollaries, social antagonisms and class struggle. The linkage of ideology and struggle points to the inseparability of knowledge as power; it emphasizes that ideology refers not only to specific forms of discourses and the social relations they structure but also to the interests they further (Gouldner 1976). Thus when Marx (1969b) linked ideology to the sectional interests of dominant groups in society he pointed to a form of ideology critique whose function is, in part, to uncover class-specific mystification and to point to concrete struggles aimed at the overcoming of class domination.

This form of ideology critique indicates the need to penetrate beyond the discourse and consciousness of human actors to the conditions and foundation of their day-to-day experiences. Critique in this sense would uncover falsifications and identify the conditions and practices that generate them. Ideology critique in this instance centers around a critical analysis of the subjective and objective forces of domination, and at the same time reveals the transformative potential of alternative modes of discourse and social relations rooted in emancipatory interests. It is also important to argue that ideology critique involves more than a critical analysis of modes of knowledge and social practices in order to determine whether they serve repressive or class interests. It is important to recognize that in addition to its functional role in the construction and maintenance of the power of dominant social formations, ideology operates as a relatively autonomous set of ideas and practices, the logic of which cannot be reduced merely to class interests. Again, its meaning and specificity cannot be exhausted by defining its functional relation to class interests and struggle. In this case, ideology critique would not only focus on whether a specific ideology functioned to serve or resist class domination (or any other form of domination, for that matter); it would also identify the contents of the ideologies in question and judge the truth or falsity of the contents themselves (Adorno 1976). That is, if the notions of ideology and ideology critique are really to serve emancipatory class interests, ultimately they cannot be separated from the question of truth claims. It is important to maintain this understanding of the transformative and active quality of ideology when we consider the link between ideology and human agency. As both the medium and the outcome of lived experience, ideology functions not only to limit human action but also to enable it. That is, ideology both promotes human agency and at the same time exerts force over individuals and groups. The latter transpires through the "weight" ideology assumes in dominant discourses, selected forms of sociohistorical knowledge, specific social relations, and concrete material practices. Ideology is something we all participate in; yet we rarely understand either the historical constraints that produce and limit the nature of that participation, or what the possibilities are for going beyond existing parameters of action to be able to think and act toward a qualitatively better existence. This issue points not only to how ideologies are to be explained, but also to their "location" and their function. The nature of ideology and its usefulness as a critical construct for radical pedagogy can be further illuminated by focusing on these within what I choose to call its *operational field*. In the most general sense, ideology operates at the level of lived experience, at the level of representations embedded in cultural artifacts, and at the level of messages in material practices produced within certain historical, existential, and class traditions. I want to examine briefly the relations between ideology and each of these respective "locations," while concentrating primarily on how ideology functions at the level of lived experience. In doing so, I will further delineate a notion of ideology critique and its relevance to radical pedagogy.

Ideology, Human Experience, and Schooling

Central to understanding how ideology functions in the interest of social reproduction is the issue of how ideology works on and through individuals to secure their consent to the basic ethos and practices of the dominant society. Equally important for an understanding of how ideology functions in the interest of social transformation is the issue of how ideology creates the terrain for self-reflection and transformative action. I do not believe that the concept of ideology can be located either in the sphere of consciousness, as in traditional Marxism, or exclusively within the realm of the unconscious, as Althusser (1969, 1971) and his followers argue. Following Gramsci (1971), I want to argue that human behavior is rooted in a complex nexus of structured needs, common sense, and critical consciousness, and that ideology is located in all of these aspects of human behavior and thought so as to produce multiple subjectivities and perceptions of the world and everyday life. That is, the referent point for the interface of ideology and individual experience can be located within three specific areas: the sphere of the unconscious and the structure of needs, the realm of common sense, and the sphere of critical consciousness. Needless to say, these categories cannot be neatly defined, nor do they exist in isolated fashion. But the value of using them is that they raise the level of analysis of consciousness to a new theoretical plane. Instead of providing referent points for the question of whether consciousness is true or false, these categories raise the more fundamental issue of what consciousness is and how it is constituted. Moreover, the argument that ideology exists as part of the unconscious, common sense, and critical consciousness points to an ideological universe in which contradictions exist both within and outside of the individual. Williams (1977) is helpful here when he argues that the ideological field in any given society is saturated with contradictions within and between what he calls emerging, residual, and dominant ideologies. Meaning, as it is produced and received in this complex of ideologies and material forces, is clearly not reducible to the individual and has to be understood in its articulation with ideological and material forces as they circulate and constitute the wider society. In other words, ideology has to be conceived as both the source and the effect of social and institutional practices as they operate within a society characterized primarily by relations of domination—a society in which men and women are basically unfree in both objective and subjective terms. This becomes clearer if we examine the relations between ideology and these three spheres of meaning and behavior separately.

IDEOLOGY & THE UNCONSCIOUS

In chapter 1 I argued that one of the major flaws of Marxist theory was its failure to develop a link between the social and the psychological. Marxism limited the parameters of nature and ideology almost exclusively to the realm of consciousness and the concept of domination. Lost from these approaches was any attempt to analyze the effects of ideology on the personality. In other words, there were very few attempts to examine how ideology produced effects, not only the level of knowledge, but also at the level of needs and desires. Locked within a theoretical strait-jacket that defined power as "merely" oppressive, orthodox Marxism failed to explore how people acted against their own interest and shared in their own oppression, or what compelled them to stand up and resist oppression in the face of intolerable odds. Foucault raises this point poignantly: "What enables people . . . to resist the Gulag[?] What can give [them] the courage to stand up and die in order to utter a word or a poem[?]" (Foucault 1980).

Within the last few decades, Marcuse (1955), Althusser (1969), and others have attempted to reconstruct the meaning of ideology and to resituate its location and effects so as to include the sphere of the un-conscious and the structure of needs. As I have mentioned repeatedly in the last few chapters, Althusser's (1969, 1971) insistence that ideology is grounded unconsciously represents a major contribution in redefining the meaning and workings of the concept. It points to the limits of consciousness in explaining the nature of domination while simultaneously pointing to the power of material practices and social relations as me-diating forms through which people live their experiences and generate meanings. But although Althusser provides a service in linking ideology to the unconscious, he is still trapped within a notion of domination that leaves little room for resistance or, for that matter, for a dialectical notion of ideology.

The work of the Frankfurt School, especially Marcuse's (1955) analysis of how ideology becomes sedimented as second nature in the structure of needs, represents a much more productive starting point for investi-gating the link between ideology and its unconscious grounding. As I mentioned in Chapter 1, Marcuse claims that domination is rooted his-torically not only in the socioeconomic conditions of society, but also in the sedimented history or structure of needs that constitute each person's disposition and personality. For Marcuse, ideology as repression is a his-torical construct rooted in the reified relations of everyday life—relations characterized by "the submission of social reality to forms of calculability and control" (Feenberg 1981). Lukacs (1968) points to the social character of repressive ideology in his notion of reification, in which concrete re-lations between human beings are made to appear as objectified relations between things. Adorno (1967b, 1968) and Marcuse (1955) capture the subjective dynamic of reification in the concept of second nature. Ideology as reification was a form of unconsciousness in which the historically contingent nature of social relations under capitalism had been "forgotten" and took on the appearance of mythic permanence and unchanging reality. Ideology as second nature was history congealed into habit, and rooted in the very structure of needs. Thus ideology not only shapes consciousness but also reaches into the depths of personality and reinforces, through the patterns and routines of everyday life, needs that limit "the free self-activity of social individuals and . . . their qualitatively many-sided system of needs" (Heller 1974).

Unlike Althusser (1971) and Bourdieu (1977b), who cast the connection between ideology and the unconscious in modes of iron-clad domination from which there appears no escape, Marcuse (1955) and Heller (1974) treat the linkage dialectically and posit its dominating as well as its emancipatory possibilities. For instance, both theorists argue that since needs are historically conditioned, they can be changed. Moreover, the unconscious grounding of ideology is not only rooted in needs that are repressive but also in needs that are emancipatory in nature, i.e., needs based on meaningful social relations, community, freedom, creative work, and a fully developed aesthetic sensibility. What emerges from this locus of contradictory needs are tensions both within the personality structure and within the larger society. Inherent in these contradictory tensions are possibilities for the full and many-sided development of "radical" needs, and the elimination of the conditions that repress them. Thus ideology, as located in the unconscious, is a moment of self-creation as well as a force for domination.

A number of important questions emerge from this analysis, two of which will be explored here. First, what particular elements of ideology critique can be developed from the analysis provided by the Frankfurt School theorists and Heller? Second, what is the relevance of this type of ideology critique for a theory of schooling?

The critique of ideology as grounded in the unconscious provides the basis for an analysis of those aspects of everyday life that structure human relations in order to reveal their historical genesis and the interests they embody. What appears as "natural" must be demystified and revealed as a historical production, both in terms of the unrealized claims or distorting messages of its content, and the elements that structure its form. Ideology critique becomes historical in a double sense: on the one hand, it reaches into the history of social relations and reveals the truth or falsity of the logic underlying it; on the other hand, it probes the sedimented history of the personality and attempts to illuminate the sources and influences at work in the very tissue of the need and personality structure. In addition, it points to the importance of identifying, analyzing, and transforming the social practices that sustain the gap between economic and cultural wealth and the real scope of human impoverishment. Furthermore, ideology critique in this perspective suggests the importance of educating people to recognize the interest structure that limits human freedom, while simultaneously calling for the abolition of those social practices that are its material embodiment. Heller (1974) is quite correct in arguing that for radical needs to be developed, individuals and groups have to nurture an ongoing self-critical awareness of their existence while developing qualitatively different social relations to sustain them.

What is crucial to recognize is the role that needs play in structuring our behavior, whether it be in the interest of social and cultural reproduction or in the interest of self-determination. If we are to take human agency seriously, we must acknowledge the degree to which historical and objective societal forces leave their ideological imprint upon the psyche itself. To do so is to lay the groundwork for a critical encounter between oneself and the dominant society, to acknowledge what this society has made of us and decide whether that is what we truly want to be. Finally, ideology critique as it is applied to the unconscious grounding of human behavior is ultimately meaningful only if it is explored in relation to consciousness and a critical monitoring of the relationship between consciousness and the structures and ideologies that make up the dominant society.

The implications of this form of ideology critique for educational theory and practice center primarily around the development of a depth psychology that can unravel the way in which historically specific experiences and traditions get produced, reproduced, and resisted at the level of daily school life. This approach points to two major concerns. First, it points to the need to identify the tacit messages embodied in the day-to-day routines of the school experience, and to uncover the emancipatory or repressive interests these routines serve. It also suggests developing a mode of critique that comprehends the forces that mediate between the structural relations of schooling and their lived effects. Students bring different histories to school; these histories are embedded in class, gender, and race interests that shape their needs and behavior, often in ways they don't understand or that work against their own interests. To work with working-class students, for instance, under the purported impetus of a radical pedagogy would mean not only changing their consciousness, but simultaneously developing social relations that sustain and are compatible with the radical needs in which such a consciousness would have to be grounded in order to be meaningful. A case in point would be developing a pedagogy that made working-class sexism an object of analysis and change. It would be essential that such a pedagogy not only interrogate the language, ideas, and relations inherent in the logic of sexism, but that it be developed within classroom social relations based on non-sexist principles and concerns. Second, this approach to radical pedagogy points to the need for an understanding by teachers of the relation between cultural capital and ideology as a basis for confirming the experiences that students bring with them to the school. Students must first view their own ideologies and cultural capital as meaningful before they can critically probe their strengths and weaknesses. The point here may be obvious. Students cannot learn about ideology simply by being taught how meanings get socially constructed in the media and other aspects of daily life. Working-class students also have to understand how they participate implicitly in ideology through their own experiences and needs. It is their own experiences and needs that have to be made problematic to provide the basis for exploring the interface between their own lives and the constraints and possibilities of the wider society. Thus, a radical pedagogy must address the task of providing the conditions for changing subjectivity as it is constituted in the individual's needs, drives, passions, and intelligence, and for changing the political, economic, and social foundation of the wider society as well.

In short, an essential aspect of radical pedagogy is the need for students to critically interrogate their inner histories and experiences. It is crucial for them to be able to understand how their own experiences are reinforced, contradicted, and suppressed as a result of the ideologies mediated in the material and intellectual practices that characterize daily classroom life. Clearly, the goal of this form of analysis is not to reduce ideology and its effects to the sphere of the unconscious as much as it is to argue for the importance of ideology as a major component of educational theory and radical praxis. For it is in the dialectical relations between consciousness and unconsciousness, experience and objective reality, that the basis for critical thought and action has to be grounded and developed. The prevailing system of needs in capitalist society—or any repressive society—must be understood in terms of its historical genesis and the interests it embodies and serves. For radical educators, this is the first step in breaking with the logic and institutions of domination. It must be followed by a radicalization of consciousness and the reconstruction of social relations that materially reinforce the logic of emancipatory interests.

IDEOLOGY & COMMON SENSE

One of the major contributions of Marx was his insight that consciousness had to be explained as part of the historical mode of one's existence. That is, thought and its production could not be separated from one's world, and forms of consciousness are forms of life that are social and historical in nature. At the same time, Marx (1969b) insisted that while consciousness is an essential constituent of any activity, a critical analysis of society must look beyond the level of lived beliefs and examine the social relations in which they were embedded. For Marx (1969a), Gramsci (1971), and other Western Marxists ideology was not exhausted through its representations in the unconsciousness. While the unconscious was an important ideological sphere, it left human agents without the benefit of consciousness, not to mention critical consciousness. Gramsci, in particular, provides a brilliant insight into the location and effects of ideology in the sphere of common sense he labeled *contradictory consciousness*. He begins with the important assumption that human consciousness cannot be equated with or exhausted in the logic of domination. On the contrary, he viewed it as a complex combination of good and bad *sense*, a contradictory realm of ideas and behavior in which elements of accommodation and resistance exist in an unsteady state of tension. More specifically, the Gramscian view of common sense points to a mode of subjectivity characterized by forms of discursive consciousness imbued with insights into the social reality as well as with distorting beliefs that mystify and legitimate it. In addition, common sense effects and manifests itself in non-discursive behavior marked by the same combination of elements of accommodation and resistance. What both of these contradictory moments share is that as conditions for knowledge and behavior they function without benefit of critical interrogation. In spite of the truth content of these moments, or their force as elements of domination, it is the grounding of common sense in an uncritical mode of mediation—a mode unconscious of its relation to the larger social totality as medium and product of its effects—that represents its singular characteristic.

Common sense represents a limited mode of self-consciousness, contradictory in nature and ill-equipped to grasp either the force behind it or its effects on the social totality. In contrast to a notion of ideology that exists either solely in the unconsciousness as an undiluted form of hegemony or that finds its presence in consciousness as simply false and distorting ideas, common sense represents a realm of consciousness informed by a complex of contrasting subjectivities. Disorder, rather than harmony, characterizes common sense; it contains a dialectical interplay of hegemonic and insightful beliefs and practices. While agency does not disappear in this account, it lacks the self-consciousness dynamic needed to resolve its contradictions and tensions or to extend its partial insights into a coherent critical perspective through which it can engage its own principles. Gramsci points to this issue in his comment on contradictory consciousness:

> The active man-in-the-mass has a practical activity, but has no clear theoretical consciousness of his practical activity, which nonetheless involves understanding the world insofar as it transforms it. His theoretical consciousness can indeed be historically in opposition to his activity. One might almost say that he has two theoretical consciousnesses (or one contradictory consciousness); one which is implicit in his activity and which in reality unites him with all his fellow workers in practical transformation of the real world; and one, superficially explicit or verbal, which he has inherited from the past and uncritically absorbed [Gramsci 1971].

Underlying this perspective are a number of assumptions and implications that have relevance for educational theory and practice. First, Gramsci rescues the human subject by positing a notion of ideology that does not obliterate the mediating faculties of ordinary people. At the same time, he does so in a way that situates human agency within a preexisting field of domination that is open-ended in its effects and outcomes. Thus, contradictory consciousness does not point primarily to domination or confusion, but to a sphere of contradictions and tensions that is pregnant with possibilities for radical change. Ideology in this sense becomes a critical concept to the degree to which it reveals the truths as well as the concealing function of common sense.

Second, Gramsci posits a notion of ideology and common sense that addresses an important dialectical relation between discourse and practical activity. In this case, ideology is located not only on the level of speech and language, but also as lived experience, as practical conduct in everyday life. What Gramsci argues for is a mode of analysis that uncovers the contradictory moments in discourse so they can not only be used to reveal their own underlying interests but also so they can be restructured into a form of critical consciousness that can, in Gramsci's words, "make coherent the problems raised by the masses in their practical activity" (Karabel 1976). In this case, the "mystical" character of common sense no longer speaks for itself, but becomes subjected to a critical interrogation via its own thought processes and practical activity as these constitute and reproduce the conduct of everyday life. In pedagogical terms, this suggests taking the typifications and attendant social relations of educational discourse and stripping them of their objective or so-called natural character. In short, these must be viewed within historical and social relations that are produced and socially constructed. This leads to a final insight about common sense, one drawn directly from the work of Frankfurt School members such as Adorno, Horkheimer, and Marcuse.

For the Frankfurt School, the notion of common sense could only be understood by analyzing its dialectical relation to the wider social totality. Inherent in the form and substance of common sense was the logic of the commodity structure; that is, common sense was constituted by taken-for-granted categories and practical activity divorced from the agents and conditions that produced them. These appeared objectified, as unquestioned "givens" cut off from the sociohistorical processes and interests through which they had evolved and which they helped sustain. In this perspective, ideology critique functioned to unmask the messages revealed in common sense, to locate historically the interests that structured them, and to interrogate their truth claims and societal functions. There is an important dimension of ideology critique in this formulation, one that is indispensible for a radical pedagogy. Radical practice begins, in this case, with a break from the positivist emphasis on the immediacy "which daily deludes individuals with a nature-like invariance of their life relationships" (Schmidt 1981). Ideology critique takes on an added dimension here. It posits the need for a historical consciousness—one that begins with an analysis of the reifications of daily life and takes the rigidified, congealed relations that reduce teachers and students to "bearers" of history as the basis for probing into history to discover the conditions that generated such conditions in the first place. Historical consciousness, as an instance of ideology critique and radical pedagogy in this perspective, functions "so as to perceive the past in a way that [makes] the present visible as a revolutionary moment" (Buck-Morss 1981a). This leads us to the relationship between ideology and reflective consciousness, the most potentially radical of the three spheres in which ideology is located.

IDEOLOGY & CRITICAL CONSCIOUSNESS

The notion that ideology has a place in the realm of critical thinking presents a direct challenge to most theories of ideology. As I have mentioned previously, these theories tend either to reduce ideology to false consciousness or to disparage it by contrasting it against what is termed science. I want to argue here that ideology can act as a critical moment in the production of meaning by illuminating the rules, assumptions, and interests that structure not only the thinking process but also the objects of analysis. The ideological dimension that underlies all critical reflection is that it lays bare the historically and socially sedimented values at work in the construction of knowledge, social relations, and material practices. In other words, it grounds the production of knowledge, including science, in a normative framework linked to specific interests. As Aronowitz (1980) makes clear, those who argue for dividing science and ideology reproduce the very notion of ideology they critique, i.e., ideology as mystification. He writes, "The concept of the science/ideology antinomy is itself ideological because it fails to comprehend that all knowledge is a product of social relations" (Aronowitz 1980).

To locate a theory of ideology in the sphere of critical consciousness is to highlight the normative basis of all knowledge and to point to the active nature of human agents in its construction. The underlying grammar of ideology finds its highest expression in the ability of human beings to think dialectically. To critically view both the object of analysis and the processes involved in such analysis as part of a complex mode of producing meaning represents not simply the active side of ideology, but its most critical dimension. Thus ideology implies a process whereby meaning is produced, represented, and consumed. The critical aspect of that process represents a reflexive understanding of the interests embodied in the process itself and how these interests might be transformed, challenged or sustained so as to promote rather than repress the dynamics of critical thought and action. Ideology in this sense suggests that all aspects of everyday life that have a semiotic value are open to reflection and critique, just as it points to the need for a critical attentiveness to all aspects of self-expression.

Ideology critique informs critical thinking by making it into more than an interpretative tool. It situates critique within a radical notion of interest and social transformation. Critical analysis, in this case, becomes the distinct and important precondition for radical praxis, with a dual purpose. On the one hand, it follows Adorno's (1973) insistence that the task of ideology critique is the explosion of reification—a breaking through of mystifications and a recognition of how certain forms of ideology serve the logic of domination. This means analyzing the hidden ideological elements in any object of analysis, whether it be a school, a curriculum, or a set of social relations, and revealing their social function. It also means releasing their unintentional truths, the suppressed utopian elements contained in what they include as well as in what they leave out. More specifically, this means breaking apart the ideas and structuring principles in a cultural artifact and then reassembling them in a different framework that allows the limits of specific ideas and formalistic properties to come into view, while simultaneously discovering the new and vital elements in them that could be appropriated for radical purposes. For instance, in looking at most literacy models, a radical educator would have to first identify the ideology that informs their content and methodology. It might then be possible to appropriate certain fundamental aspects of the models, but within a theoretical framework in which literacy is treated not merely as a technique but as a constitutive process of constructing meaning and critically interrogating the forces that shape lived experiences. This points to another desideratum of ideology critique, that is, that it be informed by a spirit of relentless negativity, one designed to promote the critical independence of the subject as well as the restructuring and transformation of an oppressive social reality. Ideology critique as a form of critical consciousness opposes the knowledge of technocratic rationality, and implies instead a dialectical knowledge that illuminates contradictions and informs the critical judgments needed for individual and social action.

The link between ideology and the notion of truth is not to be found in the peddling of prescriptions or in the deluge of endless recipes; instead, it is located in what Benjamin (1969) has called "the distance between the interpreter and the material," on the one hand, and the gap between the present and the possibility of a radically different future, on the other. The value of viewing ideology as a complex process in the production and critique of meaning becomes more concrete through an examination of how it functions as a constitutive force in the structuring and mediation of representations in school artifacts and in classroom social relations.

Ideology, Representations, and Classroom Material Practices

What is needed to fully grasp the relations between agency and structure as part of a radical pedagogy is a theory of ideology that is also capable of comprehending the way in which meaning is constructed and materialized within "texts", or cultural forms such as films, books, curriculum packages, fashion styles, etc. Thus, ideology critique is not limited to the hidden or visible processes in the realm of subjectivity and behavior, but is extended to the "study of observable material processes—the manipulation of signs in specific ways and specific contexts" (Bennett 1981). The work of Volosinov (1973), Eco (1976), Coward and Ellis (1977), and Kress and Hodge (1979) has been invaluable in this regard because it points to the relative autonomy of representations that function to construct the parameters within which meaning is produced, negotiated, and received. Of course, in the structuralist approach "signs" are synonymous with consciousness, and the notion that signs could be both the medium and the product of consciousness is denied. In other words, ideology as representations of expressed ways of thought, experience, and feeling is not given very much theoretical weight. This is clearly captured in Volosinov's claim that "Individual consciousness is not the architect of the ideological superstructure, but only a tenant lodging in the edifice of ideological signs" (Volosinov 1973). But while it is true that representations and signs address (interpellate) and situate individuals, the human beings they address are more than just a reflex of the texts in question. In other words, human agents always mediate through their own histories and class- or gender-related subjectivities the representations and material practices that constitute the parameters of their lived experiences. This is true within the parameters defined by the school, the family, the workplace, or any other social site. What is needed to offset the one-sided theory of ideology provided by many structuralists is a more fully developed theory of mediation and reception (Barrett 1981). Such an approach would link agency and structure in a theory of ideology so as to treat dialectically the role of the individual and group as producers of meaning within already existing fields of representation and practice. Not to do so, as Johnson (1979) suggests, runs the risk of getting trapped in modes of structuralist analyses that overlook "the moment of self creation, of the affirmation of belief, or the giving of consent."

The starting-point for developing a more dialectical theory of ideology and schooling rests with the acknowledgment that individuals and social classes are both the medium and outcome of ideological discourses and practices. Meaning is located in the various dimensions of subjectivity and behavior as well as in "texts" and classroom practices that structure, limit, and enable human action. Following on my discussion in Chapter 2, I want to present a theory of ideology critique that draws from both structuralist and culturalist positions and develop it within a notion of radical pedagogy. The organizing principles for such an analysis will be the notions of reproduction, production, and reconstruction, all of which will be delineated within the context of this analysis.

Reproduction refers here to texts and social practices whose messages, inscribed within specific historical settings and social contexts, function primarily to legitimate the interests of the dominant social order. I want to argue that these can be characterized as texts and social practices *about* pedagogy (Lundgren Forthcoming), and refer primarily to categories of meaning constructed so as to legitimize and reproduce interests expressed in dominant ideologies. The acts of conception, construction, and production that characterize texts *about* pedagogy usually have little to do with the contexts in which such texts are applied, and the principles that structure them almost never lend themselves to methods of inquiry that encourage dialogue or debate. Such texts and practices objectively represent the selection, fixation, and legitimation of dominant traditions. For instance, both the form and content of such texts tend to treat teachers and students as reified elements in the pedagogical processes. Even in the more sophisticated versions of such texts, such as the Humanities units Carol Buswell examined, the logic of powerlessness prevailed, albeit in recycled forms. Buswell writes:

> The texts directed pupils to books and information kept elsewhere which was part of the aim of teaching them to "learn." But a "particular" answer was still required and finding it became a complicated orienteering exercise conducted through the printed word whereby acquiring any content was made more difficult. The emphasis in all the units was on following the precise instructions and replicating what someone else had produced, very little creativity was required [Buswell 1980].

This reified view of knowledge is a classic example of Freire's (1973) "banking model" of schooling and is found not only in the structuring principles that inform such texts but also in their content as well. For instance, Joshua Brown (1981) in an extensive examination of recent children's history books, attempted to find texts that recognized human agency; that related past experiences to the present so as to stimulate intellectual curiosity; that linked material conditions to social relations; that did not simply present history as dressed-up figures and facts; and, finally, that treated history as open-ended and subject to interpretation. What he actually found were books that contained an anti-urban bias, promoted their content in "commercial studio aesthetics," celebrated technology outside of the human relations in which it functions and collapsed history into great moments, while simultaneously using a language that suppressed conflict (Brown 1981).

At another level, there is a growing amount of research that points to the increased use of prepackaged curriculum materials that accentuate delivering instruction while at the same time removing conception and critique from the pedagogical act. Apple (1982) argues that such curriculum material represents a new form of control over both teachers and students, one that indicates a process of de-skilling and the emergence of more powerful forms of rationality that embody changing modes of control within the nature of capitalist relations of production. Control in this case is removed from face-to-face contact and is now situated in the impersonal processes and logic of highly rationalized managerial relations. The effects on schooling represent a new dimension in the reproduction of texts and material practices *about* pedagogy. This is evident in Apple's claim:

> Skills that teachers used to need, that were deemed essential to the craft of working with children—such as curriculum deliberation and planning, designing teaching and curricular strategies for specific groups and individuals based on intimate knowledge of these people—are no longer as necessary. With the large-scale influx of prepackaged material, planning is separated from execution. The planning is done at the level of production of both the rules for use of the material and the material itself. The execution is carried out by the teacher. In the process, what were previously considered valuable skills slowly atrophy because they are less often required [Apple 1982].

Each of these examples provides a mode of ideology critique that reveals how reproductive ideologies work. Buswell (1980) illustrates how specific principles structure the text and classroom social relations so as to legitimate modes of learning that promote passivity and rule-following rather than critical engagement on the part of teachers and students. Brown (1981) both points to the structural silences in a text, those ideas and values that are left out and thus devalued, and at the same time analyzes the social function of existing texts. Apple, on the other hand, shows the way in which the principles that structure the production and use of curriculum materials are rooted in specific interests that reinforce a division of labor separating conception from execution at the level of teaching itself. In all of these cases, texts relating to pedagogy suppress human agency while legitimating the management and control functions of the dominant classes. What is missing from these analyses and must complement them are forms of historical critique that move beyond simply registering the ideologies embedded in the form and content of curriculum materials and practices. Moreover, it is imperative to link such ideological representations to historically constituted social relations that highlight the force and effects that some stereotypes and social relations might have as they appear in schools. Barrett (1980) illuminates this issue when she argues that female models are more persuasive to male customers than male models in similar roles are to female customers because the female stereotype bears the weight of social relations that have a long history. Clearly, the only way to understand such stereotypes is to situate them in the social relations that have constituted them historically.

As important as this mode of ideology critique is, however, it has failed to develop a *theory of production*. That is, it has failed to analyze how reproductive ideologies in texts and social practices are mediated. It is particularly important to acknowledge that texts are always mediated in some fashion by human subjects; meanings are always produced by human agents when they confront and engage cultural forms such as curriculum texts, films, and the like. As Arnot and Whitty (1982) and Jameson (1979) have stressed, educational meanings and practices are "read" by teachers and students through interpretative and selective principles that bear the weight of pre-existing situations and constituted ideologies. The relation between inscribed messages and lived effects is a tenuous one indeed and cannot be viewed through a reductionist logic that collapses one into the other. That is, the way in which a teacher or student engages a text or specific social relation is, in fact, a "function of his or her place in society" (Barrett 1980). Ideology critique in this instance would have to locate the various ideological discourses and multiple subjectivities that construct and constitute meaning for students from different classes, genders, and racial backgrounds (Therborn 1981). This demands being attentive to the cultural capital that characterizes different student experiences and to the wars in which students actually produce meanings via their historical, positional, family, and class backgrounds. By penetrating these ideologies and cultural forms, it becomes possible for teachers to unravel the mediations that give meaning to school experience and to understand how they might function in the interest of accommodation, resistance, or active change.

This leads to my final point regarding the relations among ideology, texts, and social practices. The principle of *reconstruction* shifts the theoretical terrain from the issues of reproduction and mediation to a concern for critical appropriation and transformation. This suggests a mode of ideology critique in which the interests that underlie texts, representations, and social practices would not only be identified but also disassembled and refashioned with the aim of developing social relations and modes of knowledge that serve radical needs. The task of reconstruction is not simply to analyze knowledge and social relations for dominating ideologies or subversive unintentional truths, but to appropriate their useful material elements and skills, and to restructure them as part of the production of new ideologies and collective experiences. Knowledge production is linked to transformative activities in this case, and is situated within a problematic that takes as its ultimate aim the development of forms of radical praxis both within and outside of schools. John Brenkman captures a critical aspect of this issue in his call for the development of a Marxist cultural hermeneutics:

> Its project is twofold. Interpretations which read cultural texts in relation to their historical situations and effects must conserve or subvert meanings according to their validity not for an already constituted tradition but for a community in process. And, secondly, interpretation must be connected to the project of reclaiming language practices that unfold the horizon of this community. Such a hermeneutics becomes valid only as it serves to construct oppositional cultural experiences, an oppositional public sphere. It has a political task. The dominant tendency of our cultural institutions and practices—from the organization of the learning process in the schools and the academic modes of knowledge which support them to the mass mediated forms of communication which pre-empt speaking itself—is to undermine the very possibility for human beings to interpret the discourses that found their identities, shape their interactions and regulate their activities. Only a process of interpretation which counters this tendency, actively and practically, can preserve the possibilities of a historical consciousness founded on collective experience [Brenkman 1979].

A reconstructive perspective would promote the conditions necessary for the development of what Lundgren (Forthcoming) calls texts *for* pedagogy. These would be curriculum materials and school practices appropriated and/or produced by the teachers and educators who use them. Such texts refer to both a process and a product. As a process, they embody and demonstrate principles that link conception and execution while simultaneously promoting a critical attentiveness to forms of knowledge and social practices informed by principles that promote enlightenment and understanding. Such texts would be attentive to procedures that locate knowledge in specific historical contexts and would attempt to uncover the human interests in which it is grounded. As products, such texts become the medium for a critical pedagogy aimed at providing students with the knowledge, skills, and critical sensibility they need to be able to think dialectically. That is, students need to be able to grasp the ways in which the concrete world opposes the possibilities inherent in its own conditions; they need to be able to reach into history so as to transform historical into critical thought; and finally, they need to be able to critically penetrate the categories of common sense and begin to move beyond a world constituted through such categories. In short, whereas texts *about* pedagogy, along with the social relations engendered by them, are rooted in the logic of authoritarianism and control, texts *for* pedagogy contain interests that may promote modes of schooling based on the critical dimensions of an emancipatory ideology.

Culture, Schooling, and Power

Ideology is a crucial construct for understanding how meaning is produced, transformed, and consumed by individuals and social groups. As a tool of critical analysis, it digs beneath the phenomenal forms of classroom knowledge and social practices and helps to locate the structuring principles and ideas that mediate between the dominant society and the everyday experiences of teachers and students. As a political construct, it makes meaning problematic and questions why human beings have unequal access to the intellectual and material resources that constitute the conditions for the production, consumption, and distribution of meaning. Similarly, it raises questions about why certain ideologies prevail at certain times and whose interests they serve. Hence, ideology "speaks" to the notion of power by accentuating the complex ways in which relations of meaning are produced and fought-over.

By acknowledging that ideologies are always produced, conveyed, and received within particular social practices organized around specific social systems with access to various degrees of sophisticated technology, it becomes clear that ideology as a construct reveals a limited, though essential, aspect of the relations that characterize the interface among ideology, culture, and schooling. That is, if we are to unravel the relationship between ideology and culture, it is necessary to expand the theoretical terrain from an exclusive focus on meaning to include the material determinants and principles through which antagonistic classes and groups construct their daily experiences.

As I have pointed out previously, if radical pedagogy is to incorporate a critical notion of culture and culture critique into its theoretical calculus, it will have to reject mainstream-liberal and sundry Marxist notions of the meaning of culture. More specifically, traditional social theory has reduced the notion of culture to an all-embracing category of social science by defining it as everything and anything that the members of a society produce in order to maintain themselves (Tyler 1981; Shapiro 1960). Or it is seen in the Matthew Arnold sense, as the best that has been thought and said. Conservative educators such as Bantock (1968) have fallen back on the latter usage to uphold the distinction between high and low culture, and proceed to argue that there should be two curriculums in the schools. A high-culture curriculum would be designed for the specially talented students; it would be informed by the knowledge and skills that characterize the ruling classes. On the other hand a low-culture curriculum would be a non-literary curriculum for the vast majority of students. Both positions distort the notion of culture by either depoliticizing it or by refusing to acknowledge the legitimating interests that it embodies and reproduces to maintain certain distinctions of a class, race and gender in society. Equally problematic is the fact that Marxists have politicized the notion of culture and revealed the political logic at its core, but in so doing have viewed it as epiphenomenal to the mode of production, and in effect have reduced it to a set of principles that uniformly promote domination (Adorno & Horkheimer 1973; Bourdieu & Passeron 1977a). Or, as in the case of culturalists such as Williams (1965), they have limited its scope to a class-specific focus on experience and struggle without the benefit of analyzing the structural determinants and constraints in which such struggles are embedded.

In order to rescue the concept of culture from these perspectives, it must be redefined and used as a construct that points to the notions of both social and culture reproduction *and* production. Since I have already discussed this idea in detail in Chapter 3, and will delineate it still further in chapters 5 and 6, I shall here present a brief analysis of a "critical" Marxist orientation toward the meaning and use of culture in radical pedagogy.

In the most general sense, culture is constituted by the relations between different classes and groups bounded by structural forces and material conditions and informed by a range of experiences mediated, in part, by the power exercised by a dominant society. Two important conditions are at work in this definition. The first centers around the material conditions that arise from asymetrical relations of power and the principles emerging from different classes and groups who use them to make sense of their location in a given society. The second condition refers to the relations between capital and its dominant classes, on the one hand, and the cultures and experiences of the subordinate classes, on the other. In this relationship, capital is constantly working to reproduce the ideological and cultural conditions essential to maintain itself, or the social relationships needed to produce the rate of profit.

Within these two conditions, culture is constituted as a dialectical instance of power and conflict, rooted in the struggle over both material conditions and the form and content of practical activity. It is not only the lived experiences of different classes and groups, but also the practical activity embedded in the ownership, control, and maintenance of institutions and resources that constitute the nature and meaning of culture. Moreover, the structures, material practices, and lived relations of a given society do not in themselves comprise a culture, but represent an ensemble or complex of dominant and secondary cultures that are functional to the society itself. That is, they are forged, reproduced, and contested under conditions of power and dependency that primarily serve the dominant culture or cultures.

By making a distinction between dominant and subordinate cultures, we can locate the characterizing moment of culture in the way in which power is used in a society to mediate between the reproductive ideologies and structures of the dominant classes and the complex of reproductive and transformative practices, structures, and principles of subordinate classes and groups. Within this framework, culture moves beyond the terrain of ideology with its focus on the production, reproduction, and reconstruction of meaning. That is, culture takes a related but different object of analysis in unraveling the interplay between reproduction and transformation, and focuses on the struggle over institutions and mode of production as well as on the struggle between groups and social classes who act to either maintain the existing society or change it.

As presently defined, culture doesn't exist on some Mount Olympus, removed from the dynamics of history and society; nor does it collapse into a one-sided theory of domination. Instead, it is a complex of traditions, institutions, and formations situated within a social sphere of contestation and struggle, a sphere rooted in a complex of power relations that influence and condition lived experiences without dictating their results (Williams 1977). Culture, in this instance, does not suppress human agency, nor does it eliminate the notion of determination. Determination and human agency presuppose each other in situations that represent a setting-of-limits on the resources and opportunities of different classes. Men and women inherit these predefined circumstances, but engage them in a "process of meaning-making which is always active" (Bennett 1981), and leaves their results open-ended.

Culture becomes a critical construct when it is used to analyze the concrete existences that characterize the relations between different social formations as they evolve through time and place. Such situations need to be understood not only in terms of the principles and values that inform the "radical heterogeneity" of, for instance, working-class groups, but also in terms of how these combine with the weight of institutional forms to promote or repress the ways in which subordinate groups become active participants in the quest for political change. Culture, as used here, takes on a dialectical quality that suggests both its repressive and transformative qualities. In the Gramscian sense, culture becomes the raw material for either domination or liberation, while ideology is seen as the active processes human subjects exercise in producing, mediating, and resisting the moral, political, and intellectual leadership that characterize the interests of the dominant classes (Gramsci 1971).

In the first instance, culture represents the ensemble of institutions, beliefs, and practices that unify ruling-class interests. In addition, it represents the attempt on the part of dominant groups to penetrate the cultures of subordinate classes in order to win their consent to the existing order. In the second instance, culture refers to a heterogeneous ensemble of practices, beliefs, and resources that may accommodate, resist, and even remain indifferent to the dominant culture. The issue here is that the lived experiences of the masses are always a problematic. Moreover, the sexual and social divisions of labor, the heterogeneity of different traditions, the differing degree of complexity of various work and social sites, along with the complexity of human life in general, make it nearly impossible to reduce the form and content of culture to a simple matter of class categories. Class cultures are clearly not all of one piece, but at the same time members of the working class, for instance, do share a set of experiences that are partly informed by the fact that they belong to a culture of subordination—in this case, a culture that exists in a particular relation to the wage-labor system and that constitutes a range of experiences quite different from those experienced by ruling-class groups. It is the tension in and between these classes that provides a theoretical starting-point for unraveling how hegemonic cultures and ideologies actually work, in schools or in other social sites. For it is from forms of opposition and struggle that radical educators will be able to decipher and develop an understanding of how the mechanisms of social and cultural reproduction actually work in schools.

Human agency and structures come together most visibly at the point where oppositional practices and meanings contribute to the very nature of the hegemonic process. Such resistance not only reveals the active side of hegemony, it also provides the basis for a radical pedagogy that would make it the object of a critical deciphering and analysis. What this suggests is that beneath even forms of resistance there are underlying commonalities forged in the logic of domination. Whether they be a celebration of sexism, the reproduction of the division of labor, or the aping of the commodity fetish, they provide the ground for understanding how culture and ideology interface in the interest of domination and liberation. It is the liberatory moment that needs to be further understood and extended if a radical pedagogy is to be developed.

Within the existing definition of culture we can point to a number of distinct but related elements that constitute the cultural field. First are the institutions and social practices that characterize a given society; second, the shared principles and experiences of particular groups and social formations; third, the arena of power and struggle that situates the boundaries through which to understand the forces of reproduction as well as the possibilities for political and cultural struggle and transformation. Each of these areas suggests a distinctive object of analysis and struggle for developing a theory of cultural politics and radical pedagogy.

The first instance points to understanding and challenging the internal organization of the school, while at the same time revealing how its organization and relations reproduce a similar logic in other sites. Moreover, it would be necessary to unravel and expose how the school functions amidst all of its contradictions to reproduce the logic of capital and the state. Through such an analysis, reified work conditions could be challenged and the interests they harbor exposed. This becomes especially relevant for contesting the hierarchical relations of school organizations and the cellular structure that isolates most teachers and prevents them from working collectively.

The second instance entails uncovering the historical genesis and underlying logic in the lived relations and principles that constitute the complex ensemble of class cultures. This would demand a Freirian-style interrogation of the meaning and logic that informs, for instance, working-class cultural capital as it unfolds within specific schools, classrooms, and neighborhoods. But a radical pedagogy needs to be informed by more than an understanding of how cultural reproduction works through the discourse, practices, and routines that characterize subordinate groups—equally important is how subordinate groups engage in cultural production as well. The traditions that inform various working-class groups, coupled with the contradictions and incoherencies of school life, provide the basis and space for subordinate-cultural production. The importance of this process cannot be overestimated if we are to take seriously the question of how subordinate groups do or can come to an awareness of the nature of their own existence and their relation to other classes. Moreover, the distinction between subordinate forms of cultural reproduction and production makes it possible to differentiate the pedagogical approaches that might follow from each. Willis provides a definition of cultural production and indicates the method of inquiry needed to analyze it:

> We can provisionally say that cultural production designates, at least in part, the creative use of discourses, meanings, materials, practices, and group processes to explore, understand, and creatively occupy particular positions in sets of general material possibilities. For oppressed groups, this is likely to include oppositional forms and cultural penetrations at particular concrete sites or regions. . . [W]e may note that the uncovering of these secret, repressed, informal, half-betraying forms becomes the special province of a qualitative, ethnographic, commensurate, "living" method [Willis 1981].

McRobbie illustrates this approach in revealing how a group of working-class girls in an English school redefined the sexual code prevalent there by "jettisoning the official ideology for girls in the school (neatness, diligence, appliance, femininity, passivity, etc.) and replacing it with a more feminine, even sexual one. Thus the girls took great pleasure in wearing make-up to school, spent vast amounts of time discussing boy-friends in loud voices in class, and used these interests to disrupt the class" (McRobbie 1978). What is significant about this example is that it contains elements of both production and reproduction, each of which responds to different contexts.

The display of resistant sexual behavior, in the immediate sense, rep-resents a form of cultural production at odds with the repressive sexist practices and values of the school. Outside of the school context, it contains the logic of reproduction because it underlies traditional working-class attitudes toward beauty, family life, and marriage (heavily im-printed, of course, with the logic of gender discrimination). Clearly, the task here would be to drive a wedge between these two moments so students can understand the disabling aspects inherent in the initial act of resistance. If students are to understand how the dominant culture bears down on them, they will have to grasp how it reaches into the logic of their own resistance. But to do so means not only to understand how the forces of cultural reproduction and production operate in schools, but also how schools function as part of the larger social totality.

The third instance that constitutes the cultural field centers around an understanding of the limits and possibilities inherent in different social sites for the development of the skills and forms of knowledge needed for active social transformation. It means analyzing the complex of institu-tions and practices in terms of how they affect students from different social classes and being able to assess the level of effectivity possible for working within such institutions. This raises the central question of what the possibilities are for cultural intervention within specific schools and educational sites. Any radical pedagogy, for example, must concern itself with the question of how to determine when it may be more productive to function in some situations rather than in others. In this case, human agency is not subsumed within the logic of domination, it simply chooses the ground on which it might be operational.

In the next chapter, I will demonstrate how the notion of ideology critique can be used to analyze the subject of citizenship education.

5

Critical Theory & Rationality in Citizenship Education

In the classical Greek definition of citizenship education, a model of rationality can be recognized that is explicitly political, normative, and visionary. Within this model, education was seen as intrinsically political, designed to educate the citizen for intelligent and active participation in the civic community. Moreover, intelligence was viewed as an extension of ethics, a manifestation and demonstration of the doctrine of the good and just life. Thus, in this perspective, education was not meant to train. Its purpose was to cultivate the formation of virtuous character in the ongoing quest for freedom. Therefore, freedom was always something to be created, and the dynamic that informed the relationship between the individual and the society was based on a continuing struggle for a more just and decent political community.[1]

If we were to use citizenship education in the Greek sense against which to judge the quality and meaning of civic education in this country, a strong case could be made that, for the most part, it has been a failure.[2] This is not meant to suggest that liberal democratic theory has not supported noble ideals for its citizens, for it has. It is simply to assert that such ideals have not found their way, in general, into the day-to-day practices of schools, either historically or in more recent times.

The role that schools have played historically in reproducing the rationality of social control and class dominance has been developed extensively in previous chapters, and need not be repeated here.[3] But there is one interesting note worth mentioning. Prior to the advent of the twentieth century and the rise of the scientific management movement that swept the curriculum field, there was no pretense on the part of educational leaders as to the purpose and function of public schooling. Schools, with few exceptions, were generally training grounds for character development and economic and social control.[4] Unlike the notion of social control later articulated by Dewey (1966) in which schools provide noncoercive forms of persuasion in order to develop intellectual growth consistent with psychological development in students,[5] the educators of the early republic equated social control with obedience and conformity. Edward Ross captured the nature of this sentiment when he referred "to education as an inexpensive form of police" (Spring 1978). Moreover, the language of justification in nineteenth-century public school rationales made the intent and purpose of schooling quite clear. In other words, the "hidden curriculum" during this part of the history of American education was at least "partially" revealed in public school rationales.

> . . . for much that is today called a hidden function of the schools was previously held to be among the prime benefits of schooling. . . . A society newly in conflict over its own identity could respond to such an appeal. Education continued to be justified more as a means of social control than as an instrument of individual betterment. The quest for the one best system precluded any acknowledgement of local differences and aspired instead to a uniformity of experience. In 1891 the Commissioner of Education, William Torrey Harris, frankly admitted that a major purpose of schools was to teach respect for authority and that forming the "habits of punctuality, silence, and industry" was more important than understanding reasons for good behavior [Vallance 1973, 1974].

The comparison between the Greek and early American notions of citizenship reveal telling differences in political ideals. At the same time, the interaction among schooling, politics, and citizenship is quite clear. The visibility of this interaction was lost, however, when educational theory and practice in the twentieth century shifted the philosophical basis of schooling from the political to the technical. Schooling was no longer justified in terms of political values and concerns; the theoretical pillars upon which a new rationale was constructed were efficiency and control. With the age of scientific management came the celebration of a new rationality and the removal of "the political" from the terrain of schooling. William Lowe Boyd in his study of curriculum policy-making captures the essence of this stance with this observation:

> . . . since, the reformers believed that there was "no Republican or Democratic way to pave a street, only a right way," the business of running a city or a school system was viewed as just that, a business matter and not something appropriate for politics. The prompt, business-like dispatch of the decision-making tasks facing school boards . . . was facilitated by their view that a wide range of educational questions were essentially technical matters beyond the capacity of the laity to decide [Boyd 1978].

This philosophical shift in the purpose and function of schooling not only abstracted schools from the context of the wider society, it also ushered in a mode of rationality that relegated the political nature of schooling to the anteroom of educational theory and practice. Citizenship education became entwined in a "culture of positivism," one that displayed little interest in the ways in which schools acted as agents of social and cultural reproduction in a society marked by significant inequities in wealth, power, and privilege.[6]

This chapter argues that if citizenship education is going to revitalize itself in the interest of creating a more noble and just society, it will have to free itself from the burden of its own intellectual and ideological history. In doing so it will have to develop a new rationality and problematic for examining the relationship between schools and the wider society. Questions of technique, objectivity, and control will have to give way to a rationality based on the principles of understanding and critique; likewise, within this rationality a more critical problematic will have to be developed, one that generates new categories and raises questions that could not be raised within the old rationality.

At the core of this new rationality should be a serious attempt to reformulate citizenship education by situating it within an analysis that explores the often-overlooked complex relations among knowledge, power, ideology, class, and economics (Cherryholmes 1980). Such an appraisal would have to use and demonstrate the importance of social and political theory for its analysis of schooling and citizenship education.

In approaching this task, I will examine the following aspects of rationality, in the order listed: that which can be termed the *American ideology;* the political nature of different types of rationality; and the ways in which these particular forms of rationality roughly characterize a number of existing traditions in citizenship education. Then I will outline the foundation of a more radical rationality, one that attempts to unravel the relationship among the educational system, the economic system, and the class structure. Finally, I will explore how these rationalities might be integrated into a set of radical educational practices that might be used as a foundation for developing a more viable theory of citizenship education.

Theoretical Foundations in Educational Theory and Practice

Any notion of rationality has to be defined not only in regard to the truth claims commanded by its major assumptions and ensuing practices, but also by its relationship to what might be called the dominant rationality of a given society at a particular moment in history. This methodological approach is crucial because it illuminates the interconnections that exist between a dominant rationality and the institutions that function in a given society to reproduce it (Young & Whitty 1977; Williams 1977; Mouffe 1979). Such interconnections politicize the notion of rationality by questioning how its ideology supports, mediates, or opposes the configuration of existing sociopolitical forces that use the dominant rationality to legitimize and sustain their existence.

Rationality

By rationality, I mean a specific set of assumptions and social practices that mediate how an individual or group relates to the wider society. Underlying any one mode of rationality is a set of interests that define and qualify how one reflects on the world. This is an important epistemological point. The knowledge, beliefs, expectations, and biases that define a given rationality both condition and are conditioned by the experiences into which we enter. Of crucial importance is the notion that such experiences only become meaningful within a mode of rationality that confers intelligibility on them. Modes of rationality "bind" in a nonmechanistic way. As Althusser points out, "it is not the material reflected on that characterizes and qualifies a reflection . . . but the modality of that reflection, the actual relation the reflection has with its objects" (Althusser 1969). The importance of the notion of rationality becomes clear when its definition is extended to include the concept of the problematic.[7]

Problematic

All modes of rationality contain a problematic, which is, as I noted earlier, a conceptual structure that can be identified both by the questions it raises and the questions it is incapable of raising. The concept of the problematic suggests that any mode of rationality can be viewed as a theoretical framework, the meaning of which can be understood by analyzing both the system of questions that command the answers given as well as the absence of those questions that exist beyond the possibility of such a framework. Boyne captures the importance of this dialectical concept with this comment:

> A word or concept cannot be considered in isolation; it only exists in the theoretical or ideological framework in which it's used; its problematic . . .is centered on the absence of problems and concepts within the problematic as much as their presence. . . . The notion of absence indicates that what the problematic excludes is as important as what it includes. The problematic defines the field of the visible within which errors, oversights, and individual blindness are possible, and can be corrected. At the same time it defines the boundary of the invisible, the correlate of the visible, the realm of the necessarily absent. This invisibility relates crucially to the production of problems; within any problematic there are problems which cannot be posed [Boyne 1979].

A mode of rationality and its given problematic represent a response not simply to the problematic's internal logic, but also the objective struggles, tensions, and issues posed by the historical times in which the problematic operates. The limits of a mode of rationality, particularly one that poses as being universal, become evident when we realize that the intelligibility of its claims cannot "speak" to the issues or questions that threaten to undermine its basic assumptions. This often happens when what had been given as a solution is now posed as a problem. For instance, this happened when it became clear to Lavoisier that Priestly's new gas was not "dephlogisticated" air but oxygen, or more recently, when the new sociology of education rejected the notion of "objective" curriculum knowledge and argued for a curriculum theory based on a recognition of the social construction of knowledge and the negotiation of classroom meaning (Young 1971).

The American Ideology

Before analyzing the different modes of rationality that dominate citizenship education, I want to provide a brief description of the rationality that appears to dominate American social science (Marcuse 1964; Habermas 1971b; Bernstein 1976; Wilson 1977), the curriculum field and the social studies field in particular (Pinar 1978; Popkewitz 1980). By focusing on the dominant rationality in American society, it is possible to get a better understanding of the nature of schooling as a societal process. This approach is not meant to deny the invaluable contributions of numerous traditional studies of schools as socialization agents, it is simply a matter of acknowledging that these studies have generally failed to lay bare the complex relationships between ideology and power in the dominant society and the related, though far from mechanistic, use of knowledge and power at the level of school organization and classroom practice.

Social and Cultural Reproduction in Schools

The recognition that schools are agencies of socialization is an assumption shared by all proponents of citizenship education, but this assumption is incomplete in itself as an analytical tool for unraveling the societal functions of schooling. A more analytical approach, studied in much of the socialization literature, analyzes the socialization process as a vehicle of economic and cultural reproduction; that is, as a process that mediates the social practies and cultural beliefs necessary to maintain the dominance of certain groups and power structures (Bourdieu & Passeron 1977a; Bernstein 1977; MacDonald 1977). A more recent reconceptualization of the socialization process embedded in schools is echoed in Jean Anyon's comment that "what is important about school socialization is what school practices and assumptions it entails, and conversely, what those school assumptions and practices reveal about the society in which the schools are embedded" (Anyon 1979b).

If the perspective advocated by Anyon and others strips schools of their innocence, the more traditional studies on socialization enshrine such innocence in a position that suffers from what Nietzsche once termed "the dogma of the immaculate perception." In the latter views, school knowledge is either treated unproblematically or the focus is limited to how different forms of knowledge, usually what is narrowly termed *moral knowledge*, are acquired in school settings. Talcott Parsons (1959) and Robert Dreeben (1968a) stand out as examples of this tradition.

A more fundamentally political and critical approach to school socialization would begin with the premise that one of the critical elements in the power of a dominant class resides in its ability to impose, though not mechanistically, its own set of meanings and social practices through the selection, organization, and distribution of school knowledge and classroom social relationships. The conceptual basis for investigating such an issue requires a more precise definition than educators generally have of how power functions in distinct and interrelated ways in schools and the wider social order. One promising focus of investigation has been developed by radical theorists who claim that schools are complex sites involved in the social and cultural reproduction of society. They also argue that schools are sites of contestation and struggle, and that it is necessary to understand how the mechanisms of domination and resistance work in schools so they can be fought and transformed where possible.

The importance of this perspective, largely articulated in radical critiques of schooling, is that it not only situates the relationship between schools and other social institutions in a basically political framework, but it also makes problematic the very nature of citizenship itself. It provides the basis for analyzing how a given conception of what it means to be a citizen is conveyed through the dominant rationality in a given social order. Thus, it calls into question not simply what the school claims it does, but what in fact schools may unintentionally do as institutions that exist in a particular relationship with the state. The nature of their relationship, of course, is contained in one of the fundamental questions at the heart of any notion of citizenship education. Kant has said it as well as anyone with his proclaimed principle that students "ought to be educated not for the present but for a better future condition of the human race, that is, the idea of humanity" (Marcuse 1972).

Dominant Rationality

The dominant rationality that presently permeates American society appears to be incompatible with Kant's suggestion. The democratic labels and slogans that are echoed so cheerily at sports events and in early morning school pledges belie the reality that hides behind them. Furthermore, one finds in the practices of systems management, inquiry learning, back-to-basics, and other curriculum approaches a different set of messages that appear to dissolve the human subject and the promise of critical thinking and action into what Sartre once referred to as the "bath of sulphuric acid."

H.T. Wilson has referred to the dominant rationality as "the American Ideology":

> The American ideology is composed of the following elements: 1) an anti-reflexive and anti-theoretical bias already noted which in more "liberal" times extended to virtually *all* intellectual activity; combined, paradoxically, with 2) a more recent concern for accumulating "knowledge," understood as exploitable observations (or observations in principle) having immediate application and "relevance"; undergirded jointly by 3) a false commitment to "objectivity" in the absence of the object being aspired to, derived from scientific rationalism with its unreflexive notion of neutrality, scepticism, and freedom from values and interests: and by 4) a vision of social and political processes as the product of a "piecemeal," trial-and-error approach concerned with procedural legitimacy for its own sake and prone to value a reformist posture toward social change understood as a set of activities played out within the rules of a game which sociological and political knowledge (and knowing) *must* emulate and thereby legitimize; 5) a derived contemporary view of this "open" society as eminently exportable, a negation of this very openness which justifies itself by invoking economics, sociology, and politics as disciplines which demonstrate a coming convergence of world societies and cultures and the supremacy and longevity (not to mention permanence) of the American-type Western society [Wilson 1977].

The central issue is not how this rationality permeates and functions in American society; the literature on this issue is abundant. Rather, the issue is how this type of rationality is embedded in the rationalities that characterize major traditions of citizenship education and how the problematics raised by these rationalities are incomplete. I will examine this issue and focus on a newly emerging rationality that holds more promise for building a theory of citizenship education. Before articulating the meaning of these rationalities a few points must be clarified.

Though the models of citizenship education discussed here represent ideal types that are described in distinct terms, this should not suggest the absence of variation and subtle differences among teachers and other educational workers who might combine any one of a number of them. Nor should it suggest an inclusive coverage of all the diverse citizenship programs and models which were developed in the 1960s. Such a coverage would be impossible within the confines of this chapter. Moreover, simply because I have asserted that the essence of any approach to citizenship education can, in part, be unraveled by examining its relationship to the dominant societal rationality, that is not meant to imply that *any* rationality simply mirrors the imperatives of a dominant ideology; instead it suggests a *particular* relationship to the latter. Finally, it is important to note that the relationships and distinctions among the forms of rationality to be outlined below should not imply that any one of them should be universalized to the exclusion of the others. The important task is to identify what is progressive in each of them and to develop a higher level of synthesis where the limitations and possibilities of each become clear.

Three Modes of Rationality

Most models of citizenship education can be categorized under what can be termed three modes of rationality: the technical, the hermeneutic, and the emancipatory (Habermas 1971a, 1979; Apel 1980; Brown 1979). Each of these rationalities represents different processes of social inquiry and is determined by specific knowledge interests. They will be explained briefly, along with the models of citizenship education that correspond to each of them.

Technical Rationality

Technical rationality is linked to principles of control and certainty. Its knowledge-constitutive interest lies in "controlling the objectified environmental world" (Apel 1979). Technical rationality uses the natural sciences as its model of theoretical development, and rests on a number of assumptions that underlie its view about knowledge, human values, and the methodological nature of social inquiry. Similarly, it contains a number of interrelated assumptions which, when translated into educational theory and practice, take the following form.

First, educational theory should operate in the interest of lawlike propositions which are empirically testable. A major assumption here is that theory should contribute to the mastery and control of the environment through a set of deductively derived operations aimed at discovering the regularities that exist among isolated variables under study. In this case, theory becomes enshrined in the logic of the formula, and observation and technique become starting points for theoretical practice (Habermas 1973). This is an important point because the mediating link between theory and practice not only appears primarily as a technical one, i.e., mastery, but the foundation for such an approach also points to an epistemology in which "knowledge starts from the concrete and is raised to general propositions through a process of abstraction/generalization" (Laclau 1977). Marcuse captures the essence of this assumption in his claim that "as a result of this twofold process, reality is now idealized into a 'mathematical manifold': everything which is mathematically demonstrated with the evidence of universal validity as a pure form (*reine Gestalt*) now belongs to the true reality of nature" (Marcuse 1978).

Second, knowledge, like scientific inquiry, is regarded as value-free. Thus knowledge should be objective and described in neutral fashion. The assumption here is that knowledge can be reduced to those concepts and "facts" that exist a priori and can then be translated to operational definitions and precise meanings. Thus, the hallmarks of knowledge and theoretical inquiry become steeped in a notion of objectivity, one that measures the strength of its meaning against the degree to which it is objectively testable. "Hard" data becomes the focus of explanation and discovery, while other forms of knowledge, such as those that cannot be universalized intersubjectively, are banished to the realm of mere "speculative" wisdom. The application of this assumption to educational theory is well stated by Suppes when he argues that educators "do not need wisdom and broad understanding of the issues that confront us. What we need are deeply structured theories of education that drastically reduce, if not eliminate, the need for wisdom" (Suppes 1974).

Third, causation in this approach is linked to a notion of prediction that makes the process a linear one. That is, since knowledge of the social world is objective and consists of isolated and distinctly separable parts that interact according to lawlike regularities which simply have to be discovered, then the relationship among these variables is an empirical one that can be reduced to predictable outcomes.

Finally, there is the belief that educators themselves can operate in a value-free manner by separating statements of values from the "facts" and "modes of inquiry" which must be objective.

Technical Rationality and Citizenship Education

Two traditions in citizenship education that are strongly wedded to the basic assumptions of technocratic rationality include the citizenship transmission model and the citizenship-as-social-science model (Barr, Barth, & Shermis 1977). While it is indisputable that there are basic differences in orientations between these two models, there appears to be a nucleus of ideas that link both to the principle of technocratic rationality.

CITIZENSHIP TRANSMISSION

The citizenship transmission model represents the oldest and still the most powerful tradition in citizenship education. Historically it can be seen in the writings of Mann and many of the early proponents of the curriculum field in general.[8] It appears to have reached its heyday in the hysteria of the McCarthy period, and with the demise of the innovative curriculum and social studies movements of the 1960s it once again is gaining expression in the current back-to-basics movement.

The essence of this model is captured in the concept of transmission. Knowledge, in this view, is situated above and beyond the social realities and relationships of the people who produce and define it. It is fixed and unchanging in the sense that its form, structure, and underlying normative assumptions appear to be universalized beyond the realm of historical contingency or critical analysis. Appearing in the guise of objectivity and neutrality, it is rooted in the precious adulation of the fact or facts, which simply have to be gathered, organized, transmitted, and evaluated. We get a better sense of the implications of this model for citizenship education if it is viewed not simply as a pedagogical veil for incompetent teaching or teacher "mindlessness," but as a "historically specific social reality expressing particular production relations among men" (Young 1975). That is, if we view how this model defines notions of power and meaning as expressed in its treatment of knowledge, human beings, values, and society, we get a more accurate idea of what its political and pedagogical commitments might be.

Knowledge in this perspective resides in a notion of objectivity and detachment that renders questions concerning the production and legitimation of its form and content irrelevant (Friedman 1978). Consequently, it supports a notion of knowing that ignores that facts have to be mediated, that they are never accessible in their immediacy. The question of who legitimizes "the facts" of a given social order, in this case, is removed from the context of classroom pedagogy and discussion. This is an important point because such a posture violates one of the basic preconditions of all freedom of thought: the necessity for the mental space and reflection one needs to see "beyond" the arbitrary constructs of a society in order to understand the source and genesis of their historical development and the interests they support. The importance of this issue for a more radical notion of citizenship education is captured by Herbert Marcuse in his claim that "if 'education' is to be more than simply training for the status quo it means not only enabling man to know and understand the facts which make up reality but also to know and understand the factors that establish the facts so that he can change their inhuman reality" (Marcuse 1969).

Not only is knowledge objectified in this rationality, it is usually reduced to the mastery of technical decisions for ends already decided. Ends are affirmed rather than explained as a social reality. In the name of transmitting cherished beliefs and values, this model of citizenship education ends up supporting, through its methodologies and content, behavior that is adaptive and conditioned, rather than active and critical.

The reification of knowledge and the flawed epistemology that characterize this approach find their practical counterpart in the passive model of human behavior they support in classroom social relationships. A pedagogical model built on the transmission of a given body of information, values, and beliefs does not ask whether these are warranted, it asks under what conditions they can be maintained. Teachers and students within this context are expected to be either passive consumers or transmitters of knowledge, rather than negotiators of the world in which they work and act. Built into these pedagogical relationships are a series of messages and norms that constitute a hidden curriculum, one that in its unexamined body of knowledge and social relationships concretizes and legitimizes human powerlessness. Some critics have argued that the real significance of this approach has more to do with what it omits than what it includes, and they point out that what it really teaches is a form of unrealistic civic education (Peak & Zeigler 1970).

The citizenship transmission model expresses the core of its ideology and relationship to the dominant rationality in its view of change and stability in the wider society. Wedded to a Parsonian notion of functionalism, this model supports a notion of consensus and role socialization that plays down both the notion of social conflict and the underlying contradictions that characterize the existing society (Anyon 1979a). The roles and relationships that are worthy of attention, in this view, are those that are functional for the present social order. As one functionalist puts it: "functionalism . . . seeks to do no more than assay the place of a particular element of culture or societal institution in relation to other elements. The question may then be posed as to whether an institution leads to or assists in the perpetuation of the social entity in which it appears" (Spencer 1965).

The functionalist dimension in the citizenship transmission model not only ignores the falsehoods perpetuated in many social studies textbooks—falsehoods that present students with a view of society that is as saccharine as it is ideological—it also supports a model of role socialization which, in fact, is a "refinement of role conformity" (Turner 1962). The existential reality of teachers, students, and others in the world of schooling and the social forces that both constrain and shape that reality are lost in this model (Grace 1978). In its place stands the compromised language of "integration" and harmony.

Beneath the "olympian" harmony of the citizenship transmission model stands a perception of teachers' and students' roles as relatively fixed and permanent. This becomes particularly evident in much of the research in the educational field. That is, the economic, social, and political forces that bear on pedagogical theory and practice disappear in this research, which focuses almost exclusively on the individual and the study of cognitive processes framed within the narrow boundaries of educational psychology (Lundgren 1979).

Finally, an important failing in this citizenship education model is that it neither recognizes nor responds to social and structural dysfunctions; instead, social and institutional failings are translated into personal ones. This is manifest in those educational research studies that conjure up categories that arbitrarily absorb structural failings under a pseudoscientific litany of semiotic mystifications. As Jean Anyon says: "This concept of individual culpability . . . is embedded in educational evaluation and psychological findings that attribute to 'lack of student interest,' low 'ability,' 'different or deficient family language or culture,' or to 'teacher indifference,' what may in fact be economically compatible failure to provide all groups or social classes successful pedagogy and/or 'complete personal development' " [Anyon 1979a].

SOCIAL SCIENCE MODEL

What is paradoxical about the citizenship-education-as-social-science model is that on one level it attempts to rescue students as active and critical thinkers; but on a more significant level it falls prey to certain presumptions about knowledge and meaning that results in its mere recycling, albeit in a more sophisticated package, the very assumptions it tries to redress.

Emerging in the United States in the 1960s, the social science model[9] was heavily influenced by Jerome Bruner's (1960) structuralist notion that the essence of learning lies in understanding the basic principles governing the structure of specific academic disciplines. Learning, in this approach, is based on students mastering the basic ideas and body of knowledge that represent the "deep" structure of a particular discipline. Though initially designed for science curricula, Bruner's structuralism readily found its way into the social science field. In part by attempting to situate social studies curricula in the "rigorous" foundation of the social science disciplines, the "new" social studies provided a more sophisticated epistemological framework than the rather crude rationale provided by the transmission model of citizenship education.

Attempting to free social studies knowlege from the theoretical straitjacket of the "transmision" thesis, advocates of the new social studies put forth a number of assumptions that supported their claims to an improved approach to citizenship education. These include (1) a claim to high-status knowledge and equality with other academic disciplines based upon a firm commitment in the social sciences; (2) a claim to the "truth" based upon a view of social science knowledge as "correct" in a relatively unproblematic way; (3) support for an epistemology based on reflectionalist notions of learning in which the mastery of specific social science knowledge and skills would offset the half-truths and mystifications inherent in "common sense" knowledge; (4) support for a hierarchical view of knowledge and a concomitant view of social relationships. Experts provided the knowledge, and teachers and curriculum developers "helped" students to "discover" the answers to predesigned curricula and the problems they posed (Gleeson & Whitty 1976).

While this approach to learning was a significant improvement over the transmission model in that it attempted a more rigorous definition of social science knowledge, it failed in a number of ways to live up to its claim as a pedagogy for improved citizenship education. Since this position has been extensively criticized elsewhere, my criticisms will be limited to some of the more relevant points (Gleeson & Whitty 1976; Anyon 1979a, 1980d).

What counts as valued knowledge in this perspective is grounded in a notion of objectivity that results in a pedagogy that celebrates inquiry, concept discovery, and various other forms of inductive thinking. While this may appear at first to make this model of citizenship education incompatible with the tenets of technocratic rationality, such is not the case. Celebrating not the production of meaning but the consumption of "objective" meanings sanctified by experts, inquiry- and skill-oriented pedagogy belies its own intentions. What appears to be discovery learning ends up as a series of pedagogical methods in which knowledge is depoliticized and objectively "fixed." Having limited possibilities to question the conditions under which knowledge is socially constructed, the social science model of citizenship education ignores both the social constraints that distort knowledge and the connection between knowledge and social control. Cleo Cherryholmes raises this issue in his critique of one inquiry model: ". . . as interesting as it is in many ways, [it] does not illuminate the issues involved in citizenship education for the simple reason that the wrong question was asked. The appropriate question is, what knowledge and skills do students need in order to make predictions that will increase their individual and social effectiveness in a democratic society?" (Cherryholmes 1980).

It is by studying the contradictions of daily life that the mediations between individuals and their society take on meaning and set the stage for political action. The first step in developing a pedagogy that makes this possible involves forms of analysis that seek knowledge and social reality as a human product. Both the transmission model and the social science model of citizenship education are trapped in a problematic that separates facts from values and by doing so canonizes the very knowledge it should be questioning. To view knowledge as the priestly domain of warrior scholars is to forfeit the possibility of questioning the normative and political nature of the knowledge and social interests they legitimize. What we often find in these approaches is a gross insensitivity to the experiences and "history" that students bring with them to the classroom. As a result, this model of citizenship education often ends up substituting general concepts for social concepts, and then "hawks" the importance of "analytical" skills as the answer to critical thinking. What usually results is a process whereby the judgements made by authors who use these methods are not questioned. Instead, concepts are used along with "inquiry skills" that eventually elicit confirmation from students on problems governed by answers that can barely be challenged. Tom Popkewitz in analyzing Edwin Fenton's *Comparative Political Systems: An Inquiry Approach,* found the following:

> The instructional approach uses concepts of leadership, ideology, and decision making to compare different political systems. However, investigation of the text reveals that judgments are already made by the authors. The purpose of children's "analytical" work is simply to make the teacher's answers plausible. . . . For example, a dichotomy is established between the leaders of the Soviet Union and the United States. The personal characteristics of the U.S. political leaders are characterized as energy, tact, ability to tend to many things at once, ability to operate effectively under tension, and so on. On the other hand, a Soviet leader is described as one "not given to resistance, who is a little above average in energy and intelligence and below average in imagination." Under the guise of "social theory," a dichotomy is established which seems to prevent critical scrutiny rather than nurture it [Popkewitz 1977].

Critical thinking is not all that "slips away" in this approach; so does the concept of social conflict. This model of citizenship education easily fits Adorno's critique that "social concepts are taken 'as such' and then classified according to general concepts. In the process, social antagonisms invariably tend to be glossed over" (Adorno 1967).

Lost in these two citizenship education models are the normative, political, and historical landscapes that give them meaning. In spite of all the clatter about the importance of student choice making in these models, the latter are reduced to a faint echo that does little to illuminate how dominant values work through and are mediated by teachers, students, and curriculum materials. Lacking any vestige of critical theory, these approaches to citizenship education fail to break through their own false objectivism to examine critically the assumptions that wed them to the precepts of technocratic rationality and the "American ideology."

Hermeneutic Rationality

Paraphrasing Alvin Gouldner (1980), I think it is accurate to argue that every rationality has within it another problematic struggling to get out. The "caged" problematic that represents the Achilles' heel of technocratic rationality is the very notion of meaning itself, for it is in the struggle to unshackle the concepts of meaning and experience from the "fossilized" notion of objectivity that hermeneutic rationality is grounded.

Hermeneutic rationality does not take as its starting-point the production of monological knowledge; instead, it has a deep-seated interest in understanding the communicative and symbolic patterns of interaction[10] that shape individual and intersubjective meaning. Rather than focusing on or taking for granted the a priori forms of knowledge, its constitutive interest lies in understanding how the forms, categories, and assumptions beneath the texture of everyday life contribute to our understanding of each other and the world around us.

Meaning in this mode of rationality is not removed from the worlds of the social actors who constitute, shape, and live within its definitions. Instead, it is seen in its most crucial form as something which is constantly negotiated and renegotiated by human beings as they mutually produce and define the constitutive rules that shape their interactions. Central to this form of rationality are the concepts of appropriation, intentionality, and intersubjectivity.

Human beings are never seen as passive recipients of information. Hermeneutic rationality is sensitive to the notion that through the use of language and thought human beings constantly produce meanings as well as interpret the world in which they find themselves. Therefore, if we are to understand their actions, we have to link their behavior to the intentions that provide the interpretative screen they use to negotiate with the world. Thus, as Geoff Whitty has argued, this form of rationality rejects the wider culture of positivism and is based on an epistemology in which "truth and objectivity are seen as nothing but human products, and man rather than nature is seen as the ultimate author of 'knowledge' and 'reality.' Any attempt to appeal to an external reality in order to support claims for the inferiority of one way of seeing over another is dismissed as ideological. Knowledge is inexplicably linked to methods of coming to know and any supposed dichotomy between them is therefore false" (Whitty 1974).

Hermeneutic rationality has generated a number of important concerns for educational theory and practice. First, it has challenged many of the commonsense assumptions that teachers, students, and other educational workers use to guide, structure, and evaluate their day-to-day pedagogical experiences. Second, it has refocused attention on the normative and political dimensions of teacher-student classroom relationships. Third, it has established a relationship between epistemology and intentionality, on the one hand, and learning and classroom social relationships, on the other. In other words, knowledge is treated as a specific social act with its underlying social relationships. Finally, hermeneutic rationality has played a significant role in helping educators unravel the latent and manifest dimensions of classroom knowledge and classroom relationships.[11]

REFLECTIVE INQUIRY APPROACH

The tradition in citizenship education in the United States that has been influenced by this type of rationality falls under the general label of the "reflective inquiry approach" (Barr, Barth, & Shermis 1977). This approach relies heavily upon what has generally been called decision making in a sociopolitical context. The importance of the stress on decision making is further defined by pointing to the unique burdens imposed by this process in a "democracy." "The assumption is that democracy imposes a unique burden; we cannot escape the requirement of making decisions. Sometimes decisions relate to the making of legislation or the selecting of legislators; that is, of course, an inherent part of our government— what it means to live in a self-governing, democratic society" (ibid).

In contrast to the positivist assumptions inherent in the transmission and social science models previously mentioned, the traditions that fall roughly under a hermeneutic rationality stress negotiation, participation, and the importance of values in citizenship education. For instance, various supporters of this position invoke the general trinity of knowledge, participation in decision making, and values/attitudes as the basis for citizenship education. The pedagogical approaches following from these assumptions have recently been outlined in detail by a number of theorists and need only brief mention here.[12]

In this rationality, there is a strong emphasis on the social construction rather than the imposed nature of classroom knowledge. Students are encouraged to explore their own values and either to define problems within the context of their experiences or to relate social problems to the day-to-day texture of their lives (Barth & Shermis 1979). On the other hand, the concrete vehicle for expressing this emphasis rests on its support and use of the problem-solving process as the principal pedagogical tool. In fact, the only absolute value in this pedagogical approach appears to lie in the decision-making process itself,[13] best summed up by the notion that "the orientation of the social scientist is that of research."[14]

Reflective inquiry suggests a number of useful and constructive insights, and makes important contributions to an analysis of the meaning and purpose of citizenship education; but in the end, it is trapped in a problematic that is defined less by what it advocates than by what it ignores. As a theory that attempts to situate the meaning of schooling in a wider context, it appears as a well-intentioned, but, in the final analysis, naive and incomplete model of rationality.

On one level, some of its weaknesses can be traced to the nature of its epistemology. In celebrating the notions of intentionality in the exploration of human behavior, it has failed to move beyond a relativistic notion of knowledge. That is, although this position sees through the arbitrary division between objective and subjective forms of knowing posited by technocratic rationality, it does not analyze the history of this division or develop a form of critique that is capable of revealing the ideology embedded in it. As Cherryholmes has pointed out, in this view there is "no clearly identifiable position regarding knowledge claims" (Cherryholmes 1979).

By focusing on the subjective intentions of the individual while simultaneously encouraging the importance of the social construction of knowledge, this position fails to understand how such meanings are maintained or how they might distort rather than comprehend reality. Moreover, such a posture tends to overlook how ideological and structural constraints in the larger society are reproduced in schools so as to mediate against the possibility of critical thinking and constructive dialogue. Thus, by reducing power and democratic action to the level of an epistemology that supports a form of subjective idealism, the reflective inquiry approach emerges as a one-sided theory of citizenship education which has "miraculously" abstracted its social epistemology from such troublesome concepts as ideology, power, struggle, and oppression. As a result, the basic natures of existing social arrangements in the wider society go unquestioned or are questioned in relatively narrow terms. The limits of this position are partially identified in Elizabeth Cagen's remark that "While liberal reformers tend to use education to promote equality, community, and humanistic social interaction, they do not confront those aspects of the schools which pull in the opposite direction. Their blindness to these contradictions may stem from their class position: as middle-class reformers they are unwilling to advocate the kind of egalitarianism which is necessary for a true human community" (Cagen 1978).

I am not so sure that middle-class reformers act as intentionally as Cagen suggests they do: it is more likely that they are caught within a rationality that "blinds" them to the nature of their own ideology. This can be partly demonstrated by looking at how the reflective inquiry approach deals with a theory of the state and the concept of pluralism.

Harold Berlak (1977) has pointed out that few educators have come to terms with the notion that schooling in America takes place in one of the most powerful industrial capitalist states in the world, one that is characterized by an enormous concentration of political and economic power. In spite of this, the relationship between the state and public schools is often articulated in simplistic and one-dimensional terms. While it is stressed repeatedly in the rationales of reflective inquiry advocates that schools can and must educate students to participate in the shaping and running of the state, they say practically nothing about how the state affects and reproduces the ideology of dominant social and economic interests in the schools. A number of social theorists have raised questions about the particular relationship between schools and the wider society that put in high relief the complex relations that exist between schools and the state.

Nicos Poulantzas (1978) has argued that schools are part of an ideological state apparatus that both reproduces and mediates the social divisions of labor and the dominant ideology which supports it. Schools, by the very nature of their position in a class-based society, are politically and structurally bound to a relationship with the state and its ruling interests. This relationship must be understood if we are to be clear about what schools actually do in this society. As I have mentioned in previous chapters, the broader nature of this relationship has been explored by Althusser (1971), who claims that schools produce the modes of consciousness, know-how, and ideological dispositions necessary to function in a capitalist economy. On the other hand, Bowles and Gintis (1976) stress the importance of specific structural features of schools—the class-room social relationships—in reproducing the social relations of produc-tion. Bernstein (1977) and Apple (1980) have argued that the principles involved in both the structure and content of curriculum, pedagogy, and evaluation constitute specific message systems that are ultimately de-pendent on the allocation of power and resources of a dominant class.

It is worth repeating that Bourdieu and Passeron (1977a) take one dimension of this analysis a bit further by arguing that schools institu-tionalize, through the rules and meanings that constitute the day-to-day working of classroom experience, the dominant cultural capital. Cultural capital, in this sense, refers to those systems of meanings, linguistic and social competencies, and elements of style, manner, taste, and disposition that are permeated throughout society by the dominant class as being the most legitimate.[15] In this analysis, schools play a crucial role in repro-ducing the unequal distribution of cultural capital. Instead of providing compensatory education to the students with different cultural capital, the school, while appearing neutral, asks them to think and perform in a way that is quite alien to their own background. If Bourdieu is right, and there is a significant amount of evidence suggesting that he is, classroom knowledge has little to do with the negotiated outcomes and critical thinking skills that the reflective inquiry rationality sees as the essence of schooling; instead, its essence lies in the imposition of meanings and specific modes of behavior by the school. Of course, there are modes of resistance and contradictions in the schools. There are also ideologies that are ethnic-, gender-, and community-specific that mediate and alter the dominant ideology (Giroux 1981). But what results in the absence of political action are piecemeal and minor victories, which leave the constitutive rules of the dominant ideology unchallenged.

This mode of citizenship education is wedded to a one-sided notion of determination. It argues that schools can educate students to exert political influence on the state, but it ignores how the state places con-straints of *a specific* political, ideological, and structural nature on the schools. This becomes most evident in the support for pluralism found among advocates of this group. Arguments of this sort reveal their own ideology by denying the very conditions that make the struggle for plu-ralism imperative. Pluralism as a philosophy of equality and justice is a noble political ideal. But when the ideal is not measured against a society that rests on fundamental inequalities in wealth, power, and participation, it tilts over into ideology or empty formalism, and "presupposes that society is without those antagonisms that are of its essence" (Jacoby 1975). This concept fits badly into a view of citizenship education that is based on democratic principles of justice and political participation. Pluralism ignores the tension between political democracy and economic inequality. That is, it fails to acknowledge that equality of opportunity and the importance of human reflectiveness may be impeded by particularistic private interests in the economic sphere that use the state to impose severe constraints on certain segments of the population.[16] The limited pedagogical insistence on decision-making skills that emerges from this position is inherited from a priori assumptions about the existence of a pluralistic society. What is missed is the way the "invisible" hand of dominant political and economic interests affect the nature of what is to be decided. Peak and Zeigler in their critique of "unrealistic civic education" illuminate this issue with the argument that "Pluralists have taken a hard-headed approach in insisting that the only legitimate datum is the decision. . . . By focusing entirely upon the process whereby highly contested decisions are reached, pluralists ignore . . . the more mysterious nondecisions . . . which are of more importance upon the overall political style of a community than the more spectacular and tangible decisions" (Peak & Zeigler 1970).

This points to the "hidden curriculum" that functions to favor the reproduction of the dominant society by establishing the boundaries within which conflict can take place and questions can be raised. Of course, the emphasis on critical thought in the work of the moral development advocates under the reflective inquiry approach points to the hidden curriculum as something to be overcome in order to promote critical thinking. But by defining critical thinking as a psychological characteristic reduced to matters of cognitive developmental psychology, we are left with a perspective that lacks the benefit of critical sociology or political theory.[17] How the nature and structure of social relationships in the wider society are revealed in the political structure of classroom life and schools are missing from this perspective.

The problematic that characterizes the reflective inquiry approach fails to examine the nature of its own ideology, and consequently has not been able to raise fundamental questions about the nature of the relationship between the state and schooling, the mechanisms of ideological and structural domination in schools, or how the relationship among class, culture, and ideology in schools serves to reproduce the institutional arrangements of the status quo.

The dialectical relationship that interconnects the dynamics of the state, economics, and ideology with the concept of citizenship education demands a theoretical framework grounded in a rationality that truly challenges the existing American ideology. The foundation for such a rationality can be found in what may be called emancipatory rationality.

Emancipatory Rationality

Though hermeneutic rationality has disposed of the illusion of objectivism, it has failed to develop an analysis that unravels how the relationship among power, norms, and meaning function within a specific sociohistorical context to promote forms of self-misunderstanding as well as to support and sustain modes of structural domination. The hermeneutic mode of rationality does not ask the central question: How is it that a social system steeped in domination can legitimize itself through a set of meanings and practice that prevent the development of an open, self-critical community of inquiring citizens?

The issue here is that emancipatory rationality does not renounce the primacy of intentionality and meaning central to hermeneutic interests; instead it attempts to locate such meaning and action in a societal context in order to explore how the latter might place specific limitations and constraints upon human thought and action. Sharp and Green illuminate the problematic at the heart of emancipatory rationality:

> The correct perspective should enable one to ask the question, "Under what historical conditions can men break through the structure of determination?" Such a perspective retains the model of man as active, with intentionality, while socially locating him within a context which may resist, block, or distort his projects. To realize his values as an acting subject who seeks to control his situation, he forces the constraining effect of others in this situation, the institutionalized consequences of his and others' actions, the sanctions that can be used against him, and the conditions of his non-social environment [Sharp & Green 1975].

Emancipatory rationality, in this context, is based on the principles of critique and action. It is aimed at criticizing that which is restrictive and oppressive while at the same time supporting action in the service of individual freedom and well-being. This mode of rationality is construed as the capacity of critical thought to reflect on and reconstruct its own historical genesis, i.e., to think about the process of thinking itself. More specifically, the capacity to think about thinking points to a mode of reasoning aimed at breaking through the "frozen" ideology that prevents a critique of the life and world on which rationalizations of the dominant society are based. Similarly, emancipatory rationality augments its interest in self-reflection with social action designed to create the ideological and material conditions in which nonalienating and nonexploitative relationships exist. This suggests a view of citizenship education based on a different view of sociability and social relations than those presently existing.

Sociability will have to be rescued from the limited notion of closeness it presently occupies. In other words, sociability currently defined solely in terms of family images and relationships, against which it is difficult to conceive of strangers as social, will have to be viewed as a position at odds with a democratic notion of citizenship (Donzelot 1980). In addition, citizenship education based on an emancipatory form of rationality will have to reproduce and stress the importance of social relationships in which men and women are treated as ends and not means. Both positions represent ethical principles linked to the development of radical needs and the ideological and material conditions needed to support them (Heller 1974).

Emancipatory Rationality and Citizenship Education

A number of radical educational theories have developed under this mode of rationality and have been analyzed in previous chapters. All these theories share a critical stance toward the existing social order and support, though in different ways, what may be called theories of reproduction and transformation. Madeleine MacDonald captures the focus of these theories with this comment:

> The assumption underlying most of the "reproduction" theories is that education plays a mediating role between the individual's consciousness and society at large. These theorists maintain that the rules which govern social behavior, attitudes, morals, and beliefs are filtered down from the macro level of economic and political structures to the individual via work experience, educational processes, and family socialization. The individual acquires a particular awareness and perception

of the society in which he lives. And it is this understanding and attitude towards the social order which constitute his consciousness. The concept has therefore taken on particular significance within the context of theories of social and cultural reproduction. . . . By acquiring an awareness both of the nature of social conditioning and the potential for acting upon it, the individual or groups of individuals in a social class, it is argued, can learn not only to formulate alternatives but also to bring about change. The different emphases placed . . . on social order or social change, on macro levels or micro processes, on structural or interactional features, derive from a variety of conceptions of the ability or inability of individuals and social classes to act in and upon the social world. In the context of educational strategies for change, these theories have different implications, for in each a particular relationship between schooling and society is postulated [MacDonald 1977].

In simplistic terms, a number of important theoretical elements can be abstracted from these positions, and, if dialectically related, provide the framework for understanding how schools function, on the one hand, as institutions roughly determined by the structural requirements of the imperatives of a capitalist state. On the other hand, schools can be studied as cultural realms that exist within a particular, nonmechanistic relationship with the wider society. This means focusing on the complex way in which schools mediate on a daily basis the ideological and material forces produced directly from within the contexts and sites in which they exist. The implications this has for developing a theory of citizenship education are profound.

Notes toward a Theory of Citizenship Education

First, it is important to point out that what is put forth in this section does not represent a final program. The focus, as I have pointed out, is on larger comprehensive issues that provide the foundation for establishing a theory of citizenship education that is more adequate than those that presently occupy the field.

The major struggle to develop and implement such a theory rests, in fact, with overcoming the rather dreadful legacy that has shaped it over the last century. Notions about citizenship education are complex and rather unwieldy. Citizenship education cuts across disciplines and is rooted in a myriad of political and normative issues. Unfortunately, it has been largely influenced, as I have mentioned previously, by the culture of positivism, with its underlying technocratic rationality. Hence, educators have generally retreated from engaging its most complex issues and have reduced theorizing about this issue mainly to questions of technique, organization, and administration.

Changing Society

A theory of citizenship education will have to redefine the nature of educational theorizing as it presently exists. In its place, it will have to construct a view of theory that integrates the artificial constructs that separate the academic disciplines. It will have to draw upon a more dialectical structure of knowledge in order to establish a theoretical center of gravity that provides a comprehensive analysis of what the nature and conduct of education is all about. Hence, as I have indicated previously, such a theory will be political and social. This becomes clear if we engage citizenship education at what has to be the starting point for any further theoretical development. That is, citizenship education's own problematic must begin with the question of whether or not this society should be changed in a particular way or be left the way it is. In fundamental concrete terms, it raises important questions that each individual must confront—questions that range from issues concerning how free one is in a given society to those that inquire as to what kind of understanding is necessary regarding the political basis, nature, and consequences of one's actions. Regardless of the answer, the core of the issue is fundamentally political and normative; it speaks to the need to confront assumptions concerning the aims of education—assumptions regarding who is going to be educated, and assumptions about what kinds of knowledge, values, and social relationships are going to be deemed legitimate as educational concerns.

These questions are not meant to be simply abstractions; their significance is linked to both the history and the existing social-political conjuncture that gives them context and meaning. Educational theorists and, more precisely, a theory of citizenship education will have to combine historical critique, critical reflection, and social action. This theory will have to recover the political determinants of what citizenship education has become and then decide what it does not want to be in order to emerge as a more viable mode of theorizing. In part, I have traced its history, and indicated what it has become. If it is going to provide both vision and hope for the citizens of this country, it will have to be redefined so that it can work in the interest of changing this society. In other words, it will have to measure the promise against the reality and then demonstrate the viability of such a struggle. This may not be an easy task, but it is certainly a necessary one.

Teacher Consciousness

In addition to being committed to building a better society, the next step in developing a notion of citizenship education that focuses on schools will have to address concerns about expanding the theoretical perceptions of teachers and other educational workers. That is, teachers rather than students should represent a starting point for any theory of citizenship education. Most students exercise very little power over defining the education experiences in which they find themselves. It is more appropriate to begin with those educators who both mediate and define the educational process. This is not meant to deny that students represent an important concern in both the development and effects of such a theory; in fact, it is precisely this concern that demands that we construe a theoretical framework giving teachers and others involved in the educational process the possibility to think critically about the nature of their beliefs and how these beliefs both influence and offset the day-to-day experiences they have with students. Similarly, it is important that teachers situate their own beliefs, values, and practices within a wider context so that their latent meanings can be better understood. This dialectical situating, so to speak, will help illuminate the social and political nature of the structural and ideological constraints that teachers face daily. What is needed then is a more comprehensive theory of totality, to which issue I will now turn.

THEORY OF TOTALITY

A theory of totality would avoid the pitfall of treating schools as if they existed in a political and social vacuum. Instead, schools would be analyzed, both historically and sociologically, in regard to their interconnections with other economic and political institutions. In concrete pedagogical terms, this means that educators need to situate the school, curriculum, pedagogy, and the role of the teacher within a societal context that reveals both their historical development and the nature of their existing relationship with the dominant rationality. Central to this analysis is that teachers view the evolution of schools and school practices as part of a historical dynamic in which different forms of knowledge, social structures, and belief systems are seen as concrete expressions of class-specific interests. Of course, this is not meant to reduce schooling to a reflex of the imperatives of certain powerful groups. Such a characterization ignores the active nature of resistance in human beings and often flattens out the complex relationship between schools and the dominant society. What is at stake here is the need to provide a theoretical focus for developing more critical categories that can be used to understand the linkages between how a society is controlled and organized and the principles that structure school experience. Inherent in this approach is the notion that schools act as agents of social and cultural reproduction. But if the concepts of reproduction and the notion of totality are to move beyond a "radical" functionalist account, it will be necessary to develop a more comprehensive analysis of the interconnections between culture, power, and transformation.

On one level, this means that if the notion of totality is to be defined as more than a science of interconnections, it has to illuminate how the ideological and structural dimensions of existing school practices can be traced to their social, political, and economic determinants in the wider society. This approach not only helps us to see educational practices as historical and social products, it also raises questions as to how these determinants reveal themselves in the commonsense perceptions of teachers, in the social relations of the classroom, and in the form and content of curriculum materials. In a society marked by the pervasive presence of social class and inequality, the relevance of such questions to a notion of citizenship education concerned with economic and social justice is no small matter. Sharp and Green cite the importance of developing a notion of totality specifically related to the concept of transformation:

> [We] want to stress that a humanist concern for the child necessitates a greater awareness of the limits within which teacher autonomy can operate and to pose the questions, "What interests do schools serve, those of the parents and children, or those of the teachers and headmaster?" and "What wider interests are served by the school?" and, possibly more importantly, "How do we conceptualize interests in social reality?" Therefore, instead of seeing the classroom as a social system

and as such insulated from wider structural process, we suggest that
the teacher who has developed an understanding of his [or her] location
in the wider process may well be in a better position to understand
where and how it is possible to alter that situation. The educator who
is of necessity a moralist must preoccupy himself with the social [and
economic] preconditions for the achievement of his ideals [Sharp &
Green 1975].

Hence, schools can be seen as part of the universe of wider cultural
meanings and practices. This perception becomes a powerful heuristic
and political tool for a theory of citizenship education only if we rescue
the concept of culture from the depoliticized status it now occupies in
mainstream social science theory.

POLITICS OF CULTURE

In short, a reform of citizenship education involves a reform of educators
as well; this is a political task whose purpose is to make educators better-
informed citizens and more effective agents for transforming the wider
society. It also points to and increases the possibility for helping students
develop a greater social awareness as well as a concern for social action.
An important step in realizing both tasks is, as I have pointed out
previously, to politicize the notion of culture. This is a critical imperative
for a theory of citizenship education. As I have indicated throughout this
book, culture as a political phenomenon refers to the power of a specific
class to impose and distribute in society specific meanings, message systems, and social practices in order to "lay the psychological and moral
foundations for the economic and political system they control" (Dreitzel
1977). Within the dominant culture, meaning is universalized and the
historically contingent nature of social reality appears as self-evident and
fixed. Of course, there are conflicts within the dominant cultural capital
just as there is resistance from classes who stand in opposition to the
dominant view of the world; but this should not be interpreted in ways
to either relativize the different forms of culture capital or to underestimate
the significance of the dominant culture as a moment "in the process of
social domination and capital accumulation" (Wexler, 1982).

As a heuristic tool for an emancipatory form of citizenship education,
the politicization of culture provides the opportunity for teachers to reformulate the concept of power in terms of both its meaning and its use
as a vehicle of domination or praxis. Power as a form of cultural domination

has been captured in Gramsci's (1971) concept of ideological hegemony, a concept that helps to reassert the centrality of the interconnection among politics, culture, and pedagogy, and one I have discussed in detail earlier.

The implications of this concept for teachers become clear if the notion of culture as ideological hegemony is qualified. Hegemony does not simply refer to the content found, for instance, in the formal curriculum of schools. It is that and much more; it also refers to the way such knowledge is structured. In addition, it refers to the routines and practices embedded in different social relationships; finally, it points to the notion of social structures as natural configurations which both embody and sustain forms of ideological hegemony. If we translate this insight into specific forms of pedagogy for citizenship education, the following theoretical practices for educators could be developed.

SCHOOL KNOWLEDGE AND CITIZENSHIP EDUCATION

Teachers would have to analyze school knowledge as part of a wider universe of knowledge and try to determine to what degree it reflects class interests. For instance, Anyon's work points to "a whole range of curriculum selections [that] favor the interest of the wealthy and powerful" (Anyon 1979a). Next, school knowledge must be analyzed to determine to what degree its form and content represent the unequal presentation of the cultural capital of minorities of class and color: that is, how does classroom knowledge embody modes of language, systems of meaning, and cultural experiences so as to invalidate directly or indirectly other forms of cultural capital. This suggests that educators who assign a false equivalency to "all cultures" may be falling into the trap of cultural pluralism. That is, they depoliticize the notion of culture by abstracting the concept from the societal formations that give it meaning. The real issue to be raised focuses less on the equivalency of all cultures than on the question of how the dominant culture, as a form of power and control, mediates between itself and other secondary cultures. This kind of inquiry focuses on questions aimed at understanding what kind of reproductive functions exist between the dominant culture and the culture institutionalized by the schools.

Teachers must also attempt to unravel the ideological principles embedded in the structure of classroom knowledge. Wexler (n.d.) argues that teachers must learn to identify the structuring concepts that lurk silently within a text, film, or any other form of curriculum material. These materials must be decoded not only in terms of their content but in terms of their form and composition as well, for the rigid boundaries between categories and different forms of knowledge carry messages of social control by reducing ways of knowing to static and seemingly unrelated representations of reality (Bernstein 1977).

HIDDEN CURRICULUM AND CITIZENSHIP EDUCATION

The dominant culture is not simply embedded in the form and content of knowledge. It is also reproduced through what I have in previous chapters called the hidden curriculum. The hidden curriculum in schools refers to those underlying norms, values, and attitudes that are often transmitted tacitly through the social relations of the school and classroom. By stressing rule conformity, passivity, and obedience, it comprises one of the major socialization forces used to produce personality types willing to accept social relationships characteristic of the governance structures of the workplace.

If teachers are going to implement a more comprehensive notion of citizenship education they will have to understand not only the linkages that exist between the hidden and formal curricula, but also the complex connections that exist between both curriculum and the principles that structure similar modes of knowledge and social relationships in the larger society. We can illuminate the nature of these complex linkages through an ethnographic portrayal of citizenship education in a kindergarten class analyzed by Ray Rist (1977a).

Mrs. Caplow, the teacher, as part of her unit on citizenship has appointed a student to be the "sheriff" for a trip her kindergarten class is to take. (Caplow told Rist that the point of the lesson was to teach the children "respect for the law.") Frank willingly accepts this role and literally pushes, shoves, and yells at other students who step out of line. Frank, in this case, happens to be a middle-class student, while the other students are from the "lower class."

Rist interprets this in the following way: "When the rhetoric of 'learning respect for the law' is stripped away, it is obvious that middle-class children were learning how to shuffle in the face of superior power" (Rist 1977). The ideology underlying this notion of citizenship education should be clear. But the interrelationship between the classroom social relationships that Mrs. Caplow established, and the message she wanted to reinforce, come into sharper focus in this exchange among Mrs. Caplow, another student, and Frank:

"David, can you tell Mr. Rist why you are wearing the star?" David responds, "Cause I the sheriff." Mrs. Caplow continues, "Can you tell him how you got to be the sheriff?" "By being a good citizen." "David, what do good citizens do?" "They check up on others." Mrs. Caplow: "Well, that is not all they do. . . ." Caplow repeats the question for Frank. Frank stands up and says, "Good citizens obey the rules." Mrs. Caplow responds, "Yes, that is right, Frank. Good citizens obey the rules, no matter what they are" [ibid.].

This suggests that if teachers are going to be able to analyze the nature and degree of distributive injustice in schools, they will have to pay close attention to those basic, tacit, constitutive rules that establish the more obvious factors that structure classroom choices. It is the constitutive rules that silently structure and make impervious the conditional nature of the grouping, tracking, and labeling that goes on in schools. The nature of these rules must be analyzed in light of the political choices they reflect. For this type of analysis to emerge, teachers will have to pay close attention to the type of rationality that shapes their own assumptions and how it mediates between the "rules" of the dominant culture and the classroom experiences provided for students.

POWER AND TRANSFORMATION

Finally, an analysis of power and transformation must be made an integral part of a theory of citizenship education. Teachers must attempt to understand the meaning of the contradictions, dysfunctions, and tensions that exist in both schools and the larger social order. Moreover, they must focus on the underlying conflicts in both schools and society and investigate how these can contribute to a more radical theory of citizenship education. Too often, as I have pointed out, radical theorists have portrayed the use of power in schools in strictly negative and one-dimension terms.[18] This not only distorts the reality of schools; it ends up being a more "radical" version of management ideology which sees human beings as infinitely malleable. Power in the service of domination is *never* as total as this image suggests. Richard Johnson writes insightfully about the dialectical nature of domination and resistance in schools: " . . . typically, under capitalism, schools seem to reproduce, instead of the perfect worker in complete ideological subjection, much more the worker as bearer of the characteristic antagonisms of the social formation as a whole. Schools, in other words, reproduce forms of resistance too, however limited or corporate or unselfconsious they may be" (Johnson 1979).

Neither students nor teachers resemble the "social puppet" image that emerges in the writings of the reproduction theorists. Both teachers and students demonstrate forms of resistance in the context of cultural hegemony. Willis (1977) and others have provided research on how the informal culture, for instance, of working-class students rejects consistently the sum of the messages and values embedded in the formal and hidden curricula. Likewise, there is a great deal of evidence pointing to the wide scope and degree of worker resistance that takes place at the site of production itself (Aronowitz 1973; Edwards 1979). The similarities in the different modes of resistance should be studied both historically and sociologically to see how they have been diffused in the past and how their radical potential can be developed for the future. The crucial question is how do these contradictions offer the possibility for raising the consciousness of both teachers and students? In other words, how can they be used to reveal the workings of power and domination in the school culture? Madeleine MacDonald puts the question another way when she argues that educators must develop an " . . . understanding of how stability occurs despite conflict, how order is maintained over and above the face of change. Any system of reproduction in so far as it operates within a cultural hegemony must be struggled for, won and maintained in the context of opposition. The nature of the victory is uncertain unless we can define the source and the force of the opposition" (MacDonald 1977).

As we have seen, much of the opposition in both schools and the workplace represents forms of symbolic resistance, i.e., the struggle is thereby limited to the world of cultural symbols of dress, taste, language, and the like. In order for such opposition to move to a more effective level of action, it will have to be extended into a form of resistance linked to political action and control. This is not simply a call for classroom consciousness raising. Subjective intentions alone pose little threat to the concrete and objective structures of domination that underlie the existing sociopolitical order. Social action is needed, but it must be preceded by those subjective preconditions that make the need for such action intelligible. Thus, social awareness represents the first step in getting students to act as "engaged" citizens willing to question and confront the structural basis and nature of the larger social order. It is also an important step in teaching students about the complex nature of power itself. Power in this case is extended far beyond the subjective confines of thought itself.

Hence, conflicts and contradictions must be studied and analyzed by teachers as issues to be problematized and used as points for classroom discussion and vehicles for connecting classroom practices to larger political issues. As mentioned, these contradictions exist not only in the competing forms of cultural capital unevenly distributed in schools, but also in the daily practices and life experiences of different classes outside the schools. These contradictions must be linked and used as an integral dimension of citizenship education. Such an approach would take more seriously the ways by which students and teachers define their experiences within specific classroom settings. It would be more sensitive to the nature of their discourses, their *own* views of school activities, their modes of resistance, and the way in which they serve to reproduce and sustain the dominant ideology. Within this theoretical framework, citizenship education would be better able to highlight how specific institutional practices both restrict and offer possibilities for citizenship growth and action.

In conclusion, citizenship education must be grounded in a reformulation of the role that teachers are to play in schools. As suggested, a new theoretical model that includes a theory of totality, a redefinition of culture and power, and a more insightful understanding of the contradictions and mediations that lie beneath the surface of educational theory and practice must be developed. Needless to say, these theoretical elements only become meaningful if they are wedded to a firm commitment to the development of economic and political justice in both schools and the wider social order. I now want to turn briefly to some classroom practices that follow from the above theoretical assumptions.

Classroom Pedagogy and Citizenship Education

If citizenship education is to be emancipatory, it must begin with the assumption that its major aim is not "to fit" students into the existing society; instead, its primary purpose must be to stimulate their passions, imaginations, and intellects so that they will be moved to challenge the social, political, and economic forces that weigh so heavily upon their lives. In other words, students should be educated to display civic courage, i.e., the willingness to act *as if* they were living in a democratic society. At its core, this form of education is political, and its goal is a genuine democratic society, one that is responsive to the needs of all and not just of a priviledged few. Agnes Heller illuminates the meaning of civic courage in the following comment: " . . . one should think and act as if one were in a real democracy. The fundamental bravery of this way of life is not military heroism but civic courage. Whoever says no to the dominant prejudices and to the oppressing power, and when necessary (and it is often necessary) to public opinion, and practices this throughout his life and in his life-conduct has the virtue of civic courage" (Heller 1967).

In more concrete terms, students should learn not only how to weigh the existing society against *its* own claims, they should also be taught to think and act in ways that speak to different societal possibilities and ways of living. But if the development of civic courage is the bedrock of an emancipatory mode of citizenship education, it will have to rest on a number of pedagogical assumptions and practices that need to be somewhat clarified. I have elaborated on these earlier in this book, but will recapitulate briefly here:

First, the active nature of students' participation in the learning process must be stressed. This means that transmission modes of pedagogy must be replaced by classroom social relationships in which students are able to challenge, engage, and question the form and substance of the learning process. Hence, classroom relations must be structured to give students the opportunity to both produce as well as criticize classroom meanings. Under such conditions, knowing must be seen as more than a matter of learning a given body of knowledge; it must be seen as a critical engagement designed to distinguish between essence and appearance, truth and falsity. Knowledge must not only be made problematic, stripped of its objective pretensions, it must also be defined through the social mediations and roles that provide the context for its meaning and distribution. Knowledge in this sense becomes the mediator of communication and dialogue among learners.

Second, students must be taught to think critically. They must learn how to move beyond literal interpretations and fragmented modes of reasoning. Not only must they learn to understand their own frame of reference, they must also learn how the latter has developed and how it provides a "map" for organizing the world. Depending of course upon grade levels, students can learn to juxtapose different world views against the truth claims that each of them makes. Facts, concepts, issues, and ideas must be seen within the network of connections that give them meaning. Students must learn to look at the world holistically in order to understand the interconnections of the parts to each other. As Maxine Greene says, students must learn an epistemology that allows them to draw from different subject areas and to "engage in new kinds of questioning and problem posing appropriate to an overly dominated human world" (Greene 1978).

Third, the development of a critical mode of reasoning must be used to enable students to appropriate their own histories, i.e., to delve into their own biographies and systems of meaning. That is, a critical pedagogy must provide the conditions that give students the opportunity to speak with their own voices, to authenticate their own experiences. Once students become aware of the dignity of their own perceptions and histories, they can make a leap to the theoretical and begin to examine the truth value of their meanings and perceptions, particularly as they relate to the dominant rationality.

Fourth, students must learn not only how to clarify values, they must also learn why certain values are indispensable to the reproduction of human life. Moreover, they must comprehend the source of their own beliefs and action. They must learn how values are embedded in the very texture of human life, how they are transmitted, and what interests they support regarding the quality of human existence.

Fifth, students must learn about the structural and ideological forces that influence and restrict their lives. Denis Gleeson and Geoff Whitty speak to this issue when analyzing the role social studies can play in addressing it:

> A radical conception of social studies starts with the recognition that social processes, both within school and outside it, influence and restrict the life chances of many students. What social studies can do is to help them become more aware of their assumptions and more politically articulate in the expression of what it is they want out of life. This can direct them towards an active exploration of why the social world resists and frustrates their wishes and how social action may focus upon such constraints [Gleeson & Whitty 1976].

Inherent in Whitty's suggestion are a number of valuable insights that can be used here. Students must be taught how to act collectively to build political structures that can challenge the status quo. Fred Newmann (1980) has both actively pursued this line of reasoning and rightly criticized other educators for ignoring it. Moreover, this kind of pedagogy must be infused by a passion and optimism that speak to possibilities. Too much of the literature in the citizenship education field borders on despair; not only does it lack any vision, but it seems "frozen" by its own inability to dream, imagine, or think about a better world. The endless studies on the sad state of citizenship education and the existing political consciousness of students are paraded before us as if there was nothing that could be done. These should be treated as starting points and not as terminal commentaries on the state of the nation's health.

The vitality of any field is measured, in part, by the intensity of the debate that it wages about its most basic assumptions and goals. Citizenship education is in dire need of such a debate. The prize to be gained goes far beyond the merits of intellectual dialogue and insight. What appears to be at stake at the present moment in history is the ability of future generations of Americans to think and act in ways that speak to age-old precepts of freedom and democracy. The task of developing a mode of citizenship education that addresses this issue appears awesome. But when one looks at the consequences of not addressing it, there appears the possibility of a barbarism so dreadful that we can do nothing less than act quickly and thoughtfully, in the spirit of what is just, necessary, and possible, to meet the challenge.

6

Literacy, Ideology, & the Politics of Schooling

Literacy is an issue that in the current debate regarding the role and purpose of schooling appears to have "escaped" from the ideologies that inform it. At first glance, there is a curious paradox in the fact that while the subject of literacy has once again become a major educational issue, the discourse that dominates the debate represents a conservative retreat from dealing with the issue in a significant way—the scope and widespread interest in literacy and schooling has served generally to flatten the debate rather than enhance it. With few exceptions, the issue of literacy has been removed from the broader social, historical, and ideological forces that constitute the conditions for its existence.[1] Within the boundaries of conventional discourse, literacy appears to exist beyond the specificities of power, culture, and politics; as such, it represents both a flight from critical thinking and an ideological prop for the existing relations of domination characteristic of the larger society.

A critique of the current debate surrounding literacy and schooling is important because it points to a consideration of the ways in which the production of school knowledge and meanings are, in part, determined by broader power relations. Moreover, such a critique reveals an instru- 205 mental logic and positivistic ideology that dominates the debate while simultaneously pointing to the socio-political interests that are served by it. For instance, within the context of the existing debate literacy is defined primarily in mechanical and functional terms. On the one hand, it is reduced to the mastery of fundamental "skills"; in this case, literacy is presented as "certain skills for using the written language that include skills concerned both with the written language as a second representational system for the spoken language and as an external, visual memory."[2] On the other hand, literacy becomes completely subsumed within the logic and needs of capital, and its worth is defined and measured against the demand for those reading and writing skills necessary for that growing sector of the labor process involved in the "mass production of information, communication, and finance" (Aronowitz 1981b). Literacy, in this case, becomes the new admission ticket for the poor in their attempt to enter an economy that regards them as second-class citizens.

The ideology that informs conventional conceptions of literacy has stripped it of its function as a vehicle for critical reason, as a mode of thought and assemblage of skills that allow individuals to break with the predefined. Consequently, literacy in conventional terms has collapsed under the weight of the operational ideology that informs and legitimates the logic of the dominant society; it has been reduced to the alienating rationality of the assembly line, a mastery without benefit of comprehension or political insight. What is equally startling is that even the dominant version of liberal discourse on literacy appears to have "forgotten" its own recent concerns for the tenets of critical thinking and democratic principles. No longer content to define literacy against the goal of political self-determination, dominant liberal discourse[3] has shifted its interests and now embraces notions of schooling and literacy "subsumed under the goal of fitting students into the economic order" (Aronowitz 1981b). The political conservatism of this approach is conveniently ignored under the self-proclaimed insight that literacy should now include the mastery of not only reading and writing skills but computer technology skills as well. What we generally end up with are expanded definitions of literacy that celebrate learning methods reduced to procedural operations.

Needless to say, the implications that conservative and liberal approaches to literacy have for educational theory and practice represent an issue that needs to be examined critically. This is an important task, not only because it provides the opportunity to understand the changes that schools are presently undergoing, but also because it provides opportunities to develop theoretical perspectives and modes of inquiry that may serve to counteract such changes.

The relationship between literacy and schooling becomes clear if we consider that while a child may first enter a language through his or her family, it is primarily in the school that literacy is learned. There, the child learns how to read, write, and organize communication skills systematically. More significantly, school is also the site where students from different socioeconomic groups become aware that literacy is intimately connected to forms of knowledge, ways of communicating, and classroom social practices through which they define themselves as subjects (Donald, in press). Literacy, in this case, is interconnected with language practices and modes of learning that can only be understood in terms of their articulation with the power relations that structure the wider society. What this suggests, and what I shall pursue in this chapter, is that literacy, like schooling itself, is a political phenomenon and, in part, represents an embattled epistemological terrain on which different social groups struggle over how reality is to be signified, reproduced, and resisted. Foucault captures this issue in his comment:

> Education may well be, as of right, the instrument whereby every individual, in a society like our own, can gain access to any kind of discourse. But we well know that in its distribution, in what it permits and what it prevents, it follows the well-trodden battle lines of social conflict. Every education system is a political means of maintaining or of modifying the appropriation of discourse. . . . What is an educational system after all, if not the ritualization of the word; if not a qualification of some fixing roles for speakers; if not the distribution and an appropriation of discourse, with all its learning and its powers [Foucault 1972].

If Foucault is right—and I believe he is—then it can be argued that the existing mainstream approaches to literacy ignore a point stressed throughout this book: that schools are not neutral institutions that prepare students equally for social and economic opportunities in the wider society. Similarly, the failure to recognize that schools are political sites is matched by the refusal to acknowledge that underlying any one approach to literacy are historical and cultural influences which, of necessity, impose an ideological cast. That is, the dominant discourse has failed to recognize that the issue of literacy cannot be removed from the historical process or the ideological interests that constitute its meaning.

But to argue that literacy cannot be reduced to a technical skill should not suggest that traditional approaches to literacy can or should be challenged strictly in terms of methodological considerations. Instead, existing approaches to literacy must be challenged in terms of their ideological assumptions and the interests such assumptions implicitly or explicitly support. What is needed is a mode of analysis that reveals the dominant assumptions at the center of a given problematic on literacy as well as a critical attentiveness that locates the roots of such assumptions and the interests they support within a given ideology (Laclau 1977). If we are to unravel the linkages between schools and the wider society so that we can identify and transform the structural and ideological forces that tie the schooling process to the reproduction of class, gender, and racial inequities, we must recognize how ideologies are constituted and inscribed in the discourse and social practices of daily classroom life. The study of literacy provides a productive starting point for such an analysis.

I want to argue in this chapter that any analysis of the notion of literacy has to begin by identifying the assumptions and practices that tie it to a specific configuration of knowledge, ideology, and power. This configuration, which characterizes all models of literacy, represents its conceptual structure, the meaning of which is to be found in the ideological source "that lies beneath the choice of what is considered legitimate and important or illegitimate and irrelevant in a particular instance of practical deliberation" (Simon 1982). Such a mode of analysis is important because it reveals the deep ideological grammar that structures various approaches to literacy. It is also important because it renders, though problematically, the dialectical interplay between schools and the political and economic interests that govern the dominant society.

One precondition for the construction of a theory and pedagogy of critical literacy is the development of a theory of ideological struggle. Such a theory involves fashioning the conceptual tools that provide both a critique of existing modes of literacy as well as the production of oppositional forms of knowledge and practices. I shall attempt such a task first by analyzing the major approaches to literacy in terms of the ideologies that inform them and the interests they support. In addition, I shall examine how the ideology that characterizes each approach places it in a particular relationship to the dominant society. I shall assess the shortcomings in each of these positions, and, finally, I shall attempt to delineate those concepts and practices that offer a general foundation for developing a radical pedagogy and notion of critical literacy.

I have distinguished three basic ideologies that characterize the various approaches to literacy. The ideologies may be categorized as: (a) instrumental, (b) interactionist, and (c) reproductive. Needless to say, these are ideal-typical categories and have been compressed for the sake of clarity. Moreover, these categories should not suggest the absence of a high level of variation and subtle differentiation among teachers, educators, and others who, in general terms, might subscribe to any one of them.

As I have used the concept in this book, ideology does not simply refer to a specific set of doctrines or meanings. It is a much more dynamic concept that refers to the way in which meanings and ideas are produced, mediated, and embodied in forms of knowledge, cultural experiences, social practices, and cultural artifacts. Ideology, then, is a set of doctrines as well as the medium through which human actors make sense of their own experiences and those of the world in which they find themselves. Ideology as a system of meaning, whether inscribed in consciousness, cultural forms, or lived experiences, exists in a dialectical relation with reality. That is, it is a mediating force that can either distort or illuminate reality, therefore resisting reductionist accounts that simply limit it to false consciousness. Treated in dialectical terms, ideology becomes a useful construct for understanding not only how schools sustain and produce meanings, such as what counts as literacy, but also how individuals and groups in concrete relations produce, negotiate, modify, or resist them as well.

Instrumental Ideology and Literacy

Instrumental ideology rests on a number of assumptions that tie it to the "culture of positivism" that dominates American social theory, and to the various modes of technocratic rationality that underlie most school practices (Giroux 1981). Instrumental ideology has a complex history and takes several forms; while it is impossible to reduce its meaning to a specific school of thought or a well defined perspective, it is possible to speak of instrumental ideology in terms of a number of general assumptions.

The major premises of instrumental ideology are drawn from the logic and method of inquiry associated with the natural sciences, especially the principles of prediction, efficiency, and technical control derived from eighteenth-century natural science. Underlying these interests is the assumption that there is a unitary scientific method which recognizes no distinction between the physical world and the human world. At the center of this ideology is an operational view of theory and knowledge. That is, in this perspective theory is reduced to a linear notion of causality whose explanatory power resides in its use of rigorous empirical techniques to uncover the logic and potential for analysis of so-called natural laws. Central to the logic of instrumental ideology and its view of theory is the notion that all social relations shall be subject to quantification, since the "book of nature," including human nature, is held to be written in the language of mathematics. Knowledge in this view is seen as objective, outside of the existence of the knower, and subject to the demands of exact and precise formulation. Neatly severed from the world of values, knowledge finds its most important distinction within the category of the "fact." It is in the collection, quantification, and celebration of fact in the neutral observation discourse of instrumental ideology that knowledge finds its highest expression. In other words, knowledge consists of a realm of "objective facts" to be collected and arranged so that they can be marshalled in the interest of empirical verification. As a result, knowledge is relevant to the degree that it can be viewed ". . . as description and explanation of objectified data, conceived—a priori—as cases of instances of possible laws" (Apel 1977).

Instrumental ideology, like all ideologies, has to be assessed not only by the assumptions that govern the questions it raises, but also by the issues it ignores, the questions it *does not* raise. For example, its insistence on a definition of truth that is synonymous with empirical verification and "objective methodological" inquiry renders it powerless to identify the normative interests that shape its view of theory and social inquiry. That is, behind its facade of value-freedom stands a reductionist logic that displays no interest in the grounds of knowledge (Habermas 1971). Instrumental ideology's silence regarding the normative grounding of knowledge results in a discourse that suppresses the notion of ethics and the value of history. Since knowledge in this perspective is valued for its utility and practical application, there is little room for questions concerning the ethical nature and consequences of the use of knowledge. Moreover, if theory and knowledge are subordinated to the imperatives of efficiency and technical mastery, history is reduced to a minor footnote in the priorities of "empirical" scientific inquiry. In my view, instrumental ideology touches only the surface of reality. Unconcerned with the hidden principles that structure the deep grammar of reality, it is wedded to treating history externally. And, as Russell Jacoby points out, it "tends to eliminate history as so much slag or intellectual baggage . . ." and thus does not "know the fundamental historical categories: consciousness and self-consciousness, subjectivity and objectivity, appearance and essence" (Jacoby 1980).

Instrumental ideology, in both historical and contemporary terms, has had a powerful and pervasive influence on American education. Curriculum theory and practice as well as more specific pedagogies of literacy have been largely structured by the values and assumptions inherent in instrumental ideology. It is to this issue that I will now turn.

The strength and pervasiveness of the logic of instrumental ideology in the curriculum field can be seen historically in the early work of educators like Franklin Bobbitt (1918), W.W. Charters (1923), D.S. Sneeden (1921), and others. Rooted in models of industrial psychology and control patterned after the scientific management movement of the 1920s, educators in the curriculum field conceptualized students as raw material, schools as factories, and learning as a sub-set of the tenets of behavioral psychology (Kliebard 1979a). That this view is deeply ingrained in the ideology of schooling can be seen in the powerful support given by educators to competency-based systems of instruction, behaviorist models of pedagogy, and the various versions of systems theory approaches to curriculum theory and policy development.

It is hardly surprising that functionalist accounts of schooling, with their emphasis on the transmission of a "common culture," their consensus view of the relations between schools and society, and their apolitical view of school culture, have dominated educational theory and continue to do so. Nor is it surprising that in the curriculum field itself the influence of Ralph Tyler (1950) has been paramount. The Tyler rationale distinguishes itself by its use of "guiding" curriculum principles and its relatively apolitical and atheoretical celebration of the pragmatic. Its behavioral approach to learning provides clear cut "steps" to measure, control, and evaluate the "learning experience" in conjunction with predefined objectives. There is no concern in this perspective with the normative principles that govern the selection, organization, and distribution of knowledge, particularly as these are related to issues of power and conflict. Nor is there any concern with the ways in which the structural principles of the school curriculum and classroom social practices articulate with those capitalist social processes that characterize the wider society.

Literacy approaches fashioned under the principles of instrumental logic, particularly in the areas of writing, reading, and language practices, exist almost exclusively within a theoretical framework the guiding interest of which has been primarily procedural, that is, to find the best means to reach prechosen ends. The pedagogy of reading is therefore dominated by mechanical approaches abstracted from the crucial issues of ideology and power (Walmsley 1981). In addition, writing models fashioned under the rubric of this perspective are mostly tied to the mastery of the mechanics of grammatical structures;[4] finally, language practices, or the issue of what is considered the legitimate use of discourse, represent an unproblematic and conservative endorsement of standard English. I now want to turn briefly to each of these areas in order to illuminate how instrumental ideology structures the specific meanings and practices associated with them.

There are two basic ideologically related notions of reading that dominate this tradition. The first notion speaks to the needs and interests of students from the dominant classes. Reading in this instance is defined through an emphasis on mastering certain forms of knowledge. Aligned with those who would argue that reading is a process of understanding, this group reduces the notion of understanding to learning content deemed appropriate to the well-educated citizen. What is regarded as appropriate knowledge in this tradition amounts to the classics and the "great books" of Western civilization.

If the first notion reduces reading to a mode of pedagogy designed to reproduce the values and ideology of the dominant culture, the second moves from an emphasis on reproducing a body of knowledge to an emphasis on teaching the rudimentary processes of reading, i.e., vocabulary skills, word identification and study skills, etc. The second notion is geared primarily to working-class students whose "cultural capital" is considered less compatible, and thus inferior in terms of both complexity and value, with the knowledge and values of the dominant class. In her study of how elementary schools sometimes function to produce social-class distinctions, Jean Anyon provides a telling example of how instrumental ideology functions in the interest of social and cultural reproduction in working-class schools:

> Predominant patterns of work activity that I observed in the two fifth grades in this working-class school involved repetitive rote procedures and copious mechanical activity such as copying teachers' notes from the chalkboard . . . following grammatical rules for filling in words

on language arts dittoes, and answering teachers' questions; most of these questions were rather to ascertain whether children had done the assigned work than to invite reflection or sustained creative thought on a problem or task. . . . School knowledge . . . was not so much bodies of ideas or connected generalizations, as fragmented facts and behaviors. Teachers spoke of knowledge as the basics and indicated that by this they meant behavior skills such as . . . how to syllabify, how to sound out words and write sentences, and how to follow directions. One teacher explained that this kind of "stuff" was "all the children would understand or use" [Anyon 1981].

The relation of literacy to writing fares no better in this approach. Instrumental ideology expresses itself through a purely formalistic approach to writing characterized by a strict emphasis on rules, exhortations about what to do or not to do as one writes. Instead of treating writing as a process that is both the medium and product of one's experience in the world, this approach strips writing of its normative and critical dimensions and reduces it to the learning of skills, which at the most reductionist level focuses on the mastery of grammatical rules. On a more sophisticated level, but one that is no less positivistic, the emphasis is on the formalistic mastery of complicated syntactical structures, often regardless of their content.

Language practices represent another important aspect of literacy. In this area the child uses forms of speech rooted in a history of lived experiences. These practices are often used to affirm his or her identity and to give meaning to the wider society. What must be stressed here is that while language practices are primarily class-specific, they are never formed within the limited confines of a given class; they are anchored in what might be called a selective affinity to class-specific experiences. But it is important to note that such practices form and establish themselves amidst class relationships of dominance and domination. In other words, language practices are a fundamental part of class identity, but that identity is mediated within socioideological contexts such as the family, the school, and the workplace. It is within these contexts that language practices and subjectivities are formed through relations of struggle and resistance. But, as James Donald (forthcoming) reminds us, they are not formed so as to insure that the struggle between social and cultural formations will be fought out on equal terms. This is an important issue to stress because it points to the assumption that a dominant class has the power to produce and define language practices which serve to legitimize its own cultural capital while it reifies the language practice of subordinate cultures and social formations. For example, as Pierre Bourdieu (1977a), Basil Bernstein (1977), and others have shown, schools play a powerful role in legitimating the values and language practices of the dominant culture, particularly through the mechanisms of overt and hidden curriculums. What gets produced and valorized in schools, though not without resistance and struggle, are the values, styles, taste, and culture of the favored classes. Similarly, through the legitimation of certain language practices, the school functions, in part, to both produce and repress cultural identities via the hidden referents of class, gender, and ethnicity embodied in the school curriculum and classroom social relations. Again, James Donald cogently captures this issue: "The really significant power of schools is not [simply] to repress but to produce cultural identities. Through their practices they set up a hierarchy of values for different forms of knowledge, language, and taste, and it is within such discursive regimes that people take up their subject regimes" (Donald, forthcoming).

In essence, language practices represent one feature of the dominant culture that schools legitimate in varying degrees. When such practices are rooted in the logic of instrumental ideology, they give full support to the dominant culture and its existing power relations. This becomes more understandable when we examine the way in which language practice mediates between the student and the teacher in the pedagogies informed by instrumental ideology. It unnecessarily anticipates the mastery of predefined knowledge and skills. By emphasising the transmission of information, the pedagogy used in this approach represents a top-to-bottom model that removes the student from any active participation in either the construction of knowledge or the sharing of power. Not only is the subject of literacy treated like a commodity, the student is reified as well. In other words, by defining literacy as the mastery and appropriation of predefined knowledge and skills largely removed from the background and cultural capital of the students, instrumental ideology provides the context for a pedagogy that disconfirms the historical and cultural experiences of students from the working class or any other group that is not part of the dominant class.

Needless to say, within the context of such a pedagogy dominant-class students are also treated as objects. But it is a form of reification in which they have the "advantage" of moving within a school culture that contains an element of familiarity, one that has a select affinity to their own. While they may be reified at the level of individual participation, at another level they receive constant support and confirmation. One might say it is a form of objectification experienced from a position of assurance, assurance that beneath *their* cultural capital lurks the logic of power and class affirmation. Conversely, not only does such a pedagogy contain a logic that suggests that subordinate class experiences and language practices do not count for very much; it is also mediated in such a way that working-class students receive it from the vantage point of powerlessness, even when such students succeed in mastering its formalistic demands. As Tony Bennett points out:

> The bourgeoisie, by virtue of the facility acquired from an understanding of its mechanisms, experiences [the dominant] language as its own. It is at home with it, familiar with its workings. The subordinate classes, by contrast, receive that language in an administered form, handed down from above within the education system. Familiar only with its shell, they experience the language as an exclusion and limitation in relation to the "superior" . . . language by which they are by virtue of their class formally excluded [Bennett 1979].

Finally, the relation between instrumental ideology and the "needs" of the state becomes strikingly evident when we examine the concept of functional literacy, in which the reduction of literacy to instrumental needs finds its quintessential expression in the concept of functional literacy. Defined originally by William Gray in 1956, the term and model of pedagogy derived from it have become widely used by UNESCO in its literacy programs in developing countries. Moreover, functional literacy has become one of the primary goals of the back-to-basics orientation currently so prevalent in the United States. Within this concept, literacy is defined in relation to the financial and economic needs of a given society. UNESCO, for instance, is quite clear on the meaning and purpose of functional literacy programs: ". . . [L]iteracy programs should preferably be linked with economic priorities. . . . [They] must impart not only reading and writing, but also professional and technical knowledge, thereby leading to a fuller participation of adults in economic life." (UNESCO 1966).

Literacy in this perspective is geared to make adults more productive workers and citizens within a given society. In spite of its appeal to economic mobility, functional literacy reduces the concept of literacy and the pedagogy in which it is suited to the pragmatic requirements of capital; consequently, the notions of critical thinking, culture, and power disappear under the imperatives of the labor process and the need for capital accumulation.

Interaction Ideology and Literacy

I have argued that instrumental ideology expresses a view of literacy that posits an undialectical relation between knowledge, skills, and the human subject. In this account, knowledge and skills are given high priority as value-free, objective elements in the literacy process. Similarly, students are relegated to a relatively passive role in the pedagogical process; that is, human agency is ignored.

Interaction ideology, however, is situated in interests that contrast sharply with the notions of prediction, control, and efficiency. At the center of this account is an interest in recovering the subject and the human dimensions of knowledge. Thus, learning is viewed as a dialectical interaction between the person and the objective world, and knowledge is seen as a social construction. The question of meaning rather than the issue of mastery constitutes the central problematic underlying interaction ideology. While the goal of learning certain literacy skills is seen as important, such a task is given low priority next to the overarching question of how students construct meaning. Yet, although the question of meaning is central to the adherents of this ideology, there are significant differences among its proponents. Some support a notion of meaning that extols the problem-solving process and its concurrent emphasis on cognitive and developmental growth; meaning, in this sense, is strongly tied to epistemological concerns. Others espouse a view of meaning that is primarily psychologial and person-centered. In this perspective, meaning is situated in a concern for personal growth, inner happiness, and interpersonal relations which affirm the dignity and autonomy of the self.

The cognitive-developmental tradition represents one aspect of interaction ideology, and the romantic tradition characterizes the other aspect. For the sake of theoretical convenience I shall discuss these traditions separately, and I shall conclude this analysis of interaction ideology by positing a critique of the underlying ideological notions shared by both positions.

The cognitive-developmental approach to literacy is influenced heavily by the early work of John Dewey (1916) and the stage theorizing of Jean Piaget (1970). In Piagetian terms, the child's interaction with the wider society is portrayed through a process of assimilation and accommodation. Similarly, it is argued that the basis of logical thinking is rooted in the development of a person's cognitive abilities as he or she moves from lower to higher "stages" of complexity. Kohlberg and others have argued that there are six stages of moral-cognitive development and that the aim of education should be to help students attain the highest stage compatible with their physical and cognitive structures. A curriculum fostering modes of reading and writing that examine moral dilemmas will presumably teach students, through the process of cognitive conflict, to move on to higher forms of moral reasoning.

The discourse of liberal ideology is deeply ingrained in this perspective. Humanistic in tone and social democratic in practice, it views schools as the central agencies for the development of democratic life. In effect, critical thinking and cognitive development are portrayed as the epistemological equivalent of democratic action.

Rejecting the positivist conception of knowledge as objective and value-free, cognitive developmental ideology calls for both a restructuring of knowledge and a democratization of the pedagogy in which it is communicated. Lawrence Kohlberg sums this up cogently in his comments on the importance of the cognitive-developmental approach to schooling as it is used in the social studies curriculum:

> The foundation of the old civic educator was the transmission of unquestioned truths of fact and of unquestioned consensual values to a passively receptive child. . . . In contrast to the transmission of consensual values, the new social studies have been based on Dewey's conception of the valuing process [which] postulates the need to focus upon situations which are not only problematic but controversial. . . . These objectives spring from the Deweyite recognition of social education as a process with forms of social interaction as its outcome. A Deweyite concern about action is not represented by a bag-of-virtues set of behavioral objectives. It is reflected in an active participation in the social process. This means that the classroom, itself, must be seen as an arena in which the social and political process takes place in microcosm [Kohlberg 1973].

The cognitive developmental approach focuses primarily on reading as an intellectual process. The issue of process is crucial here because inherent in this view is the assumption that content is of minor importance. Analysis, comprehension, and problem solving become operations divorced from the object of critique. Content is not ignored; it is simply considered less important than the goal of developing higher stages of thinking in students. As Sean Walmsley comments: "In general, the cognitive developmental approach to . . . reading stresses the importance not of . . . comprehension of an author's message (although this maybe an important by-product) but rather [of] the development of new cognitive structures that allow the student to progress toward the understanding of increasingly complex materials" (Walmsley 1981).

On the surface, it appears that the student is an agent in the literacy process, since he or she has to draw upon prior knowledge and cognitive skills to move successfully to increasingly complex levels of understanding. Furthermore, the reading process is seen as one aspect of a pedagogy in which the problems raised in the text serve to promote dialogue in order to enable students to think and analyze issues at higher levels of reasoning. Language practices become important here to the degree that they exhibit the skills needed to analyze and decode the problems. Thus the index of what constitutes acceptable language practice appears to be its adequacy as a medium for problem solving. I shall return to the political and ideological significance of this approach after I analyze what I call the *romantic tradition in interaction ideology.*

The romantic approach underlying interactionist ideology in the area of literacy has its roots in a long tradition of thought that includes the work of such diverse notables as Rousseau, A.S. Neill, Carl Rogers, and Joel Spring.[5] Inherent in this tradition is a deep regard for the individual's ability to construct his or her own meaning through a process of renewed self-affirmation.

Rejecting the overly cognitive rationales embedded in most literacy approaches, the romantic view insists on the importance of the affective dimension in the reading and writing process.[6] This position finds clear expression in Rosenblatt's goals for reading, which include "the intimate reliving of fresh views of personality and life implicit in the work [of literature]; the pleasure and release of tensions that may flow from such an experience . . . the deepening and broadening of sensitivity to the sensuous quality and emotional impact of day-to-day living" (Rosenblatt 1949).

The view of writing that emerges from this tradition is one that rests on the premise that there is a causal relationship between making students feel good and improving their writing abilities. Writing, like reading, appears to gain in validity to the degree that it constitutes both the medium and the outcome of a catalytic discharge of joyful emotion.

Accordingly, the pedagogy of writing often focuses on having students write in journals, engage in autobiographical writing and free-expression writing exercises, etc. Simon, Hawley, and Bretton clarify this approach in the introduction to their own text on the subject, the title of which lays bare its ideology. In *Composition for Personal Growth,* they comment:

> The activities are designed to produce written responses which may consist of anything from one word to a complete essay. The student records his responses in a private journal. Some of these responses may be recorded by another member of the peer group in his own journal with other members of the peer group. Although the data in journals is unorganized, it is all more or less relevant to questions such as "Who am I? How am I perceived by others? Which of my characteristics are common and which are unique? What do I value" [Simon, Hawley, & Bretton 1973].

In this view, language practices are evaluated through the double lens of authenticity and the promise of unfettered spontaneity. The substance of such discourse is legitimated through its use as a medium of psychic redemption and personal growth. As a constituting medium that relates the individual to social practices situated in issues of class, gender, and race that shape every day experience, discourse does not count for much in this approach.

Needless to say, the romantic approach to literacy presents a counterpoint to top-to-down authoritarian modes of pedagogy, and contains an implicit critique of the overly cognitive rationalities that inform most literacy approaches, particularly those steeped in the logic of instrumental ideology. However, both the romantic and cognitive developmental traditions hide more than they reveal, and it is the "structured silences" in these approaches to which I shall now turn. While both approaches to literacy represent different aspects of interactionist ideology, whatever differences exist between them are ultimately dissolved in the political orientation that they both share. This becomes clear through an examination of a number of issues that provide the ideological cement that ties them together.

Both positions subscribe to a truncated notion of power and praxis. In the cognitive developmental model, power is reduced to a struggle or interaction between "man" and the natural world. Thus the notion of conflict between different class formations, or the assumption that power may be structured socially to place unequal economic and political constraints on different social classes, is ignored. In the romantic approach, power is reduced to the discourse of psychological categories and ends up becoming synonymous with concepts such as "self-fulfillment", "becoming", and "self-actualization".[7] Power and freedom in this perspective collapse into an exaggerated notion of human will as well as into a blindness towards those larger social forces that promote economic and cultural disintegration. In both positions, power is reduced either to the exercise of cognitive problem solving or to the journey into the "self". The emphasis may be different in each approach, but the result is the same, i.e., the antagonisms and conflicts that characterize the wider society are dissolved in an ideology that perpetuates the very problems it attempts to resolve.

Literacy practices in both accounts are rooted in forms of pedagogy that divorce theory from practice and consciousness from social action. For example, both positions reduce the relationship between content and context either to the imperatives of feeling good or to the safety of the classroom debate. That is, in the romantic view the notion and search for truth get obscured within the overiding emphasis on pedagogical practices that promote positive interpersonal experiences. It is the experience and not the interpretation of the experience that receives high priority. In contrast, in the cognitive developmental model the pedagogical emphasis on cognitive dissonance and moral development exhibits little concern for the content of students' life experiences or the class, racial, and gender histories of the different groups of students exposed to this approach. In fact, there is an abstract and naive simplicity to the content of the moral dilemmas used in this approach, just as there is a kind of political naivete in reducing struggles over power to the "just community school" concept. There is also a revealing paradox: on the one hand, truth is thought to be grounded in a form of social practice, while on the other hand social practice is reduced to forms of relations devoid of even the hint of social and class conflict. Class is simply an abstract category. Thus, social practice finds its highest expression in the cognitive developmental model in the structured debates of the classroom encounter and the liberal issues that define school governance issues.

Finally, both approaches support a view of language practice that strips it of political and cultural significance. By relegating dialogue to its functional requirements in modes of pedagogy designed either to increase cognitive problem-solving skills or heighten interpersonal sensitivity, language appears merely as a vehicle to organize and express either ideas or emotions. But language is not a tool neutrally available to all students who engage in classroom discussions. Language, as James Donald reminds us, is " . . . a practice of signification and also a site for cultural struggle and . . . a mechanism which produces the antagonistic relations between different social groups" (Donald forthcoming). By ignoring this insight, cognitive developmental and romantic perspectives construct a view of language practice that legitimates the relations of dominance behind different forms and modes of discourse. In other words, both approaches support a view of discourse and classroom social relations that presume a false equality of language practices. Ignoring the gender, class, and racial inequalities that infuse the relations and practices of language use, both approaches promote classroom pedagogies that are abstracted from the different historical and cultural backgrounds of a significant number of students. The result is a view of literacy that celebrates an abstract condition regarding language usage, intellectual growth, and psychosocial development. Such a view removes the notions of roles, rationality, and culture, all of which deeply structure the school experience, from the benefit of sociological and historical analysis.

One consequence of this approach is a failure to examine how different literacy pedagogies are structured so as to work to the advantage or disadvantage of the cultural competencies of specific social formations. By not acknowledging that each of the respective methodologies supported by the traditions I have described may embody cultural values and class- and gender-specific ideologies, the adherents of such approaches fail to recognize that the form and content of their own discourse may serve to alienate large numbers of their students. Moreover, by failing to recognize the ideology that informs their discourse and the discourse of different students, teachers who work in these perspectives have no clear way of understanding why certain groups of students may succeed, fail, or resist classroom encounters characterized by language practices removed from or close to their own lives (Morely 1981).

As an important postscript to this analysis, it must be stressed that the logic of interaction ideology supports approaches that point to the disadvantage of being illiterate while simultaneously decrying the failure of the family, the school, and the public sphere to promote literacy. But such concern for the plight of "illiterates" becomes empty chatter and false empathy when it comes to analyzing the social and political conditions that promote and support the problem. A recent example of this form of analysis can be found in a recent issue of *Daedalus,* from which a comment will suffice:

> . . . [S]chools that accept a broad range of students are reluctant to admit to any single overriding aim. . . . They have in common an inability to make all their pupils literate. To expect high schools, then, to adopt the goal of literacy is to ask them to depart from their traditional pattern. For this they will need informed support from the public, not the carping criticism that has been much more common, and they will need to provide evidence that their students are achieving literacy [Graham 1981].

Behind this grave concern and call for high schools to promote literacy programs, there is a curious silence. That is, questions concerning how power, ideology, and the forces of social and cultural reproduction operate both within and outside of schools to promote "illiteracy" are absent from this analysis. In this light, it is not surprising that an appeal is made to the medicinal bath of pretended harmony and consensus in order to renounce what is labeled "carping criticism." This is rather ironic, considering that what is needed are precisely those criticisms that reveal the social antagonisms at the root of the literacy crisis.[8] Fortunately, there have been approaches to schooling and the issue of literacy that search out such antagonisms rather than ignore them, and it is these approaches that I will examine in the final section of this essay.

Reproductive Ideology and the Pedagogy of Critical Literacy

The logic and values that inform reproductive ideologies are drawn from a wide variety of sources and movements, all of which have emerged within the last decade in the United States and in Europe. In general terms, reproductive approaches can be analyzed as three distinct yet interrelated theoretical positions. The first position, loosely categorized as the social reproduction perspective, develops a radical analysis of pedagogy that focuses around those social, economic, and political determinants of schooling whose interests are rooted in the dynamics of capital accumulation and the reproduction of the labor force. In these accounts, schools are viewed relationally as part of an ideological state apparatus, the function of which is to secure the ideological and social relations necessary for the reproduction of capital and its institutions.[9] In the second perspective, a number of historical and sociological accounts have appeared that reveal how the social structure of the workplace is replicated through the daily routines and practices that shape classroom social relations or that promote the hidden curriculum.[10] More recently, we have accounts of schooling that illuminate how cultural resources are selected, organized, and distributed admidst complex relations of conformity and resistance in order to promote social and cultural reproduction. This perspective is sometimes categorized as the cultural reproduction position. Since I have dealt with these theories in depth in Chapter 3, I shall here focus briefly on a number of theoretical issues that point to the unique contribution they make to a radical theory of literacy.

Reproductive ideology takes as its central concern the question of how a social system reproduces itself and how certain forms of subjectivity get constituted within such a context. Whereas instrumental and interactive ideologies view the relation between the individual and society in either highly conservative or unproblematic terms, reproductive ideology views the relation as one steeped in domination and conflict. Underlying the reproductive perspective is the important question of what constitutes those structural and ideological mechanisms that sustain systems of class, gender, and racial domination both within and outside of schools. Equally important is the question of why the oppressed do not recognize such structures and why they often participate in reproducing them. Thus it can be argued that while different versions of reproductive ideology postulate differing modes of analysis regarding the relationship between schools and society, each of these perspectives is rooted in interests based on the principles of critique and social transformation.

While many of these accounts do not deal directly with the issue of literacy, they do provide a number of theoretical constructs that could be useful for developing the ideological foundation for a model of critical literacy. On the one hand, these approaches have stripped the schools of their political innocence by focusing on the social and material conditions that tie schools to the state, to the labor process, and to domestic life. Such approaches, while restricting themselves to analyses of ideologies about education, provide a theoretical framework for *locating outside of schools* the origins of class and gender divisions and their articulation with forms of knowledge, literacy, and pedagogy in the school curriculum (Giroux 1981). On the other hand, reproductive theorists have attempted to illuminate how the dominant ideology inscribes itself in the culture of the school and how the form and content of such an ideology are maintained and resisted in the internal discourse of the curriculum and the lived antagonistic relations that make up school culture.

The concepts of power, culture, resistance, and social change are central theoretical elements in the reproductive account of schooling. Before turning to the work of Paulo Freire (1973) and examining its importance to the concept of critical literacy, I want to analyze how these theoretical elements might prove useful in developing a theory of critical literacy and pedagogy.

Reproductive ideologies argue that schools cannot be understood either in terms of their relation to the wider society or in terms of how they function daily as agencies of social and cultural reproduction, unless the complex interplay of power and control is critically analyzed. It is in this context that the connection between power and culture becomes important. For instance, in the work of theorists such as Willis (1981) and Bourdieu (1977a) culture is seen as a political phenomenon that functions, in part, to support and legitimate existing power relations. In these accounts, dominant power relations are not sustained simply through the one-sided imposition of authority, but primarily through the mediations and power of dominant ideologies inscribed in the selected cultural forms and representations that are legitimated and distributed throughout society. In this case, schools are seen as mediators of society, not merely the instrument of it; but what is generally mediated under the guise of "neutrality" and the promise of social mobility represents the most valued forms of cultural capital. That is, knowledge, language practices, ways of viewing the world, cultural styles, and the like. Culture, in this perspective, becomes the mediating link between the system of power relations and the processes and outcomes that characterize the system of schooling. Knowledge, in this perspective, is linked to power in terms of the ideology inscribed in its messages and content. Rather than simply being transmitted, knowledge functions as a reproductive force that partially serves to locate subjects within the specified boundaries of class, gender, and race.

What is crucial to this analysis is the added assumption that the dominant culture functions within a network of social relations marked by a wide variety of antagonisms and contradictions. The point is that the material and ideological forces that promote social and cultural reproduction also *produce* forms of resistance. The existence of dominant ideologies and structural constraints in schools do not mean that educational outcomes are simply a passive reflex. As Rob Moore points out, "It [is] reasonable to argue that educational knowledge and practice are organized on class principles, but that the transmission process is mediated by the cultural field of the classroom in such a way that determinate effects cannot be guaranteed" (Moore 1978, 1979).

What this suggests is that modes of analysis which separate questions of knowledge from those of power have failed to see how the assumptions and practices embedded in any view of literacy are essentially political and cannot be abstracted from the ideological interests they support.

The reproductive theories briefly analyzed in this essay provide some important contributions to developing a theory of critical literacy. First, by situating schools within the wider network of power relations, they demonstrate the need for educators to develop a theory of society in order to understand the complex role that schools play as agencies designed to mediate and sustain the logic of the state and the imperatives of capital. Second, they have politicized the relationship among culture, knowledge, and power. In doing so, reproductive theories have helped us to recognize that the production of knowledge and classroom social relations represent significant moments in the process of social domination. Third, implicit in these critiques is the assumption that literacy can be neither neutral nor objective, and that for the most part it is inscribed in the ideology and practice of domination.

The reproductive theories analyzed thus far have made substantial contributions to establishing a theoretical framework in the development of critical literacy; but, as I have mentioned before, they are not without some significant theoretical limitations. The most obvious limitation is that they are characterized by an undialectical notion of power. Power, in these perspectives, appears mostly as an instance of domination. Even where resistance and contradictions are highlighted in the analyses, they appear to be nothing more than faint bursts of misplaced opposition that eventually incorporate the very logic they struggle against. As a result, the notion of agency is played down in these accounts, and what we are left with are analyses that demonstrate how power works on people rather than through them. It is in the attempt to build a more dialectical and potentially radical theory of literacy that the work of Paulo Freire (1970, 1973, 1978a, b) gains enormous significance.[11]

Paulo Freire and the Notion of Critical Literacy

In the reproduction theory accounts, the notion of culture is reintroduced into the concept of power. As a result, culture is seen as an ideological and political category, not as an anthropological construct that can be defined as an all-embracing neutral category of social science. But while culture is politicized in these views, it is also seen one-sidedly; that is, it is viewed almost exclusively as a medium for social and class control. Thus we are presented with analyses that emphasize how the dominant culture works to legitimize existing modes of social relations and production. Freire's (1973) account moves beyond this theoretical position by viewing culture in dialectical terms. At the core of his notion of literacy is the insight that culture contains, not only a moment of domination, but also the possibility for the oppressed to produce, reinvent, and create the ideological and material tools they need to break through the myths and structures that prevent them from transforming an oppressive social reality. In essence, Freire (1978a) has defined and used his theory of literacy to critique the process of cultural reproduction while simultaneously linking the notion of cultural production to the process of critical reflection and social action.

Freire's critique of mainstream literacy approaches provides the theoretical landscape against which to understand his notion of literacy as a mode of radical cultural production. Inherent in his analysis is the assumption that traditional literacy approaches reduce the processes of reading, writing, and thinking to alienating, mechanical techniques and reified social practices. Instead of being a critical response to the plight of the oppressed, Freire claims, traditional literacy approaches ignore the culture, language skills, and issues that both inform and dignify the everyday life of the poor. Such approaches are not simply repressive and alienating, they also produce among the oppressed identities and subjectivities that reinforce the dominant ideology's view of them as inferior and responsible for their location in the class structure. In this case—largely as a result of what it does not say—literacy promotes powerlessness, making people voiceless and denying them the tools they need to think and act reflectively.

In his approach to literacy, Freire moves from critique to cultural production to social action by linking these notions of culture and power within the context of a radically informed pedagogy. Central to Freire's (1973) approach to literacy is his notion of "conscientization." The term refers to the interface of critical reflection and action as two separate but interconnected moments in the process of individual and collective emancipation. Literacy, in this context, becomes both a medium and a constitutive force for human agency and political action.

Literacy, for Freire, is a quality of human consciousness as well as the mastery of certain skills. The uniqueness of this approach is that it is situated in a critical perspective that stresses the transformation of relations between the dominated and the dominant within the boundaries of specific historical contexts and concrete cultural settings. In this view, the ideology of a given form of literacy is inextricably linked to the way it addresses the possibility of people becoming actors in the process of social change and how it might provide them with the support and tools necessary to promote a critical dialogue among themselves regarding their relationship to the larger society. This issue becomes more concrete if we examine Freire's notion of pedagogy.

Freire (1973) believes that the role of the literacy educator is to enter into dialogue with the people around themes that speak to the concrete situations and lived experiences that inform their daily lives. Literacy, in this sense, is not merely linked to the notion of relevance; instead, it is grounded in a view of human knowledge and social practice that recognizes the importance of using the cultural capital of the oppressed to authenticate the voices and modes of knowing they use to negotiate with the dominant society. What is at stake here is the goal of giving working-class students and adults the tools they need to reclaim their own lives, histories, and voices. For it must be remembered that the dominant culture and its attendant literacy approaches do not simply teach the mechanics of reading and writing; they also teach people how to live passively amidst alienating structures. It is a pedagogy and ideology that disconfirms the traditions and lived experiences of the oppressed. It does so not through the self-conscious exercise of authority, but often unconsciously through the mechanisms of a dominant ideology that constitute the "small change" of everyday existence. Bourdieu elaborates:

> The whole trick of pedagogic reason lies precisely in the way it extorts the essential while seeming to demand the insignificant: in obtaining the respect for form and forms of respect which constitute the most visible and at the same time the best-hidden (because that most "natural") manifestations of submission to the established order, the incorporation of the arbitrary abolishes . . . "lateral possibilities," that is, all the eccentricities and deviations which are the small change of

madness. The concessions of politeness always contain political concessions [Bourdieu 1977b].

Freire has rightly stressed that the historical and existential experiences that are devalued in everyday life by the dominant culture must be recovered in order to be both validated and critically understood. To be voiceless in a society is to be powerless, and literacy skills can be emancipatory only to the degree that they give people the critical tools to awaken and liberate themselves from their often mystified and distorted view of the world. But it must be emphasized that literacy as defined by Freire only becomes relevant if it is grounded in the cultural milieu that informs the context of the learners' everyday lives. Freire makes this quite clear in his claim that students need to be able to decode their own lived realities before they can understand the relations of dominance and power that exist outside of their most immediate experiences.

The principles underlying Friere's pedagogy are essential to any radical theory of literacy. The relationship between teachers and students would have to be mediated by forms of discourse and content rooted in the cultural capital of the learners and made problematic through modes of critical dialogue. Second such a view of literacy would have to politicize the notion of culture. This task is two-fold. On the one hand, students would have to learn to assess critically how culture functions in the interest of the dominant classes. This would require examining the form and content of various cultural "texts" in order to reveal the ideologies inscribed in their techniques and in the images and ideas they present. In a pedagogical sense, the words, settings, and images contained in school materials have to be reevaluated so that such materials can be seen as bearers of certain meanings and views. This certainly expands the notion of literacy to include not only print culture but visual and oral culture as well. The latter is particularly important at a time when the visual culture, as it is used within capitalist social relations, threatens the very foundation of critical thinking at all levels of society.[12] On the other hand, culture must be analyzed as something that students can construct and appropriate in order to understand themselves as agents who can engage in the task of social and political reconstruction. That is, they must learn to speak with their own voices, draw from their own experiences, and produce classroom "texts" that reflect the social and political issues important to their lives. Nan Elsasser and Vera John-Steiner describe these goals:

The aim of the best literacy programs has been to challenge the myths of our society, to perceive more clearly its realities, and to find alternatives and, ultimately, new directions for action. Basic literacy is not sufficient to achieve these far-reaching ends. People must reach a level of mastery of language skills from which they can critically examine and theoretically elaborate their political and cultural experiences. Simultaneously, literacy must be adequately developed so as to provide increasing numbers of men and women with access to technological and vocational skills and information [Elsasser & John-Steiner 1977].

Finally, it is crucial that radical theories of literacy understand how dominated groups are formed within relations of both domination and resistance. What this suggests is that radical educators will have to avoid two different but equally damaging assumptions about subordinate classes and the language practices that characterize many radical approaches to literacy and pedagogy in general. On one side, some theorists argue that the language practices and cultural capital of the working class are merely different from, rather than inferior to, the language practices and cultural capital of the dominant classes. This view indirectly supports a radical form of cultural relativism and argues that any attempt by educators to criticize or promote changes in working-class culture is a form of cultural imperialism.[13] Others contend that the language practices of working-class students are governed by a restricted code that makes them inferior to the language practices of the dominant classes.[14] Some "radical" theorists have gone even further, and argue that working-class culture is a distinctly inferior culture that needs to fully appropriate the knowledge and skills of the dominant classes.

Questions about the value of standard English as well as about the role of working-class culture in education become meaningful only if it is remembered that the skills, knowledge, and language practices that roughly characterize different classes and social formations are forged within social relations marked by the unequal distribution of power. Subordinate cultures are situated and recreated within relations of domination and resistance, and they bear the marks of both. To argue that working-class language practices are just as rule-governed as standard English usage and practice may be true, but to suggest at the same time that *all* cultures are equal is to forget that subordinate groups are often denied access to the power, knowledge, and resources that allow them to lead self-determined existences. Certainly, there are radical and important elements in subordinate cultures, and these speak in important

ways to the development of social relations and knowledge forms invaluable to both a radical theory of literacy and the notion of social transformation. At the same time, it must be stressed that the dominant
culture contains an ethos and a set of social relations that are often
dehumanizing and life-threatening. One could argue that while the language practices of the dominant classes contain valuable elements for
analytical and decontextualised thought, the formalistic qualities characteristic of these practices are often informed by an ideology that strips
them of the possibility for *conceptual literacy;* that is, formalistic skill
mastery (reading, writing, speaking, etc.) may exist without the benefit
of sustained theoretical insight. Put another way, the language and literacy
practices of the dominant class may provide the basis for functional literacy
within the context of advanced industrial capitalism, but they are often
simultaneously informed by modes of thought that represent a form of
political illiteracy.

Pedagogically, this means that once it becomes clear that subordinate
groups are formed in language practices and class identities constituted
within relations of dominance and subordination, we can begin to unravel
why students may resist cultural practices that are necessary for critical
literacy. We can also begin to develop ways to help them appropriate
elements of the dominant culture that are fundamental to the notion of
conceptual literacy. This approach rests on the assumption that subordinate groups must be given the opportunity to develop analytic and
practical skills that they can use to understand and transform the relations
that underlie the dominant culture, rather than simply being incorporated
into its logic. The complex interplay of domination, resistance, and literacy becomes clear in the work of Finlay and Faith (1981). Teaching
English in a university attended primarily by working-class students, they
discovered that their students refused to write, not because they were
"stupid" or careless, but because they viewed writing as a mode of discourse that was alienating and whose logic appeared to have little to do
with their own lives. The elaborated code and the process of writing
represented the domain of "the other," that is, it was reduced to "teacher
talk" or writing for a grade. Needless to say, these students harbored a
deep distrust of the dominant language codes and practices as important
bearers of meaning. They saw literacy skills, not as different, but as
something to be refused; thus, their own forms of discourse, and concept
of "literacy" were not "different-but-equal", but "different-and-antago-
nistic" (Donald, forthcoming).

A radical theory of literacy must search through the cultural meanings and practices of different groups and begin to ascertain how their contradictory natures can be used to promote a critical comprehension of reality. For example, while resistance to literacy exposes an exploitive moment in the logic of the dominant culture, it also fails to understand how skills such as reading and writing can be used in the service of critical analysis and social construction. Students must be given critical literacy skills that not only help them understand why they resist, but also allow them to recognize what this society has made of them and how it must, in part, be analyzed and reconstituted so that it can generate the conditions for critical reflection and action rather than passivity and indignation. Literacy skills, in this case, become tools that enable working-class students to appropriate those dimensions of their history that have been suppressed, as well as those skills that will reveal and explode the false attractions and myths that hide the deep divisions and inequities of the capitalist state. This task must become the basis and goal for a critical literacy.

CONCLUSION

Toward a New Public Sphere

. . . {T}he view that the schools can build a new society is akin to the idea that the world will be redeemed by children or that the children will somehow save us adults. I believe that both those ideas are incorrect. We cannot give our children the responsibility for redeeming the world we either messed up or at least witnessed being destroyed. . . . I don't believe a new social order can be built through the schools. I do believe that schools will be an essential part of a new order that is built through the cooperative effort of all of us: teachers, miners, factory-workers, professionals—all the people who believe in the social and moral imperative of struggling toward a new order. Thus I find that the crucial question should not be, "Do the schools have the power to change society?" so much as, "What small power can we use in working with others to change society?" And if we do begin to change society what will be the role of us as teachers in building a lasting new order? {Kohl 1980}.

KOHL'S QUOTATION IS IMPORTANT BECAUSE IT RAISES SIGNIFICANT QUES-tions about the nature of schooling and the role that teachers might play in the building of a more democratic society. Implicit in his remarks is the assumption that schools, like most social sites, are marked by con-tradictions and struggles which, while primarily serving the logic of domination, also contain the possibilities for emancipatory practice. But in this case there is an important qualification. The roles that schools and teachers might have in developing radical modes of pedagogy can only be understood within the broader historical, social, and economic con-ditions that characterize the wider society. Kohl's further development of this assumption is correct on two fronts. First, schools cannot by 234 themselves change society; second, teachers have a dual role to play in the struggle for a new society. That is, they can work both within and outside of schools to help illuminate both the value and the limitations of radical teaching. Within this dialectic of domination and resistance and the contradictory experiences and meanings that schools provide for political work, there exists a theoretical gap regarding the value and limitations of a critical pedagogy whose aim is the transformation of society and the relations of everyday life.

It is to Kohl's credit that he has raised the right questions. But as I have argued throughout this book, the answers to such questions will not be found in the theoretical legacies that constitute either the dominant or radical discourses on schooling. Radical theorists, in particular, have made important contributions to unravelling the relations between schools and the dominant society. But in the long run they have failed to escape either from a crushing pessimism or from the inability to link in a dialectical fashion the issue of agency and structure. That is, radical theorists have established the groundwork for a pedagogy that often disables rather than enables emancipatory hopes and strategies. Thus it is particularly essential for the development of radical theories of schooling to move from questions of social and cultural reproduction to issues of social and cultural production, from the question of how society gets reproduced in the interest of capital and its institutions to the question of how the "excluded majorities" have and can develop institutions, values, and practices that serve their autonomous interests. In more specific terms, it is crucial that a critical discourse be established around the distinction between radical forms of schooling and radical modes of education, both of which are essential to the development of what I have previously labeled civic courage and the public sphere. In other words, radical pedagogy needs a discourse that illuminates the ideological and material conditions necessary to promote critical modes of schooling and alternative modes of education for the working class and other groups that bear the brunt of political and economic oppression. The starting point for such a discourse, I believe, centers around the notion of the public sphere and the implications this has for radical pedagogy and political struggle both within and outside of the schools.

As Habermas (1964) and others[1] have pointed out, the notion of the public sphere is not new. Historically, the public sphere arose during the early stages of capitalism in the seventeenth century, and originally represented those ideological and material spaces constructed by the bourgeoisie to interpret, reason, and mediate, through rationally informed discourse, questions of culture and everyday life, and questions of politics and the state. The value of the public sphere, in its classical liberal form, rested in its definition and function as an instrument of political change and emancipation. That is, as a set of practices, institutions, and values, it provided a mediating space between the state and private existence. Moreover, it was rooted in an interest aimed at promoting emancipatory processes through collective self-reflection and discourse. The liberal public sphere, in one sense, can be understood as a specific form of political practice that takes as its central concern the organizing of human experience so as to enable individuals to formulate interpretations of social reality in a critical and emancipatory fashion. Hohendahl's analysis of the public sphere is illuminating on this issue:

> The bourgeois public sphere . . . constituted itself in the 17th and 18th centuries as a sphere *(sui generis)* situated between the absolutistic state and bourgeois society, i.e., between the world of social labor and commodity trade. It consists of discoursing *(rasonierende)* private persons who critically negate political norms of the state and its monopoly on interpretation. The object of discourse is, on the one hand, questions of literature and art and, on the other, the theory and practice of absolutistic domination. Public opinion institutionalizes itself with the goal of replacing decisionistic secret politics with a form of domination that is legitimated by means of rational consensus among participating citizens. This model of public sphere recognizes neither social differences nor privileges. Equality of the members and general accessibility are assumed, even if they cannot be realized in specific situations. The revolutionary potential of the model is attributed to the fact that it makes possible, even demands, its application to all social groups. The public sphere sees itself clearly distinguished both from the state and from the private domain [Hohendahl 1979].

The notion of the public sphere represents both an ideal and a referent for critique and social transformation. As an ideal, it posits the need for the ideological and cultural conditions necessary for active citizenship. That is, it signifies the need for an enlightened citizenry able to rationalize power through the medium of public discussion under conditions free from domination. As a referent for critique, it calls into question the gap between the promise and the reality of the existing liberal public spheres. In one sense, the concept of the public sphere reveals the degree to which culture has become a commodity to be consumed and produced as part of the logic of reification rather than in the interest of enlightenment and self-determination. Rooted in market interests and benefiting the process of capital accumulation, culture no longer serves as the object of discussion, i.e., as a vehicle for individual and social critique. Instead, "it has become a commodity and is consumed accordingly as leisure-time activity. Its goal is to reproduce labor power" (Hohendahl 1979). It is equally important to recognize that the structural alterations of capitalist societies in the West during the nineteenth and twentieth centuries has vitiated, in great part, the conditions for a democratic public sphere. Formal democracy has subsumed substantive democracy in bourgeois society, and behind the facade of elections and plebescites hide economic and political interests that depoliticize the masses while simultaneously exploiting them. Collective discussions have given way to publicity campaigns, advertisements, and other forms of legitimation; furthermore, class, gender, and racial inequalities vitiate the possibilities for unrestricted discourse and the possibility for all social groups to "participate in public life in accordance with [their] self-conscious interests" (Aronowitz 1973). As a referent for social transformation, the public sphere provides new opportunities for reformulating the dialectical relationship between the sociocultural realms and the power manifested in the state and the control of the means of production. In other words, it constitutes the sociocultural realm of society as an important terrain in the ideological battle for the appropriation of the state, the economy, and the transformation of everyday life. I shall now turn to this issue, focusing primarily on the role that teachers can assume in such a struggle.

If a radical pedagogy is to become conscious of its own limitations and strengths within the existing society, it must be viewed as having an important but limited role in the struggle for oppressed groups to reclaim the ideological and material conditions for organizing their own experiences. In other words, schools will have to be seen as only one significant site providing an "opening" for revealing capitalist (and other oppressive) ideologies, and for reconstructing more emancipatory relations. For teachers, this suggests developing a critical understanding of those economic and political interests outside of schools that directly infringe upon the processes of schooling via policy enactments, the distribution of resources, and tax-cuts. Struggles within the schools have to be understood and linked to alliances and social formations which can effect policy decisions relating to the control and content of schooling. In effect, radical teachers will have to establish organic connections with those excluded majorities who inhabit the neighborhoods, towns, and cities in which schools are located. On the one hand, such an alliance points to the need to get working-class people, minorities of color, and women actively involved in the shaping of school policies and experiences. Rather than being the object of school policy, these groups must become the subject of such policy making. Moreover, although such a view runs counter to the conservative logic of teacher professionalism and expertise, particularly in the United States, it provides new possibilities for democratizing the schools and broadening the opportunities for community support of teacher struggles. On the other hand, radical teachers will have to be deeply involved in struggles outside of the apparatuses of the state to develop alternative public spheres and counter-educational institutions that provide the conditions and issues around which people could organize in ways that reflect their own needs and actual experiences. Johnson's notion of being actively educative captures the essence of this strategy:

> Being actively educative is not just a question of "carrying a policy to the public" or destroying myths about education. It involves learning too. It involves really listening to popular experiences of formal education. It involves research, centering around particular struggles and local issues. It involves making links with other local agencies—researchers, community activists, black groups, women's groups—not to take them over, but to learn from their experiences and practices. It involves creating a real branch life at the level of ward and constituency, something actively to look forward to, energizing rather than deadening, developing socialist understandings and commitment. It involves extending this activity beyond a narrow local membership, organizing events and activities on a more open basis, not requiring immediate political commitment from those attending [Johnson 1981].

As part of this perspective, radical pedagogues will have to abandon the traditional leftist policy of treating the oppressed within the boundaries of a unitary discourse. They will have to insert the notion of the concrete back into a theory of radical pedagogy and take seriously the specific needs, problems, and concerns of everyday life. The point is, of course, to link the personal and the political so as to understand how power is reproduced, mediated, and resisted at the level of daily existence. Inherent in such an understanding are the theoretical elements of a cultural politics that establishes the preconditions for alternative public spheres.

For radical pedagogues, the dual role that emerges out of this analysis centers around a distinction between education and schooling. In effect, this distinction speaks not only to different regions or spheres of struggle, it also points to different methods of inquiry and social practices. Edu-

cation has a direct link to the creation of alternative publ
it represents both an ideal and a strategy in the service o
social and economic democracy. As the embodiment of a
to forms of learning and action based on a commitment tc
of forms of class, racial, and gender oppression. As a mode of intellectual
development and growth, its focus is political in the broadest sense;
education deals with needs and issues that arise from the groups involved,
while simultaneously drawing upon theoretical constructs that allow the
participants to situate such issues within a wider historical, social, and
economic context. In other words, education, as used in this context,
takes place outside of established institutions and spheres. Moreover, it
represents a collectively produced set of experiences organized around
issues and concerns that allow for a critical understanding of everyday
oppression while at the same time providing the knowledge and social
relations that become the foundation for struggling against such oppression. In effect, education represents the central category in the development of alternative public spheres. It refers to critique and the
restructuring of social experiences based on new forms of communicative
interaction and the reappropriation of cultural modes of communication.
As a mode of production, education "combats the influence of the school,
the workplace, and mass culture in destroying critical sensibilities"
(Aronowitz 1973). As part of an alternative public sphere, it organizes
and uses, where possible, the technology of science and the mass media
to promote dialogue and democratic forms of communication. Of course,
situating the technology of science and the mass media in new social
relations also becomes part of the task of providing a new ideology and
view of the world to others in the wider society.

For teachers, education points to the need to work with adults around
issues directly related to their lives, their cultural capital. It means acting
not simply as teachers, but as citizens, or, if you will, as "radical educators," struggling to establish a social and economic democracy. As
radical educators, we can help destroy the myths that education and
schooling are the same phenomenon; we can debunk the notion that
expertise and academic credentials are the primary qualifications of the
"intellectual", and, equally important, we can provide, discuss, and learn
from historical and contemporary examples in which working-class people
and others have come together to create alternative public spheres. Clearly,
the elements of a democratic pedagogy can be exhibited not only through
the social relations that radical educators may help to establish, but also

through an examination of historically specific examples in the various organizations, clubs, cultural activities, and media productions developed by, for instance, the English working class in the nineteenth and twentieth centuries (Thompson 1966; Hakken 1981),[2] or the traditions of worker education developed in the United States throughout the beginning of the twentieth century, etc. Needless to say, such educational work would also promote critical analyses of schooling itself and its relation to other institutions included in the liberal public sphere.

The concept of radical educator also points to a view of theory and practice that needs to be redefined and restructured if the goal of creating alternative public spheres is to be taken seriously. All too often, the theory and practice relation has been recycled on the terrain of political pedagogy so as to reproduce the division between conception and execution. Teachers and other such "intellectuals" are seen as theorists, and the people who are alleged to benefit from such theorizing are the objects and agents of practice. Such a view is demeaning to the concept of radical pedagogy and struggle, and it suffers from a thorough misunderstanding about how human agents mediate and act on the world. In effect, it fails to comprehend that people in different structural and social positions are constantly theorizing at different levels of abstraction and within different sets of ideological assumptions and discourses about the nature of social reality. The interface between theory and practice is not at the point where "radicals" provide prescriptions and parents, workers, and the oppressed receive and utilize them; instead, it is at the point where these various groups come together and raise the fundamental question of how they may enlighten each other, and how through such an exchange (of theoretical positions) a mode of practice might emerge in which all groups may benefit. This is not meant to suggest that all theories should be given equal weight—such a view is a form of relativistic nonsense. It does mean that the human subject should be reintroduced into the process of theorizing. The truth claims of specific theoretical perspectives have to be analyzed and mediated through dialogue and democratic social relations (it is assumed that university academics, for instance, can listen and learn something from teachers, staff workers, etc.). Central to such a process is the fundamental notion of critique, a notion that should inform such exchanges and processes. More specifically, critique should be organized around historical and sociological modes of analysis. That is, the "self" and the wider society must be understood as socially constructed and historically constituted through social practices that are contradictory in nature but anchored in a totality of dialectical relations, i.e., society. Moreover, analyses of the social, political, and economic conditions that characterize a given society, and the constraints they promote, should be judged against ethical concerns regarding whether the existing totality of relations in such a society should be sustained or transformed. Finally, the processes that inform theory and practice within the parameters of an alternative public sphere have to be grounded in a notion of transcendence. As used here, transcendence speaks to an affirmative vision regarding the development of a new society, a democratic notion of sociability, and the development of social conditions that maximize individual and social possibilities to expand what Bahro (1978) has called the "rich individuality" of all people.

Schooling, as I use the term, is distinct from education in that it takes place within institutions that serve the interests of the state. These are formal institutions directly or indirectly linked to the state through public funding or through certification requirements. Within these institutions, individuals assuming the role of radical teacher often find themselves working within structural and ideological constraints that both limit and enable in varying degrees their opportunities to develop critical modes of pedagogy. Since I have presented in detail throughout this book elements of what I consider to be a radical pedagogy for school settings, I will limit my remarks here on the role of radical teachers to a few concerns. First, as teachers, radicals must start with their own social and theoretical perspectives regarding their views about society, teaching, and emancipation. Teachers cannot escape from their own ideologies (and in some cases should embrace them), and it is important to understand what society has made of us, what it is we believe in, and how we can minimize the effects on our students of those parts of our "sedimented" histories that reproduce dominant interests and values. Teachers work under constraints, but within those constraints they structure and shape classroom experiences and need to be self-reflexive about what interests guide such behavior. Put another way, as teachers we need to reach into our own histories and attempt to understand how issues of class, culture, gender, and race have left their imprint upon how we think and act. Second, radical teachers must strive to make school democracy possible. This is particularly important when it comes to working with groups outside of the school so as to give them a voice, as I have previously mentioned, in the control and sharing of curriculum and school policy. The democratization of schooling also involves the need for teachers to build alliances with other teachers. Not only do such alliances lend credence to the extension of democratically informed social relations in other public spheres, they also promote new forms of social relations and modes of pedagogy within the school itself. The cellular structure of teaching is one of the worst aspects of the division of labor. The Taylorization of the work process, as it is manifested in schools, represents one of the greatest structural constraints that teachers face, i.e., it isolates teachers and reifies hierarchical forms of decision making and authoritarian modes of control. Finally, it must be remembered that radical pedagogy either within or outside of schools involves linking critique to social transformation, and, as such, means taking risks. To be committed to a radical transformation of the existing society in all of its manifestations always places the individual or the group in the position of losing a job, security, and in some cases friends. Often, as radicals, we are powerless in the face of such repercussions, and the only consolation is to know that others are struggling as well, that the values and ideas one fights for are rooted not only in ethical principles but in an obligation to the past, to our families, friends, and comrades who have suffered under these dismal systems of oppression. Of course, we also struggle for the future—for our children and for the promise of a more just society.

What this suggests is that radical pedagogy needs to be informed by a passionate faith in the necessity of struggling to create a better world. In other words, radical pedagogy needs a vision—one that celebrates not what is but what could be, that looks beyond the immediate to the future and links struggle to a new set of human possibilities. This is a call for a concrete utopianism. It is a call for alternative modes of experience, public spheres that affirm one's faith in the possibility of creative risk-taking, of engaging life so as to enrich it; it means appropriating the critical impulse so as to lay bare the distinction between reality and the conditions that conceal its possibilities. This is the task we face if we would build a society where alternative public spheres will no longer be necessary.

Notes

Chapter 1 / Critical Theory and Educational Practice

1. Of course, the notion of depth psychology as a social and political category did not make its first appearance in the work of the Frankfurt School; its historical, political, and theoretical roots were first established in the early works of Wilhelm Reich (1949, 1970, 1971, 1972). Reich's work is important because it exercised a strong influence on figures such as Erich Fromm, who was one of the first members of the Frankfurt School to display a serious interest in Freud's work. Moreover, the work of Reich and Fromm influenced in both a positive and negative manner the way in which Adorno, Horkheimer, and Marcuse developed their own perspectives on Freudian psychology.

Wilhelm Reich (1949, 1970) began with the assumption that the rise of authoritarianism in Europe in the 1920s and the willingness of sections of the working class to participate in such movements could not be explained by the breakdown of social relations into merely economic and political categories. While the latter were clearly important in any discussion of domination, they did not address the question of how domination was internalized by the oppressed. Put another way, such categories could not provide an answer to the question of how it was possible that the oppressed could participate actively in their own oppression.

In attempting to answer these questions, Reich's early work provided both a critique of orthodox Marxism and an elaboration of the role that Freudian   243 thought might play in deepening and extending a critical Marxist perspective. For Reich as well as the Frankfurt School, "crude" Marxism had eliminated the notion of subjectivity and as such had blundered both theoretically and politically. Theoretically, European Marxism in the early 1920s had failed to develop a much-needed political psychology because of its indifference to the issues of subjectivity and the politics of everyday life. On the other hand, it blundered politically because by abandoning a concern for issues such as human motivation, the nature of human desire, and the importance of human needs as fundamental components of a theory of political change, it had surrendered to Hitler and Fascism the opportunity to mobilize both working-class and middle-class groups. This was accomplished by engaging their emotions and appealing through propagandistic techniques to important psychic needs such as solidarity, community, nationalism, and self-identity. Reich is worth quoting on this issue:

> One element in the fundamental cause of the failure of socialism—only an element, but an important one, no longer to be ignored, no longer to be regarded as secondary—is the absence of an effective doctrine of political psychology. . . . This shortcoming of ours has become the greatest advantage of the class enemy, the mightiest weapon of fascism. While we presented the masses with superb historical analyses and economic treatises on the contradictions of imperialism, Hitler stirred the deepest roots of their emotional being. As Marx would have put it, we left the praxis of the subjective factor to the idealists; we acted like mechanistic, economistic materialists [Reich 1971].

For Reich, the obstacles to political change could be overcome, in part, by delineating "the exact place of psychoanalysis within Marxism" (Jacoby 1975). In Reich's (1972) terms, this meant uncovering the way in which concrete mediations, whether they be in the form of discourse, social relations, or the productions of the mass media, functioned so as to produce the internalization of values and ideologies that inhibited the development of individual and collective social consciousness. Central to Reich's (1970, 1971) early focus on explaining the role of psychoanalysis within a Marxist perspective was his emphasis on character structure, the role of the family as an oppressive agency of socialization, and the importance of sexual repression as a basis for authoritarianism.

As one of the first members of the Frankfurt School to display a sustained interest in Freud's work, Erich Fromm (1941, 1947) occupies an important place in the attempt to locate psychoanalysis within a Marxist framework. Like Reich, Fromm was interested in Freud's attempt to reveal linkages between the individual and society that illuminated the dynamics of psychological repression and social domination. Fromm's (1970) early work on the patriarchal family, as well as his modifications of Freud's ahistorical view of the unconscious, exercised a significant influence on Adorno, Horkheimer, and Marcuse. Equally important is the negative influence that Fromm had on these theorists. As Fromm later rejected many of his early formulations regarding Freud's work—particularly as he shifted his focus from a psychology of the unconscious to one of the conscious, from sexuality to morality, and from repression to personality development— the Frankfurt School began to fashion its own diverse versions of Freudian theory. This development, then, was in reaction to Fromm's revisionist reading of psychoanalysis.

Chapter 2 / Schooling and the Hidden Curriculum

1. I am heavily indebted to the work of Madeleine Arnot (formerly Mac-Donald) for this section on gender studies. Her work, in my estimation, represents the best attempt within a theory of education to develop a systematic analysis of gender and schooling. Cf. Arnot (1981, 1982); MacDonald (1980, 1981).

2. A representative example of this work can be found in Jackson (1968), Overly (1970), Dreeben (1968a), Keddie (1971), Dale (1977), Anyon (1980), and Giroux and Purple (1982).

3. I have purposely excluded the work of Anarchists such as Illich and Spring, because their work has either been incorporated into the more recent work of the new sociology of education or is outdated. For a review of this work, see Dale (1977).

4. For a good critique of this position, see Hogan (1979).

Chapter 3 / Reproduction, Resistance, and Accommodation

1. The point here is that students may display behavior that violates school rules while the logic that informs such behavior is firmly rooted in forms of ideological hegemony such as racism and sexism. Moreover, the source of such hegemony generally originates outside of the school, particularly in the family, the peer group or in the industrialized culture. Under such circumstances, schools become social sites where oppositional behavior simply gets played out. In this case, less as a critique of schooling than as an expression of ideological hegemony. This becomes clearer in McRobbie's (1978) account of sixth-form female students in England who by aggressively asserting their own sexuality appear to be rejecting the official ideology of the school with its sexually repressive emphasis on neatness, passivity, compliance, and "femininity." This takes the form of carving boyfriends' names on school desks, wearing makeup and tight-fitting clothes, flaunting their sexual preferences for older, more mature boys, and

spending endless amounts of time talking about boys and boyfriends. Rather than suggesting resistance, I think this type of oppositional behavior displays an oppressive mode of sexism. Its organizing principle appears to be linked to social practices informed by the objective of developing a sexual and ultimately successful marriage relation with a male, and, as such, it underscores a logic that has little to do with resistance to school norms and a great deal to do with the sexism that characterizes working-class life and the mass culture in general.

This leads to a related issue. Resistance theories have gone too far in viewing schools as institutions characterized exclusively by forms of ideological domination. Lost from this view is the insight that schools are also repressive institutions that use various coercive state agencies, including the police and the courts, to enforce involuntary school attendance. Consequently, in some cases, students may be totally indifferent to the dominant ideology of the school, with its respective rewards and demands. Their behavior within schools may be fueled by ideological imperatives that point to issues and concerns that have little to do with school in the most direct sense. School just happens to be the place where the oppositional nature of these concerns gets worked out. Such behavior may be oppositional but at the same time it may have little to do with registering a protest against the logic of schooling. As in the case of McRobbie's girls, the culture of aggressive sexuality displayed by them not only suggests an enormous indifference to school, but also a form of ideology that is incompatible with the task of social reconstruction. In other words, in the final analysis this form of oppositional behavior collapses under the weight of its own dominating logic and cannot be celebrated as resistance.

2. One of the major problems characterizing resistance theories, as Walker (forthcoming) points out, is that they have focused primarily on overt, publicly rebellious acts of student behavior. By limiting their analyses to this type of behavior, resistance theorists have ignored less obvious forms of resistance among students and have often misconstrued the political value of resistance displayed by the "showy rebels." For instance, some students go through the daily routines of schooling by minimizing their participation in school practices while simultaneously displaying outward conformity to the ideology of the school. That is, these students opt for modes of resistance that are quietly subversive in the most immediate sense, but potentially politically progressive in the long run. These students may resort to using humor to disrupt a class, to using collective pressure to get teachers away from class lessons, or to purposely ignoring teacher directions and doing what is necessary to develop collective spaces that allow them to escape the ethos of individualism that permeates school life. Each of these modes of behavior points to a form of resistance as long as the context out of which it emerges represents a latent or overt ideological condemnation of the underlying repressive ideologies that characterize schools in general. That is, if we view these acts as practices involving a conscious or semiconscious political response

to school-constructed relations of domination, they then can be viewed as acts of resistance that are politically more progressive than those performed by the showy rebels. In otherwords, these students are resisting school ideology in a manner that gives them the power to reject the system on a level that does not make them powerless in the future to protest it, i.e., not having access to knowledge and skills that allow them to move beyond the class-specific positions of dead-end, alienating labor that most of the showy rebels will eventually occupy (Willis 1977). Of course, in some cases students might be aware that while it is easy to display immediate subversive acts of rebelliousness, it makes more sense to challenge the system at a later date and under different circumstances. That is, students may actively resist the school on an ideological level, and see very clearly through its lies and promises but decide not to translate this insight into extreme forms of rebelliousness because to do so would make them powerless in the most immediate sense and in terms of their future lives. Of course, it is feasible that they may get through school on terms that they define and still face limited opportunities in the future. The point here is that any other alternative seems ideologically naive and limits whatever transcendent hopes for the future they may have. It is in the tension between the present reality of their lives and their willingness to dream of the possibility of a better world that makes such students potential political leaders. Of course, in some cases, students may not be aware of the political grounds of their position towards school, except for a general awareness of its dominating nature and the need to somehow escape from it, but under conditions that do not isolate them or relegate them to a future they do not want. Even this vague understanding and its attendant behavior portends a politically progressive logic. I would argue that one of the most important measures of school resistance is to be found not in the overt behavior of students but in the nature of their attitudes toward school as an hegemonic institution. The varied relations between oppositional and accommodating attitudes and behavior and the significance of each for a theory of resistance can be seen in the following analysis. Students characterized as having either an "understood" or a highly critical awareness of their own school ideology could be labeled as (S-), whereas their behavior might be slightly oppositional on the surface (B). Other students such as the showy rebels might exhibit both strongly oppositional ideologies and highly non-conformist behavior (S-) and (B-), or they may exhibit accommodating or coping subjective perceptions of school ideology (S), while simultaneously displaying a form of behavior that is strongly oppositional in nature (B-), i.e., accepting school ideology about the nature of failure, commodity logic, etc. but at the same time resisting one's involuntary presence in such schools. Moreover, students who display highly conformist postures would exhibit relatively compatible positive attitudes and behavior (S +) and (B +) toward school. Again, I believe that the students who provide the greatest potential for radical moral and intellectual leadership would be those who reject the ideology of the school (S−) and at the same time understand the need to work within social practices and relations (B) that allow them to learn eventually how to critique and organize themselves around the principles of individual and social determination. On the other hand, the showy rebels (S−) and (B−), or (S) and (B−), generally cut themselves off from this possibility by rejecting the relationship between knowledge and power and opting for forms of oppositional behavior that are exclusively symbolic and cultural in nature.

3. A theory of resistance is central to the development of a radical pedagogy because it points to those social practices in schools that are organized around hegemonic principles and the mixture of accommodating and resistant practices that accompany them. For instance, it points to the hegemonic curriculum and to its hierarchically organized bodies of knowledge, particularly the way in which working-class knowledge is marginalized (Connell, et al 1982). Furthermore, it points to the effects of such a curriculum, with its emphasis on individual rather than collective appropriation of knowledge, and how this drives a wedge between school administrators and teachers and working-class parents. Of course, the hegemonic curriculum not only divides parents from school staff, it also promotes class and gender specific relations around the production and distribution of knowledge; equally important is the way the individual appropriation of such knowledge often works to pit students from both outside and within different social classes against each other. In addition, theories of resistance illuminate the way in which teacher-student relations often work to the benefit of some groups and not others. This is evident in the social divisions between teachers and the working-class as a group, particularly as such divisions are manifested in the different forms of tracking, teaching, and evaluation procedures that differentially characterize students from the various social classes.

Chapter 5 / Critical Theory in Citizenship Education

1. For an excellent discussion of the classical doctrine of politics, see Wolin (1960), Habermas (1973), and Iglitzin (1972).

2. The literature on this issue is much too extensive to cite thoroughly. Informative summaries of these findings can be found in Franklin (1974a); Tyack (1974); Spring (1976); Torney, Oppenheim, and Farmen (1975); Brown (1977); National Assessment of Educational Progress (1978); Metzger and Barr (1978); Shaver, Davis, and Helburn (1979); and Ehrman (1979).

3. Studies that exemplify the revisionist historians' view include Katz (1968), Greer (1972), Spring (1972), and Bowles and Gintis (1976). A recent critique of the revisionist position can be found in Ravitch (1978). Some of the more recent works that use the revisionist perspective to examine classroom

practices include Apple (1979), Giroux and Penna (1979), Benet and Daniels (1980), and Anyon (1980).

4. The notion of social control is an ambiguous term and its usage needs to be qualified. Social control is not always a negative phenomenon, particularly when it is seen as an inherent part of any social system. A more precise definition of the term would focus on whether it was used to maximize democratic and economic rights in a country or to further the privileges, power, and wealth of one social group at the expense of other groups. It is in the latter sense that the term is being used in this essay. For an elaboration of this issue, see Feinberg (1975), Franklin (1974a), Kliebard (1979), and Giroux (1981).

5. This theme is developed in Dewey (1971), particularly chapters 4 and 5.

6. The term *positivism* has gone through so many changes since it was first used by Saint-Simon and Comte that it is virtually impossible to narrow its meaning to a specific school of thought or a well-defined perspective. Thus, any discussion of positivism will be broad and devoid of clearcut boundaries. However, we can speak of the "culture of positivism" as the legacy of positivistic thought, a legacy which includes those convictions, attitudes, techniques, and concepts that still exercise a powerful and pervasive influence on modern thought. In the sense that the term is used here, it appropriates the different dimensions of positivism that are both historical and epistemologically specific. That is, it refers to a legacy of thought that looks at the commonalities that join epistemological, sociological, economic, and political dimensions of positivism. Epistemologically, we can see positivism emerge from the writings of Comte to the Vienna School to the present-day writings of "reflectionist" theorists. In schools, we see the residue of this type of positivism in curricula which objectify knowledge, support a transmission form of pedagogy, and separate conception from execution. Sociologically, we see the legacy of positivism in social relationships that were first systematically structured under the notion of the scientific management movement of the 1920s. In schools, we see the legacy of this movement in those types of social encounters in which roles are hierarchically arranged in rigid fashion and where the emphasis is on individual performance rather than collective interaction. Economically, the changing nature of positivism has moved from a science of management control in which workers performed isolated tasks on machines to forms of atomized behavior which program machines designed to regulate other mechanized aspects of the labor process. Politically, the legacy of positivism carries with it changing social relationships and social formations based on a separation of power and a division of labor rooted in class specific interests. See Giroux (1979).

7. This concept has received its most extensive treatment in Bachelard (1968), Althusser (1969), Laclau (1977), and Castells and de Ipalo (1979).

8. See Apple (1979) and Franklin (1974b). An exceptional critique of the

"new technology" movement in recent curriculum writings can be found in Andrews and Hakken (1977).

9. Representative examples of the work under analysis here include Fenton (1966); Hanna and Lee (1968); and Price, Hickman, and Smith (1965).

10. The hermeneutic tradition finds its strongest philosophical expression in the works of Gadamer (1977), Schutz (1967); and Winch (1972). A good collection of writings can be found in Douglas (1973).

11. In the United States this type of work is probably best represented by a number of traditions ranging from the free school movement of the early 1960s, the open school movement, various offshoots that support a Freire-like approach to education, and various branches of humanistic pedagogy. An analysis of these traditions can be found in Giroux (1981).

12. See Remy and Turner (1979). A critical overview of these positions can be found in Newmann (1980).

13. The enthusiasm for this approach sometimes appears to reach dizzying heights. For example, Metzger and Barr (1978) seem to believe that the essence of citizenship education lies in a combination of positive political attitudes in students and the support the latter receive in open school environments which encourage decision making and participation. The concept of false consciousness and the notion that student participation may take place within narrowly defined parameters of power appear to disappear in these studies.

14. See Engle (1960). The positivist nature of this assumption, that radical decision making should assume higher priority in the social studies than Verstehen and social reconstructionism, compromises much of the hermeneutic rationality underlying this mode of citizenship education.

15. An interesting discussion of Bourdieu's notion of cultural capital and schooling can be found in MacDonald (1979/80).

16. Two excellent critiques of the notion of pluralism can be found in Wolff (1969) and Clark and Gintis (1978).

17. This is particularly true of the work of Kohlberg and his associates. See Kohlberg and Mayer (1972) and Mosher (1978).

18. I have analyzed the work of a number of these theorists in Giroux (1981). See also Bredo and Feinberg (1979).

Chapter 6 / Literacy, Ideology, and Politics of Schooling

1. I am referring to the United States in this case. Some of the insightful exceptions include Aronowitz (1977), Lazere (1975; 1977), Greene (1978), Elsasser and John-Steiner (1977); Ohmann (1976).

2. See Stricht (1978). An overview and critique of the literature in this perspective can be found in Walmsley (1981).

3. Of course, it must be stressed that liberal and conservative ideologies

have their own internal divisions and contradictions, and neither form of discourse can be viewed as homogeneous. But I would argue that in spite of such differences each ideology is in the broad sense marked by an underlying set of dominant assumptions that provide a selective affinity to either a liberal or conservative world view. See Gintis (1980).

4. An overview and critique of this position can be found in Giroux (1978).

5. For instance, see Neill (1960), Spring (1975), Pine and Boy (1977).

6. For two representative examples see Bleich (1975) and Stahl (1975).

7. A superb critique of this view can be found in Jacoby (1975).

8. For an example of a serious and illuminating approach to the development of a literacy policy in a high school in Canada, see Simon and Willensky (1980).

9. This position is reflected in the early work of Bowles and Gintis (1976).

10. See Chapter 2.

11. But there is an important qualification that must accompany the use of Freire's work in a North American context. There has been such a rapid change in the material and spiritual culture of the United States that developing forms of literacy capable of incorporating the nature and products of this transition is an enormously complex enterprise. Moreover, people need to understand the importance of appropriating these new conditions; for example, they must develop the capacity to fathom how these conditions contribute to their own oppression and how society works—that is, how much more sophisticated and complex is this type of domination compared with that which operates in Brazil.

12. See Lazere (1977), Aronowitz (1977), Giroux (1979–1980). It is important to note that ideologies are not "inscribed" in a text so that they have a clear and unequivocal meaning. "Inscribed" merely means that as a result of what they include and leave out, these texts generally support the messages and ethos of the dominant ideologies. Needless to say, all texts, in varying degrees of complexity, provide open horizons for different interpretations. Texts have to be mediated and, as such, do not simply reproduce themselves; instead they are acted upon by human subjects who mediate their messages. In this way they become part of the production of meaning at the level of consumption. This position is developed in more depth in chapter 4.

13. Representative examples can be found in Labov (1972), Bowers (1981; in press).

14. This position has been inspired by the work of Basil Bernstein (1977), who denies that this was his original intention.

Conclusion

1. In addition to Habermas's (1962, 1974) work on the public sphere, there are important commentaries on the subject by Hohendahl (1974, 1979), Knodler-Bunte (1975), McCarthy (1978), and Paris (1975).

2. Hakken's (1980) work is particularly useful in that it points to a number of organizations and educational institutions established by the workers in Sheffield, England. These include the development of trade union courses, workers research committees, day-release programs for workers to develop educational skills, independent political education groups, etc.

Bibliography

Adorno, T.W. 1967a. *Prisms*, trans. Samuel and Shierry Weber. London: Neville Spearman.

1967b "Sociology and psychology: Part I." *New Left Review*, 46.

1968 "Sociology and psychology: Part II." *New Left Review*, 47.

1969 "Scientific Experiences of a European Scholar in America." In *The Intellectual Migration*, ed. Donald Fleming and Bernard Bailyn. Cambridge, Mass.: Harvard University Press.

Adorno, T.W., and M. Horkheimer, 1972. *Dialectic of Enlightenment*, trans. John Cumming. New York: Seabury Press.

1973 *Negative Dialectics*. New York: Seabury Press.

1975 "The Culture Industry Reconsidered." *New German Critique*, 6 (Fall).

1976 "On the Logic of the Social Sciences." In *The Positivist Dispute in German Sociology*, T.W. Adorno et al. London: Heinemann.

1978 "On Culture and Administration." *Telos*, 37 (Fall).

Agger, B. 1978. "Work and Authority in Marcuse and Habermas." *Human Studies*, 2(3) (July).

Althusser, Louis. 1969. *For Marx*. New York: Vintage Books.

1970 *Reading "Capital."* London: New Left Books.

1971 "Ideology and the Ideological State Apparatuses." In *Lenin and Philosophy, and Other Essays*, trans. Ben Brewster. New York: Monthly Review Press.

Andrews, B., and D. Hakken. 1977. "Educational Technology: A Theoretical Discussion." *College English*, 39 (Sept.).

Anyon, J. 1979a. "Ideology and U.S. History Textbooks." *Harvard Educational Review,* 49.

1979b "Structure and the Power of Individuals." *Theory and Research in Social Education,* 7.

1980 "Social Class and the Hidden Curriculum of Work." *Journal of Education,* 162 (Winter).

1981a "Elementary Schooling and Distinctions of Social Class." *Interchange,* 12.

1981b "Social Class and School Knowledge." *Curriculum Inquiry,* 11(1) (Spring).

Apel, K.O. 1977. "The A-Priori of Communication and the Foundation of the Humanities." In *Understanding Social Inquiry,* ed. Fred Dallmay and Thomas McCarthy. Indiana: University of Notre Dame Press.

1979 "Types of Social Science in the Light of Human Cognitive Interests." In *Philosophical Disputes in the Social Sciences,* ed. S.C. Brown. Sussex: Harvester Press.

1980 *Towards a Transformation Philosophy.* Boston and London: Routledge & Kegan Paul.

Appelbaum, R. 1979. "Born Again in Functionalism? A Reconsideration of Althusser's Structuralism." *Insurgent Sociologist,* 9.

Apple, M.W. 1971. "The Hidden Curriculum and the Nature of Conflict." *Interchange,* 2(4).

1979 *Ideology and Curriculum.* London and Boston: Routledge & Kegan Paul.

1981 "Curricular Form and the Logic of Technical Control." In *Rethinking Curriculum Studies,* ed. L. Barton, R. Meighan, and S. Walker. Lewes, England: Falmer Press.

1982 *Education and Power.* Boston: Routledge & Kegan Paul.

Apple, M.W., and W. Feinberg. Forthcoming. "On the Dangers of Deskilling Teacher Education." *Compact: The Journal of the Education Commission of the States.*

Apple, M.W., and N. King, 1977. "What Do Schools Teach?" In *Humanistic Education.* Berkeley: McCutchan.

Arato, A., and E. Gebhardt, eds. 1978. *The Essential Frankfurt School Reader.* New York: Urizen Books.

Arnot, M. 1981. "Culture and Political Economy: Dual Perspectives on the Sociology of Women's Education." *Educational Analysis,* 3(1).

Arnot, M., and G. Whitty. 1982. "From Reproduction to Transformation: Recent Radical Perspectives on the Curriculum from the USA." *British Journal of Sociology of Education,* 3(1).

Aronowitz, S. 1973. *False Promises.* New York: McGraw-Hill.

1976 "Enzenberger on Mass Culture: A Review Essay." *Minnesota Review,* 7 (Fall).

1977 "Marx, Braverman, and the Logic of Capital." *Insurgent Sociologist,* 8 (2, 3) (Apr.).

1980 "Science and Ideology." *Current Perspectives in Social Theory,* 1.

1981a *The Crisis in Historical Materialism: Class, Politics, and Culture in Marxist Theory.* New York: Bergin.

1981b "Redefining Literacy." *Social Policy* (Sept.-Oct.).

Bachelard, G. 1968. *The Philosophy of No.* New York: Orion Press.

Bahro, R. 1978. *The Alternative in Eastern Europe.* London: New Left Books.

Bantock, G.H. 1968. *Culture, Industrialization, and Education.* London: Routledge & Kegan Paul.

Baron, S., D. Finn, N. Grant, M. Green, and R. Johnson. 1981. *Unpopular Education.* London: Hutchinson & Co.

Barr, R., D. Barth, and S.S. Shermis. 1977. *Defining the Social Studies.* Washington, D.C.: National Council for the Social Studies.

Barrett, M. 1980. *Women's Oppression Today.* London: Verso Books.

1981 "Materialist Aesthetics." *New Left Review,* 126.

Barth, J.L., and S.S. Shermis. 1979. "Defining Social Problems." *Theory and Research in Social Education,* 7(1).

Barth, R. 1957. *Mythologies.* Paris: Seuil.

1975 *S/Z.* London: Jonathan Cape.

1977 *Image, Music, Text: Essays.* London: Fontana.

Bates, R. 1981. "New Developments in the New Sociology of Education." *British Journal of Sociology of Education,* 1(1) (Mar.).

Baudelot, C., and R. Establet. 1971. *L'Ecole Capitaliste en France.* Paris: Francois Maspero.

Becker, H. 1961. *Boys in White.* Chicago: University of Chicago Press.

Bee, B. 1980. "The Politics of Literacy." In *Literacy and Revolution: The Pedagogy of Paulo Freire,* ed. Robert Mackie. London: Pluto Press.

Benet, J., and A.K. Daniels, eds. 1980. *Education: Straitjacket or Opportunity.* New Brunswick, N.J.: Transaction Books.

Benjamin, J. 1977. "The End of Internationalization: Adorno's Social Psychology." *Telos,* 32 (Summer).

Benjamin, W. 1969 In *Illuminations,* ed. Hannah Arendt. New York: Schocken.

1974 In *Über den Begriff der Geschichte: Gesammelte Schriften,* 1(2), ed. Rolf Tiedemann and Hermann Schweppenhauser, Abhandlungen, Suhrkamp Verlag, Frankfurt am Main.

1977 *The Origin of German Tragic Drama,* trans. John Osborne. London: New Left Books.

Bennett, T. 1979. *Formalism and Marxism.* London: Methuen.

1980a "Popular Culture: A Teaching Object." *Screen Education,* 34 (Spring).

1980b "The Not-So-Good, the Bad, and the Ugly." *Screen Education,* 36 (Autumn).

1981 *Popular Culture: History and Theory*. London: Open University Press.

Berggren, C., and L. Berggren. 1975. *The Literacy Process: A Practice in Domestication or Liberation*. London: Writers & Readers Publishing Cooperative.

Berlak, H. 1977. "Human Consciousness, Social Criticism, and Civic Education." In *Rationales for Citizenship Education*, ed. James P. Shaver. Arlington, Va.: National Council for the Social Studies.

Bernstein, B. 1977. *Class, Codes and Control*. Vol. 3, *Towards a Theory of Educational Transmission*, 2d ed. London: Routledge & Kegan Paul.

1982 "Codes, Modalities, and the Process of Cultural Reproduction: A Model." In *Cultural and Economic Reproduction in Education*, ed. Michael Apple. Boston: Routledge & Kegan Paul.

Bernstein, R.J. 1976. *The Restructuring of Social and Political Thought*. Philadelphia: University of Pennsylvania Press.

Best, M., and W. Connolly. 1979. "Politics and Subjects: The Limits of Structural Marxism." *Socialist Review*, 9(6).

Bisseret, N. 1979. *Education, Class Language, and Ideology*. Boston: Routledge & Kegan Paul.

Bleich, D. 1975. *Readings and Feelings: An Introduction to Subjective Criticisms*. Urbana, Ill.: National Council for Teachers of English.

Bobbitt, F. 1918. *The Curriculum*. Boston: Houghton-Mifflin.

Boggs, C. 1976. *Gramsci's Marxism*. London: Pluto Press.

Bourdieu, P. 1962. *The Algerians*. Boston: Beacon.

1967 "Systems of Education and Systems of Thought." *International Social Science Journal*, 20(4).

1968a "Outline of a Theory of Art Perception." *International Social Science Journal*, 20(4).

1968b "Structuralism and Theory of Sociological Knowledge." *Social Research*, 35(4).

1973 "The Three Forms of Theoretical Knowledge." *Social Science Information*, 12(1).

1975 "The Specificity of the Scientific Field and the Social Conditions of the Progress of Reason." *Social Science Information*, 14(6).

Bourdieu, P., and J.C. Passeron. 1977a. *Reproduction in Education, Society, and Culture*. Beverly Hills, Cal.: Sage.

1977b *Outline of Theory and Practice*. Cambridge: Cambridge University Press.

1977c "Cultural Reproduction and Social Reproduction." In *Power and Ideology in Education*, ed. Jerome Karabel and A.H. Halsey. New York: Oxford University Press.

1978 "Sport and Social Class." *Social Science Information*, 17(6).

1979 "Symbolic Violence." *Critique of Anthropology*, 4(13, 14).

1980a "The Production of Belief: Contributions to an Economy of Symbolic Goods." *Media, Culture and Society*, 2(3).

1980b "The Aristocracy of Culture: Review of the Works of E. Gombrich." *Media, Culture and Society*, 2(3).

Bowers, C.A. In press. "Reproduction of Technological Consciousness: Locating the Ideological Foundations of a Radical Pedagogy." *Teachers College Record*.

1981 "Linguistic Roots of Cultural Hegemony in Freire's Pedagogy." Mimeo. Dept. of Educational Policy and Management, University of Oregon, Eugene.

Bowles, S., and H. Gintis. 1976. *Schooling in Capitalist America*. New York: Basic Books.

1980 "Contradiction and Reproduction in Educational Theory." In *Schooling, Ideology, and the Curriculum*, ed. Len Barton et al. Sussex: Falmer Press.

Boyd, W.L. 1978. "The Changing Politics of Curriculum Policy Making for American Schools." *Review of Educational Research*, 48(4).

Boyne, R.D. 1979. "Breaks and Problematics." *Philosophy and Social Criticism*, 6(2).

Bredo, E., and W. Feinberg. 1974. "Meaning, Power and Pedagogy." *Journal of Curriculum Studies*, 11(4).

Breines, P. 1979/80. "Toward an Uncertain Marxism." *Radical History Review*, 22 (Winter).

Brenkman, J. 1979. "Mass Media: From Collective Experience to the Culture of Privatization." *Social Text*, 1.

Brown, B.F. 1977. *Education for Responsible Citizenship: The Report of the National Task Force on Citizenship Education*. New York: McGraw-Hill.

Brown, J. 1981. "Into the Minds of Babes: Journey through Recent Children's Books." *Radical History*, 25 (Oct.).

Brown, S.C., ed. 1979. *Philosophical Disputes in the Social Sciences*. Sussex: Harvester Press.

Bruner, J. 1960. *The Process of Education*. Cambridge, Mass.: Harvard University Press.

Buck-Morss, S. 1977. *The Origins of Negative Dialectics*. New York: Free Press.

1981a "Walter Benjamin—Revolutionary Writer: Part I." *New Left Review* (128).

1981b "Walter Benjamin—Revolutionary Writer: Part II." *New Left Review* (129).

Buswell, C. 1980. "Pedagogic Change and Social Change." *British Journal of Sociology of Education*, 1(3).

Cagen, E. 1978. "Individualism, Collectivism, and Radical Educational Reform." *Harvard Educational Review*, 48.

Callinicos, A. 1977. *Althusser's Marxism*. London: Pluto Press.

Carnoy, M., and H. Levin. 1976. *The Limits of Educational Reform*. New York: McKay.

Castells, M., and E. De Ipalo. 1979. "Epistemological Practice and the Social Sciences." In *Critical Sociology,* ed. J.W. Freiberg. London: Halsted Press.

Charters, W.W. 1923. *Curriculum Construction.* New York: Macmillan.

Cherryholmes, C. 1979. "Citizenship Education as Critical Decision Making." Paper presented at the annual meeting of the American Educational Research Association, San Francisco, April.

   1980 "Social Knowledge and Citizenship Education: Two Views of Truth and Criticism." *Curriculum Inquiry,* 10(2) (Summer).

Clark, B., and H. Gintis. 1978. "Rawlsian Justice and Economic Systems." *Philosophy and Public Affairs,* 7(4) (Summer).

Clarke, J., et al., eds. 1979. *Working Class Culture: Studies in History and Theory.* London: Hutchinson.

Cohen, J. 1977. "Review of Theory of Need in Marx by Agnes Heller." *Telos,* 33.

Connell, R.W., D.J. Ashenden, S. Kessler, and G.W. Dowsett. 1982. *Making the Difference.* Sydney: George Allen & Unwin.

Connell, R.W., et al. 1981. "Class and Gender Dynamics in a Ruling-Class School." *Interchange,* 12(2, 3).

Connerton, P., ed. 1976. *Critical Sociology.* London: Penguin Books.

Corrigan, P. 1979. *Schooling the Smash Street Kids.* London: Macmillan Press.

Coward, R., and J. Ellis. 1977. *Language and Materialism.* London: Routledge & Kegan Paul.

Dale, R. 1977. "Implications and Rediscovery of the Hidden Curriculum for the Sociology of Teaching." In *Identity and Structure: Issues in the Sociology of Education,* ed. Dennis Gleeson. Driffen, England: Nafferton Books.

Davies, D. 1981. *Popular Culture, Class, and Schooling.* London: Open University Press.

Derrida, J. 1977. *Of Grammatology.* Baltimore: Johns Hopkins Press.

Dewey, J. 1916. *Democracy and Education.* New York: Macmillan.

Donald, J. In press. *Language, Literacy, and Schooling.* London: Open University Press.

Donzelot, J. 1980. *The Policies of Families,* trans. Robert Hurley. New York: Pantheon.

Douglas, M., ed. 1973. *Rules and Meaning.* London: Penguin Books.

Dreeben, R. 1968a. *On What Is Learned in Schools.* Reading, Mass.: Addison-Wesley.

   1968b "The Contribution of Schooling to the Learning of Norms." *Socialization and Schools.* Cambridge, Mass.: Harvard University Press.

Dreier, P. 1980. "Socialism and Cynicism: An Essay on Politics, Scholarship, and Teaching." *Socialist Review,* 10(5) (Sept.-Oct.).

Dreitzel, H.P. 1977. "On the Meaning of Political Culture." In *Beyond the Crisis,* ed. Norm Birnbaum. New York: Oxford University Press.

Durkheim, E. 1969. *L'Évolution Pédagogique en France*. Paris: Presses Universitaires de France.

Eagleton, T. 1978. *Criticism and Ideology*. London: Verso.

Eco, U. 1976. *A Theory of Semiotics*. Bloomington: Indiana University Press.

Edwards, R. 1979. *Contested Terrain*. New York: Basic Books.

Ehrman, L.H. 1979. "Implications for Teaching Citizenship." *Social Education*. 32 (Nov.-Dec.).

Elasser, N., and V.P. John-Steiner. 1977. "An Interactionist Approach to Advancing Literacy." *Harvard Educational Review*, 47(3) (Aug.).

Engle, S. 1960. "Decision Making: The Heart of Social Studies Instruction." *Social Education*, 24 (Nov.).

Entwistle, H. 1979. *Antonio Gramsci: Conservative Schooling for Radical Politics*. Boston: Routledge & Kegan Paul.

Enzenberger, H.M. 1974. *The Consciousness Industry*. New York: Seabury Press.

Erben, M., and D. Gleeson. 1977. "Education as Reproduction: A Critical Examination of Some Aspects of the Work of Louis Althusser." In *Society, State, and Schooling*, ed. G. Whitty and M. Young. Sussex: Falmer Press.

Ewen, S. 1976. *Captains of Consciousness: Advertising and the Social Roots of the Consumer Culture*. New York: McGraw-Hill.

Feenberg, A. 1981. *Lukacs, Marx, and the Sources of Critical Theory*. Totowa, N.J.: Rowman & Littlefield.

Feinberg, W. 1975. *Reason and Rhetoric: The Intellectual Foundations of Twentieth Century Liberal Reform*. New York: Wiley.

1980 "Educational Studies and the Disciplines of Educational Understanding." *Educational Studies*, 10(4) (Winter).

Fenton, E. 1966. "A Structure of History." In *Concepts and Structure in the New Social Science Curricula*, ed. Irving Morrisett. New York: Holt, Rinehart, & Winston.

Finlay, L.S., and V. Faith. 1979. "Illiteracy and Alienation in American Colleges: Is Paulo Friere's Pedagogy Relevant?" *Radical Teacher*, 16 (Dec.).

Foucault, M. 1972. *The Archeology of Knowledge and the Discourse of Language*. New York: Harper & Row.

1977 *Discipline and Punish: The Birth of the Prison*. New York: Pantheon.

1979 *Power, Truth, and Strategy*. Sydney: Feral Publications.

1980 *Power and Knowledge: Selected Interviews and Other Writings*, ed. C. Gordon. New York: Pantheon.

Franklin, B.M. 1974a. "The Curriculum Field and the Problem of Social Control, 1919–1938: A Study in Critical Theory." Ph. D. diss., University of Wisconsin, Madison.

1974b "Education for Social Control." *History of Education Quarterly*, 14.

1976 "Technological Models and the Curriculum Field." *Educational Forum* (Mar.).

Frazier, N., and M. Sadker. 1973. *Sexism in School and Society*. New York: Harper & Row.

Freud, S. 1949. *Civilization and Its Discontents*. London: Hogarth Press.

Friedman, G. 1981. *The Political Philosophy of the Frankfurt School*. Ithaca, N.Y.: Cornell University Press.

Friedman, J. 1978. "The Epistemology of Social Practice: A Critique of Objective Knowledge." *Theory and Society*, 6(1).

Friere, P. 1970. *Cultural Action for Freedom*. Cambridge, Mass.: Harvard Educational Review Monograph (1).

1973 *Pedagogy of the Oppressed*. New York: Seabury Press.

1978a *Education for Critical Consciousness*. New York: Seabury Press.

1978b *Pedagogy in Process*. New York: Seabury Press.

Fromm, E. 1941. *Escape from Freedom*. New York: Farrar & Rinehart.

1947 *Man for Himself*. New York: Farrar & Rinehart.

1955 "The Human Implications of Instinctive 'Radicalism.' " *Dissent*, 4 (Autum).

1962 *Beyond the Chains of Illusion: My Encounter with Marx and Freud*. New York: Simon & Schuster.

1970 *The Crisis of Psychoanalysis*. New York: Holt, Rinehart, & Winston.

Gadamer, H.G. 1977. *Philosophical Hermeneutics*, trans. David E. Linge. Berkeley: University of California Press.

Giarelli, J. In press. "The Cognitive Developmental Theory of Moralization: Toward a Radical Reconstruction." *Journal of Education*.

Giddens, A. 1979. *Central Problems in Social Theory*. Berkeley: University of California Press.

Gintis, H. 1980. "Communications and Politics: Marxism and the Problem of Liberal Democracy." *Socialist Review*, 2–3

Giroux, H.A. 1978. "Writing and Critical Thinking in the Social Studies." *Curriculum Inquiry*, 8(4).

1979 "Schooling and the Culture of Positivism: Notes on the Death of History." *Educational Theory*, 29(4)

1979–80 "Mass Culture and the Rise of the New Illiteracy: Implications for Reading." *Interchange*, 10(4).

1980 "Essay Review of *Antonio Gramsci: Conservative Schooling for Radical Politics*. In *Telos*, 37 (Fall).

1981 *Ideology, Culture, and the Process of Schooling*. Philadelphia: Temple University Press.

Giroux, H.A., and A.N. Penna. 1979. "Social Education in the Classroom: The Dynamics of the Hidden Curriculum." *Theory and Research in Social Education*, 7(1) (Spring).

Giroux, H.A., and D. Purple. 1982. *The Hidden Curriculum and Moral Education: Illusion or Insight*. Berkeley: McCutchan.

Gleeson, D., and G. Whitty. 1976. *Developments in Social Studies Teaching.* London: Open Books.

Goldman, L. 1976. "Theses on the Use of the Concept of 'World View' in the History of Philosophy." In *Cultural Creation*, ed. Lucien Goldman. St. Louis: Telos Press.

Gouldner, A. 1976. *The Dialectic of Ideology and Technology: The Origins, Grammar, and Future of Ideology.* New York: Seabury Press.

1979 *The Future of Intellectuals and the Rise of the New Class.* New York: Seabury Press.

1980 *Two Marxisms: Contradictions and Anomalies in the Development of Theory.* New York: Seabury Press.

Grace, G. 1978. *Teachers, Ideology, and Control: A Study in Urban Education.* Boston and London: Routledge & Kegan Paul.

Graham, P. 1981. "Literacy: A Goal for Secondary Schools." *Daedalus*, 110(3) (Summer).

Gramsci, A. 1971. *Selections from Prison Notebooks*, ed. and trans. Quinten Hoare and Geoffrey Smith. New York: International Publishers.

Gray, W. 1956. *The Teaching of Reading and Writing.* UNESCO Monographs on Fundamental Education (10). Paris: UNESCO.

Greene, M. 1978. *Landscapes of Learning.* New York: Teachers College Press.

Gross, H. 1979. "Adorno in Los Angeles: The Intellectual Emigration." *Humanities in Society*, 2(4) (Fall).

Habermas, J. 1962. *Strukterwandel der Offentlichkeit.* Neuwied: Luchterhand.

1971a *Knowledge and Human Interest.* Boston: Beacon Press.

1971b *Toward a Rational Society.* Boston: Beacon Press.

1973 *Theory and Practice.* Boston: Beacon Press.

1974 "The Public Sphere: An Encyclopedia Article (1964)." *New German Critique*, (3) (Fall).

1975 *Legitimation Crisis.* Boston: Beacon Press.

1979 *Communication and the Evolution of Society*, trans. Thomas McCarthy. Boston: Beacon Press.

1980 "Psychic Thermidor and the Rebirth of Rebellious Subjectivity." *Berkeley Journal of Sociology*, 25.

Hahn, H. 1933. "Logik Mathematik and Naturerkennen." In *Einheitswissenschaft*, ed. Otto Neurath et al. Vienna: n.p.

Hakken, D. 1980. "Workers' Education and the Reproduction of Working-Class Culture." *Anthropology and Education Quarterly*, 11(4) (Winter).

Hall, S. 1981. "Cultural Studies: Two Paradigms." In *Culture, Ideology, and Social Process*, ed. T. Bennett et al. London: Batsford Academic & Educational.

Hall, S., and T. Jefferson. 1976. *Resistance through Rituals.* London: Hutchinson & Co.

Hanna, P., and J. Lee. 1968. "Generalizations from the Social Sciences." In *Structure in the Social Studies*. Washington, D.C.: National Council for the Social Studies.

Hargreaves, A. 1982. "Resistance and Relative Autonomy Theories." *British Journal of Sociology of Education*, 3(2).

Hargreaves, D. 1967. *Social Relations in a Secondary School*. London: Routledge & Kegan Paul.

Harty, S. 1979. *Hucksters in the Classroom: A Review of Industry Propaganda in Schools*. Washington, D.C.: Center for Study of Responsive Law.

Hebdige, D. 1979. *Subculture: The Meaning of Style*. London: Methuen.

Held, D. 1980. *Introduction to Critical Theory: Horkheimer to Habermas*. Berkeley: University of California Press.

Heller, A. 1974. *The Theory of Need in Marx*. London: Allison & Busby.

1976 "Marx's Theory of Revolution and the Revolution in Everyday Life." In *The Humanization of Socialism: Writings of the Budapest School*, ed. A. Heller et al. London: Allison & Busby.

Hirst, P. 1979. *On Law and Ideology*. Atlantic Highlands, N.J.: Humanities Press.

Hogan, D. 1979. "Capitalism, Liberals, and Schooling." *Theory and Society*, 8(3) (Nov.).

Hoggart, R. 1958. *The Uses of Literacy*. London: Pelican.

Hohendahl, P. 1974. "Jurgen Habermas: 'The Public Sphere (1964).' " *New German Critique* (4) (Fall).

1979 "Critical Theory, Public Sphere, and Culture: Jurgen Habermas and His Critics." *New German Critique*, (16) (Winter).

Holly, D. 1977. "Education and the Social Relations of a Capitalist Society." In *Society, State, and Schooling*, ed. Michael Young and Geoff Whitty. Lewes, England: Falmer Press.

Horkheimer, M. 1972. *Critical Theory*. New York: Seabury Press.

1974 *Eclipse of Reason*. New York: Seabury Press.

Iglitzin, L.B. 1972. "Political Education and Sexual Liberation." *Politics and Society* (Winter).

Jackson, P. 1968. *Life in Classrooms*. New York: Holt, Rinehart, & Winston.

Jacoby, R. 1975. *Social Amnesia*. Boston: Beacon Press.

1980 "What Is Conformist Marxism?" *Telos*, 45 (Fall).

1981 *Dialectic of Defeat: Contours of Western Marxism*. New York: Oxford University Press.

Jameson, F. 1971. *Marxism and Form*. Princeton, N.J.: Princeton University Press.

1979 "Reification and Utopia in Mass Culture." *Social Text*, 1 (Winter).

Jay, M. 1973. *The Dialectical Imagination: A History of the Frankfurt School and the Institute of Social Research 1923–1950*. Boston: Little, Brown.

Johnson, R. 1976. "Notes on the Schooling of the English Working Class, 1780–1850." In *Schooling and Capitalism: A Sociological Reader,* ed. Roger Dale, Geoff Esland, and Madeleine MacDonald. Boston and London: Routledge & Kegan Paul.

1979a "Three Problematics: Elements of a Theory of Working Class Culture." In *Studies in History and Theory,* ed. John Clarke et al. London: Hutchinson.

1979b "Histories of Culture/Theories of Ideology: Notes on an Impasse." In *Ideology and Cultural Production,* ed. Michele Barrett et al. New York: St. Martin's Press.

1981 "Socialism and Popular Education." *Socialism and Education,* 8(1) (Spring).

Karabel, J. 1976. "Revolutionary Contradictions: Antonio Gramsci and the Problem of Intellectuals." *Politics and Society,* 6(2).

Karabel, J., and A.H. Halsey, eds. 1977. *Power and Ideology in Education.* New York: Oxford University Press.

Katz, M. 1968. *The Irony of Early School Reform.* Boston: Beacon Press.

Keddie, N. 1971. "Classroom Knowledge." In *Knowledge and Control,* ed. M.F.D. Young. London: Collier-Macmillan.

Kellner, D. 1978. "Ideology, Marxism, and Advanced Capitalism." *Socialist Review,* 8(6) (Nov.-Dec.).

Kliebard, H. 1979a. "The Drive for Curriculum Change in the United States, 1890–1958: Part I, The Ideological Roots of Curriculum as a Field Specialization." *Journal of Curriculum Studies,* 11(3).

1979b "The Drive for Curriculum Change in the United States, 1890–1958: Part II, From Local Reform to National Preoccupation." *Journal of Curriculum Studies,* 11(4).

Knodler-Bunte, E. 1975. "The Proletarian Public Sphere and Political Organization." *New German Critique,* (4) (Winter).

Kohl, H. 1980. "Can the Schools Build a New Social Order?" *Journal of Education,* 162(3) (Summer).

Kohlberg, L. 1973. "Moral Development and the New Social Studies." *Social Education* (May).

Kohlberg, L., and R. Meyer. 1972. "Development as the Aim of Education." *Harvard Educational Review,* 42(4).

Kress, G., and R. Hodge. 1979. *Language as Ideology.* London: Routledge & Kegan Paul.

Labov, W. 1972. "Logic of Non-Standard English." In *Language and Social Context,* ed. Pier Paolo Giglioli. Harmondsworth, England: Penguin.

Lacan, J. 1977. *Écrits: A Selection.* New York: Norton.

Lacey, C. 1970. *Hightown Grammar: The School as a Social System.* Manchester, England: Manchester University Press.

1982 Review of *Ideology, Culture, and Schooling* by Henry Giroux, and *Dilemmas of Schooling* by Ann and Harold Berlak. *Times Literary Supplement*, 22 Jan.

Laclau, E. 1977. *Politics and Ideology in Marxist Theory*. London: New Left Books.

Lazere, D. 1975. "Literacy and Political Consciousness: A Critique of Left Critiques." *Radical Teacher* (8) (May).

1977 "Mass Culture, Political Consciousness, and English Studies." *College English*, 38(8).

Lenin, V.I. 1971. *What Is To Be Done?* New York: International Publishers.

Lévi-Strauss, C. 1972. *Structural Anthropology*. Harmondsworth, England: Penguin.

Levy, B. 1974. "The School's Role in the Sex-Role Stereotyping of Girls: A Feminist Review of the Literature," In *Demystifying School*, ed. M. Wasserman. New York: Praeger Publishers.

Lobban, G. 1978. "The Influence of the School on Sex-Role Stereotyping." In *The Sex Role System*, J. Chetwynd and O. Hartnett. London: Routledge & Kegan Paul.

Lorrain, J. 1979. *The Concept of Ideology*. London: Hutchinson.

Lowenthal, L. 1979. "Theodor W. Adorno: An Intellectual Memoir." *Humanities in Society*, 2(4) (Fall).

Lukacs, G. 1968. *History and Class Consciousness*. Cambridge, Mass.: M.I.T. Press.

Lundgren, U. 1979. "Background: The Conceptual Framework." In *Codes, Context, and Curriculum Processes*, ed. Ulf Lundgren and Stan Peterson. Stockholm: Liber.

Forthcoming *Between the Scholared and the School*. Geelong, Australia: Deakin University Press.

MacDonald, M. 1977. *The Curriculum and Cultural Reproduction*. Milton Keynes, England: Open University Press.

1979/80 "Cultural Reproduction: The Pedagogy of Sexuality." *Screen Education*, 32.

1980 "Socio-Cultural Reproduction and Women's Education." In *Schooling for Women's Work*, ed. Rosemary Deem. Boston and London: Routledge & Kegan Paul.

1981 *Gender, Class, and Education*. London: Open University Press.

Mager, R. 1975. *Preparing Instructional Objectives*. Belmont, Cal.: Fearon.

Marcuse, H. 1955. *Eros and Civilization*. Boston: Beacon Press.

1960 *Reason and Revolution*. Boston: Beacon Press.

1964 *One Dimensional Man*. Boston: Beacon Press.

1968a *Negations: Essays in Critical Theory*. Boston: Beacon Press.

1968b *An Essay on Liberation*. Boston: Beacon Press.

1969 "Repressive Tolerance." In *A Critique of Pure Tolerance*, ed. Robert Paul Wolff, Benjamin Moor, Jr., and Herbert Marcuse. Boston: Beacon Press.

1970 *Five Lectures,* trans. Jeremy Shapiro and Sheirry Weber. Boston: Beacon Press.

1972 *Counter-Revolution and Revolt.* Boston: Beacon Press.

1977 *The Aesthetic Dimension.* Boston: Beacon Press.

1978 "On Science and Phenomenology." In *The Essential Frankfurt School Reader,* ed. Andrew Arato and Eike Gebhardt. New York: Urizen Books.

Marx, K. 1947. *The Economic & Philosophical Manuscripts* of 1844, trans. Martin Milligan. New York: International Publishers.

1969a *The Eighteenth Brumaire of Louis Bonaparte.* New York: International Publishers.

1969b *Preface to the Critique of Political Economy.* New York: International Publishers.

1972 *The German Ideology.* New York: International Publishers.

McCarthy, T. 1978. *The Critical Theory of Jurgen Habermas.* Cambridge, Mass.: M.I.T. Press.

McLaren, P. 1980. *Cries from the Corridor.* London: Methuen.

McRobbie, A. 1978. "Working Class Girls and the Culture of Femininity." In *Women Take Issue.* Eds. Centre for Contemporary Cultural Studies. Boston and London: Routledge & Kegan Paul.

1980 "Settling Accounts with Subcultures." *Screen Education* (3,4) (Spring).

McRobbie, A., and T. McCabe, eds. 1981. *Feminism for Girls: An Adventure Story.* Boston and London: Routledge & Kegan Paul.

Mehan, H. 1979. *Learning Lessons: Social Organization in the Classroom.* Cambridge, Mass.: Harvard University Press.

1980 "The Competent Student." *Anthropology and Education Quarterly,* 11(3).

Merelman, R. 1980. "Democratic Politics and the Culture of American Education." *American Political Science Review,* 74(2) (June).

Merton, R. 1957. *Social Theory and Social Structure.* New York: Free Press.

Metzger, D.J., and R.D. Barr. 1978. "The Impact of School Political Systems on Student Political Attitudes." *Theory and Research in Social Education,* 6(1).

Mickelson, R.A. 1980. "The Secondary School's Role in Social Stratification: A Comparison of Beverly Hills High School and Morningside High School." *Journal of Education,* 162(4) (Fall).

Moore, R. 1978/79. "The Value of Reproduction." *Screen Education* (39) (Winter).

Morely, D. 1981. "The Nationwide Audience: A Postscript." *Screen Education* (39) (Summer).

Mosher, R. 1978. "A Democratic High School: Damn It, Your Feet Are Always in the Water." In *Value Development. . .as the Aim of Education,* ed. Norman Sprinthall. New York: Character Research Press.

Moskowitz, E., P. Wexler, and T. Whitson. 1980. "Schooling by Default: The

Changing Social Functions of Public Schooling." Mimeo. Graduate School of Education, University of Rochester, Rochester, N.Y.

Mouffe, C., ed. 1979. *Gramsci and Marxist Theory.* London and Boston: Routledge & Kegan Paul.

Mueller, C. 1973 *The Politics of Communication.* New York: Oxford University Press.

Musgrave, P.W. 1980. "The Sociology of the Australian Curriculum: A Case Study in the Diffusion of Theory." *Australian and New Zealand Journal of Sociology,* 12(2) (July).

NAEP. 1978. *Changes in Political Knowledge and Attitudes, 1969–1976.* Denver, Col.: National Assessment of Educational Progress.

Neil, A.S. 1960. *Summerhill.* New York: Hart Publishing Co.

Newmann, F.M. 1980. "Political Participation: An Analytical Review and Proposal." In *Political Education in Flux,* ed. Judith Gillespie and Derek Heater. London: Sage.

Nietzche, F. 1957. *The Use and Abuse of History,* trans. A. Collins. Indianapolis: Bobbs-Merrill.

1966 "Aus dem Nachlass der Achtzigerjahre." In *Werke,* vol. 3, ed. Karle Schleckta. Munich: Hanser.

Ohmann, R. 1976. *English in America.* Cambridge: Oxford University Press.

Olson, P. 1981. "Laboring To Learn: How Working Theory Gets Down to Classrooms and Kids." *Interchange,* 12(2,3).

O'Toole, J. 1977. *Work, Learning and the American Future.* San Francisco: Jossey-Bass.

Overly, N., ed. 1970. *The Unstudied Curriculum.* Washington, D.C.: Association of Supervision and Curriculum Development.

Paris, R. 1975. "Class Structure and Legitimatory Public Sphere: A Hypothesis on the Continued Existence of Class Relationships and the Problem of Legitimation in Transitional Societies." *New German Critique* (5) (Spring).

Parsons, T. 1949. *The Structure of Social Action.* Glencoe, N.Y.: Free Press.

1951 *The Social System.* London: Routledge & Kegan Paul.

1959 "The School Class as a Social System: Some of Its Functions in American Society." *Harvard Educational Review,* 29(4) (Fall).

Peak, W., and H. Zeigler. 1970. "The Political Functions of the Educational System." *Sociology of Education,* 43(2).

Piaget, J. 1970. *Psychology and Epistemology: Towards a Theory of Knowledge.* New York: Viking Press.

Pinar, W.F. 1978. "Notes on the Curriculum Field, 1978." *Educational Researcher,* 7 (Sept.).

1981 "The Abstract and the Concrete in Curriculum Theorizing." In *Curriculum and Instruction: Alternative Theoretical and Practical Perspectives for*

Educators, ed. Henry A. Giroux, Anthony N. Penna, and William F. Pinar. Berkeley: McCutchan.

Pine, G., and A. Boy, eds. 1977. *Learner-Centered Teaching: A Humanistic View.* Denver: Love Publishing.

Popham, W.J. 1969. *Instructional Objectives.* Chicago: Rand McNally.

Popkewitz, T.S. 1977. "The Latent Values of the Discipline-Centered Curriculum." *Theory and Research in Social Education,* 5(1).

1978 "Educational Research: Values and Visions of Social Order." *Theory and Research in Social Education,* 6(4) (Dec.).

1980 "Paradigms in Educational Science: Different Meanings and Purpose In Theory." *Journal of Education,* 162(1).

1981 "The Social Contexts of Schooling, Change, and Educational Research." *Journal of Curriculum Studies,* 13(3).

Popkewitz, T.S., 1982. *The Myth of Educational Reform.* Madison: University of Wisconsin Press.

Poulantzas, N. 1973. *Political Power and Social Classes.* London: New Left Books.

1978 *Classes in Contemporary Society.* London: New Left Books.

Price, R., W. Hickman, and G. Smith. 1965. *Major Concepts for the Social Studies.* Syracuse, N.Y.: Social Studies Curriculum Center.

Ravitch, D. 1978. *The Revisionists Revised: A Critique of the Radical Attack on Schools.* New York: Basic Books.

Reich, W. 1949. *Character Analysis,* 3d ed. New York: Farrar, Straus, & Giroux.

1970 *The Mass Psychology of Fascism,* trans. Vincent Carfango. New York: Farrar, Straus, & Giroux.

1971 "What Is Class Consciousness?" trans. Anna Bostock. *Liberation* (Oct.).

1972 *Sex-Pol Essays, 1929–1934,* ed. Lee Baxandall. New York: Vintage Books.

Remy, R.C., and M.J. Turner. 1979. "Basic Citizenship Competencies: Guidelines for Educators, Policymakers, and Citizens." *Mershon Center Quarterly Report,* 5 (Autumn).

Rist, R. 1977a. *The Urban School: A Factory for Failure.* Cambridge: M.I.T. Press.

1977b "On Understanding the Process of Schooling: The Contribution of Labeling Theory." In *Power and Ideology,* ed. J. Karabel and A.H. Halsey. New York: Oxford University Press.

Rosenblatt, L.M. 1949. "The Enriching Values of Reading." In *Reading in an Age of Mass Communication,* ed. William S. Gray. New York: Appleton-Century Crofts.

Rosenzweig, L. 1976. "A Selected Bibliography of Materials about Moral Education Based on the Research of Lawrence Kohlberg." *Social Education,* 40(4) (Apr.).

Saussure, F. 1974. *Course in General Linguistics*. London: Fontana.

Schmidt, A. 1981. *History and Structure*, trans. Jeffrey Herf. Cambridge, Mass.: M.I.T. Press.

Schutz, A. 1967. *The Phenomenology of the Social World*. Evanston, Ill.: Northwestern University Press.

Shapiro, H.L., ed. 1960. *Man, Culture, and Society*. New York: Galaxy.

Sharp, R. 1980. *Knowledge, Ideology, and the Politics of Schooling*. London and Boston: Routledge & Kegan Paul.

Sharp, R., and A. Green. 1975. *Education and Social Control*. Boston and London: Routledge & Kegan Paul.

Shaver, J.P., O.L. Davis, Jr., and S.W. Helburn. 1978. "An Interpretive Report on the Status of Pre-College Social Studies Education Based on Three NSF-Funded Studies." Washington, D.C.: National Council for the Social Studies.

1979 "The Status of Social Studies Education: Impressions from Three National Science Foundation Studies." *Social Education*, 43(2) (Feb.).

Sieber, R.T. 1982. "The Politics of Middle-Class Success in an Inner City School." *Journal of Education*, 164(1) (Winter).

Silberman, C.E. 1970. *Crisis in the Classroom*. New York: Random House.

Silberman, C.E., S. Bowles, and H. Gintis. 1976. *Schooling in Capitalist America*. New York: Basic Books.

Simon, R. "Mysticism, Management, and Marx." In *The Management of Educational Institutions*, ed. H.L. Gray. Sussex: Falmer Press.

Simon, R., and J. Willensky. 1980. "Behind a High School Literacy Policy: The Surfacing of a Hidden Curriculum." *Journal of Education*, 162(1) (Winter).

Simon, S., R. Hawley, and D. Bretton. 1973. *Composition for Personal Growth*. New York: Hart Publishing.

Snedden, D.S. 1921. *Sociological Determination of Objectives in Education*. Philadelphia: Lippincott.

Spencer, R. 1965. "Nature and Value of Functionalism." In *Functionalism in the Social Sciences*, ed. Don Martendale. Philadelphia: American Academy of Political and Social Sciences.

Spring, J. 1972. *Education and the Rise of the Corporate State*. Boston: Beacon Press.

1975 *A Primer for Liberation*. New York: Free Life Editions.

1976 *The Sorting Machine: National Education Policy since 1945*. New York: McKay.

1978 *American Education*. New York: Longman.

Stahl, A. 1975. "Creative Writers on the Effects of Reading." *Journal of Reading Behavior*, 7(2) (Summer).

Stewart, J. 1980. "Jurgen Habermas's Reconstruction of Critical Theory." In *Current Perspectives in Social Theory*, vol. 1. Greenwich, Conn.: JAI Press.

Stinchombe, A. 1964. *Rebellion in a High School.* New York: Quadrangle Books.

Stricht, T.G. 1978. "The Development of Literacy." *Curriculum Inquiry*, 8(4).

Sullivan, E. 1977. "A Study of Kohlberg's Structural Theory of Moral Development: A Critique of Liberal Social Science Ideology." *Human Development*, 20.

Sumner, C. 1979. *Reading Ideologies.* London: Academic Press.

Suppes, P. 1974. "The Place of Theory in Educational Research." *Educational Researcher*, 8 (June).

Therborn, G. 1981. *The Ideology of Power and the Power of Ideology.* London: New Left Books.

Thompson, E. 1961. Reviews of Raymond Williams's *The Long Revolution. New Left Review*, (9, 10).

1966 *The Making of the English Working Class.* New York: Vintage Press.

1975 *Whigs and Hunters.* London: Allen Lane.

1977 *William Morris: Romantic to Revolutionary.* New York: Pantheon.

1978 *The Poverty of Theory.* London: Merlin Press.

Torney, J.V., A.N. Oppenheim, and R.F. Farmen. 1975. *Civic Education in Ten Countries.* New York: Wiley.

Turner, R.H. 1962. "Role Taking: Process *vs.* Conformity." In *Human Behavior and Social Processes*, ed. A. Rose. London and Boston: Routledge & Kegan Paul.

Tyack, D.B. 1974. *The One Best System.* Cambridge, Mass.: Harvard University Press.

Tyler, E.B. 1891. *Primitive Culture.* London: John Murray Publishers.

Tyler, R.W. 1950. *Basic Principles of Curriculum and Instruction.* Chicago: University of Chicago Press.

UNESCO. 1966. "An Asian Model of Educational Development: Perspectives for 1965–1980." Paris: UNESCO.

Vallance, E. 1973. "Hiding the Hidden Curriculum." *Curriculum Theory Network*, 4(1).

1980 "The Hidden Curriculum and Qualitative Inquiry as Stages of Mind." *Journal of Education*, 162(1) (Winter).

Vogel, D. 1979. "Business's New Class Struggle." *Nation*, 229(20) (Dec).

Volosinov, V.V. 1973. *Marxism and the Philosophy of Language.* New York: Seminar Press.

Walker, J. Forthcoming. "Rebels with Our Applause: A Critique of Resistance Theories of Schooling." *Journal of Education*.

Walkerdine, V. 1981. "Sex, Power, and Pedagogy." *Screen Education* (30) (Spring).

Walmsley, S.A. 1981. "On the Purpose and Content of Secondary Reading Programs: Educational Ideological Perspectives." *Curriculum Inquiry,* 11(1).

Weitzman, L., D. Eifler, E. Hokada, and C. Ross. 1972. "Sex-Role Socialization in Picture Books for Pre-School Children." *American Journal of Sociology,* 77(6).

Wellmer, A. 1974. *Critical Theory of Society,* trans. John Cumming. New York: Seabury Press.

Wexler, P. 1977. *The Sociology of Education: Beyond Equality.* Indianapolis: Bobbs-Merrill.

1981 "Body and Soul: Sources of Social Change and Strategies of Education." *British Journal of Sociology of Education,* 2(3).

1982 "Structure, Text, and Subject: A Sociology of School Knowledge." In *Cultural and Economic Reproduction in Education,* ed. Michael Apple. Boston and London: Routledge & Kegan Paul.

Forthcoming *A Critical Social Psychology.* London: Routledge & Kegan Paul.

Whitty, G. 1974. "Sociology and the Problem of Radical Educational Change." In *Educability, Schools, and Ideology,* ed. Michael Flude and John Ahier. London: Croom Helm.

1981 *Ideology, Politics, and Curriculum.* London: Open University Press.

Whitty, G., and M. Young. 1977. *Society, State, and Schooling.* Sussex: Falmer Press.

Williams, R. 1963. *Culture and Society, 1790–1950.* London: Penguin.

1965 *The Long Revolution.* London: Penguin.

1973 "Base and Superstructure in Marxist Cultural Theory." *New Left Review* (82).

1977 *Marxism and Literature.* London: Oxford University Press.

Willis, P. 1976. "The Class Significance of School Counter-Culture." In *The Process of Schooling,* ed. Martyn Hammerstay and Peter Woods. London: Routledge & Kegan Paul.

1977 *Learning To Labor.* Lexington, Mass.: D.C. Heath.

1978 *Profane Culture.* Boston and London: Routledge & Kegan Paul.

1981 "Cultural Production Is Different from Social Reproduction Is Different from Reproduction." *Interchange,* 12(2).

1982 "Cultural Production and Theories of Reproduction." Mimeo. Center for Contemporary Cultural Studies, University of Birmingham, Birmingham, England

Willis, P., and P. Corrigan. 1980. "Cultural Forms and Class Mediations." *Media, Culture, and Society* (2).

Wilson, H.T. 1977. *The American Ideology: Science, Technology, and Organizations as Modes of Rationality in Advanced Industrial Societies.* London: Routledge & Kegan Paul.

Winch, P. 1972. *The Idea of Social Science and Its Relation to Philosophy.* London: Routledge & Kegan Paul.

Wolff, R.P. 1969. "Beyond Tolerance." In *Critique of Pure Tolerance,* ed. Robert Paul Wolff, Benjamin Moore, Jr., and Herbert Marcuse. Boston: Beacon Press.

Wolin, S.S. *Politics and Vision.* Boston: Little, Brown.

Woods, P. 1979. *The Divided School.* London: Routledge & Kegan Paul.

Young, M.F.D. 1971. "Knowledge and Control." In *Knowledge and Control,* ed. Michael F.D. Young. London: Collier-Macmillan.

   1975 "Curriculum Change: Limits and Possibilities." *Educational Studies* (2).

Young, M.F.D., and G. Whitty, eds. 1977a. *Society, State and Schooling.* Sussex: Falmer Press.

   1977b "Towards a Critical Theory." In *Society, State, and Schooling,* ed. Michael F.D. Young and Geoff Whitty. Lewes, England: Falmer Press.

Index